T·H·E
ART & CRAFT
·O·F·
TECHNOLOGY
BUSINESS
INCUBATION

Best Practices, Strategies, and Tools from More Than 50 Programs

Louis G. Tornatzky, Ph.D.
Southern Technology Council

Yolanda Batts
Southern Growth Policies Board

Nancy E. McCrea
Southern Growth Policies Board

Marsha S. Lewis
Institute for Local Government Administration and Rural Development
Ohio University Center for Public and Environmental Affairs

Louisa M. Quittman
North Carolina State University

For information, please contact:

Southern Technology Council
P.O. Box 12293
Research Triangle Park, NC 27709
(919) 941-5145
(919) 941-5594 fax

National Business Incubation Association
20 East Circle Drive, Suite 190
Athens, Ohio 45701
(614) 593-4331
(614) 593-1996 fax

Institute for Local Government Administration
    and Rural Development
Ohio University Center for Public and Environmental Affairs
143 Technology and Enterprise Building
Athens, Ohio 45701
(614) 593-4388
(614) 593-4398 fax

To order additional copies, please contact:

National Business Incubation Association
20 East Circle Drive, Suite 190
Athens, Ohio 45701
(614) 593-4331
(614) 593-1996 fax

Printed in the United States of America

10 9 8 7 6 5 4 3 2 1

ISBN 0-927364-04-2

Table · of · Contents

Summary of Tables

ACKNOWLEDGMENTS

A number of individuals and organizations made this project possible. Early on, when the effort was being planned and conceptualized, Gregg Lichtenstein, president of Collaborative Strategies, Inc., was a strong advocate, organizer, and participant in the design of the research. Peter Bearse, president of Development Strategies Corporation, also played a significant role. On a *pro bono* basis, Peter was heavily involved in the development of the data collection approach, in organizing support within the incubator community, and in crafting the project plan.

The project would never have seen the light of day without the organizational support of the National Business Incubation Association (NBIA) and the personal advocacy of Dinah Adkins, executive director of NBIA. Dinah was invaluable in gaining support and participation from her members and in providing good advice to the project leader in times of stress and strain. In a similar manner, Mark Weinberg, director of the Institute for Local Government Administration and Rural Development (ILGARD) at Ohio University, provided early intellectual input and ongoing in-kind participation in the actual execution of the project.

Many project organizers may seek the advice and continued support of an advisory committee, but few are fortunate enough to truly receive it. We would like to extend a sincere thank you to Bob Calcaterra, Arizona Technology Incubator; Bob Thomson, NET Ben Franklin Technology Center; Mary Ferguson, Technology Development Center; Glenn Doell, Rensselaer Polytechnic Institute Incubator Center; and Melody Brown, First Flight Venture Center, for their work on this effort. I hope the results are pleasing to each of you.

The state and corporate members of the Southern Technology Council deserve a strong thank you. The Council not only provided ongoing financial support for the project team, but individual members provided valuable advice and guidance over the course of a long and complex effort.

The core project team was the epitome of intelligence, perseverance, and grace under pressure. Yolanda Batts, Nancy McCrea, Louisa Quittman, and Marsha Lewis were true research professionals throughout. Annette Roper deserves a special credit for organizing and managing the production of the text and integrating the many elements. Leah Totten designed this edition.

Finally, we would like to express our gratitude to our 50 managers throughout North America for their patience, participation, and wisdom. They gave of their time, they released the tricks of their trade, and they stayed with the project through the long months of editing, revising, and fine-tuning that resulted in a final product.

PREFACE

REGIONAL ECONOMIC DEVELOPMENT THROUGH TECHNOLOGY VENTURING

The world is changing in terms of how business is conducted. In many respects, economic transactions in the past have been an economic exchange of money for goods, materials, or services. In some cases, the exchange involved countertrade. But as we look to the future, the more important economic transactions will be those that involve knowledge-building transactions. Knowledge transactions encompass more than money or goods. Technology business incubation is an important economic development strategy that can be leveraged to facilitate academic, government, and business collaborations at the community level as well as between emerging global regional centers.

Traditional measures of comparative advantage have to be broadened to include knowledge—or put another way, innovation and technology. This in turn requires that communities, companies, and firms—as well as academic institutions—implement newer approaches as well as business models that will account for globally competitive market systems.

Competing successfully in a hypercompetitive, knowledge-based marketplace is fundamentally different from the past in two key respects. First, the process of change in science, invention, marketing, and financing has been dramatically accelerated. Second, new economic market systems are emerging as a result of the paradox of competition and cooperation. Furthermore, business operations in all communities now must compete in a global marketplace where national boundaries are disappearing. The classical factors of comparative advantage have been those of ownership of low-cost labor, natural resources, capital, arable land, and markets. Increasingly, wealth is not measured in terms of possession of fixed physical assets, but rather in ease of access and timely control of knowledge-intensive, value-added capabilities to produce leading-edge, next-generation systems. This shift in the nature of comparative advantage is being driven by the liquidity of capital and the rapid development and transfer and commercialization of advanced technology.

Technology Business Incubation

Technology business incubation involves the commercialization of science and technology through newer community-institutional arrangements which can be thought of as technology venturing. It concentrates on alliances as an economic development strategy. Technology venturing is based on creative and innovative ways of linking public-sector initiatives and private-sector resources within and across regional and national boundaries for promoting economic growth.

Technology incubation can foster corporate and community collaborative efforts, while nurturing positive government-academic-business relationships. These new types of organizational alliances incorporate a dynamic private sector; a creative role for government through technology policies, initiatives and development programs; and innovative academic relationships. The science and technology policies that promote and flow from these technology alliances are redefining the role and scope of the wide variety of institutions involved in advancing economic growth through technology.

Critical Linkages

Technology venturing through incubator activity is an integrative strategy. It links corporate and community collaborative efforts while accelerating the transfer and commercialization of technology through innovative and cooperative efforts. These efforts in turn enhance the competitiveness of a company, a community, and a nation. In short, technology venturing is based on business, academic, and government alliances but the appropriate innovative activities for implementation take place at the community or regional level.

Technology venturing activities within a community are based on linking four critical factors: 1) talent—people; 2) technology—ideas; 3) capital—resources; and 4) know-how—knowledge. Entrepreneurial talent results from the perception, drive, tenacity, dedication, and hard work of special types of individuals—people who make things happen. Where there is a pool of such talent, there is the opportunity for growth, diversification, and new business development. But talent without ideas is like a seed without water. When talent is linked with technology, when people recognize and push viable ideas, the entrepreneurial process is underway. Every dynamic process needs to be fueled. The fuel is capital. Capital is the catalyst in the technology venturing chain reaction. The final key element is "know-how," the ability to leverage business or scientific knowledge by linking talent, technology, and capital in emerging and expanding enterprises. This expertise may involve management, marketing, finance, accounting, production, and manufacturing, as well as legal, scientific, and engineering skills.

Each of these critical factors needs to be nurtured and supported at the community and regional levels by creating conditions that build an environment that promotes innovation, technology, and economic development. Support for each factor includes:

- Expanding the talent pool. These conditions include quality of life, infrastructure, access and communication to other areas domestically and internationally, recognition of successful role models, and development of a culture conducive to innovation as well as support for education and research.

- Accelerating the transfer of technology. These conditions include governmental funding programs for research and development (R&D), technology transfer, science parks, R&D consortia, centers of excellence, and intellectual property.

- Increasing the availability of capital. These conditions include creative governmental programs, traditional venture and private sector capital pools, tax advantages for investing in R&D and new companies, small business R&D programs, and creation of state and governmental as well as private new venture capital pools.

- Improving availability of managerial, technical, and business know-how. These conditions include establishment of R&D programs, projects, institutes, and business incubators; availability of educational programs for international management training and assistance; development of technical support and assistance programs; development of organized networks of experienced people, local advisors, and professional associations and support groups, as well as support for small and medium technology-based firms to determine their individual global strategies policies.

Technology Transfer Gap

The most critical gap in technology transfer is linking talent (entrepreneur/champions), technology, and capital with market pull—the ability to leverage business or scientific knowledge by new and expanding enterprises. Know-how is a human dimension that involves person-to-person contact with conceptual understanding and shared information based upon knowledge and experience. Technology incubators can adjust to fill the technology transfer gap, but it requires a willingness to experiment with new processes and structures. Equitable partnerships or workable relationships with industry, financial institutions, and universities are required.

The primary drivers of technology business incubation are entrepreneurs/champions—people who make things happen—and technologies or ideas that have a potential to be commercialized within a reasonable period of time. Center management must have a support system that provides access to quality capital, extended know-how networks, cost-effective facilities, and a capable, reactive administration. Successful incubators provide a framework for focusing and leveraging critical success factors for timely and effective technology transfer. The benefits for tenant companies can be summarized in terms of four categories: developing credibility, shortening the learning curve, solving problems faster, and providing access to business know-how networks. Start-up technology-based firms face a particularly difficult challenge in today's hypercompetitive environments: They must quickly establish credibility as a viable company.

Technology incubators can help accelerate the learning process through entrepreneurial education, peer counseling, know-how networks, and university ties. Tenant companies can solve problems faster by targeting the right problem and leveraging resources to achieve a workable solution. Technology transfer to successful product/process commercialization is significantly enhanced by access to regionally-based know-how networks and by the center's entrepreneurs utilization of these networks. Technology business incubators can benefit public and private participants, technology transfer processes, and regionally based economic development.

George Kozmetsky, Ph.D.
IC2 Institute
The University of Texas at Austin
Austin, Texas
January 1996

CHAPTER 1

INTRODUCTION AND OVERVIEW

This book is the product of an 18-month research effort involving several dozen organizations. Its goal is to improve the craft and practice of technology business incubation, primarily in the United States but wherever it might be beneficial. It is also part of a larger mission shared by all of the partner organizations: to improve the quality of life and future opportunities for individuals in our communities through the creation of a robust entrepreneurial economy. The balance of this chapter describes some of the conceptual underpinnings of the project, its rationale in terms of program development needs, our approach to methods and procedures, and last but unfortunately not least, some of the limitations.

THE ECONOMIC CONTEXT

While perhaps too much has been written of late about the "new economy," it is nonetheless useful to briefly review some of the recent economic and sociopolitical trends that have driven this study project. After all, it is not obvious to some observers why a benchmarking project on technology business incubation programs should take precedence over other topics or issues. For our purposes, there are three significant events or trends that have guided the research: 1) the increasing role of science and technology in economic growth worldwide; 2) the growing prominence of the entrepreneurial and small business economy; and 3) changes in economic development strategies and programs pursued by various levels of government.

The Role of Science and Technology

It has become increasingly clear that science and technology are important and growing components of economic growth. The world economy has become one in which the relative advantage of companies and nations is a function of their ability to rapidly commercialize leading science and technology in new products and processes (Mokyr, 1990). Many international markets are now dominated by products and/or companies that simply did not exist 20 years ago and which have clear intellectual lineage to recent research advances (Mansfield, 1991). While this is especially true in the case of some industries (e.g., chemicals, pharmaceuticals, instruments) and with certain technologies (e.g., genetic engineering, artificial intelligence), it is becoming the norm across the economy. In the future, most products, processes, and industries will rely on a core of advanced science and technology. The implication for both theoretical understanding of economic events and for practical intervention is that enterprise is not simply a combination of labor and capital, but also includes the intellectual property of science and technology embedded in new products and processes. In fact, the proficiency with which companies build and manage their technology-based intellectual property will become a primary source of competitive advantage in the future.

The Entrepreneurial Economy

Some years ago, a then relatively obscure researcher (Birch, 1979) revised much of conventional wisdom on sources of economic vitality (as measured by job growth) in the U.S. economy. While that original research has been criticized on some methodological grounds (Harris, 1984), the fundamental conclusion is still valid: Most of the growth and vibrancy in the national economy is among start-ups and entrepreneurial small companies. This has been echoed in more recent studies, which, for example, point to the importance of entrepreneurial companies in the commercialization of university-based inventions (General Accounting Office, 1992) and in the development of health-care technologies (Health Care Technology Institute, 1992). A parallel development has been the emergence of an entrepreneurial support industry, as represented by the phenomenal growth of business incubation programs throughout the past decade (National Business Incubation Association, 1993).

New Economic Development Strategies

Since the early part of this century when the practice of economic or industrial development was launched, it has been characterized by a dominant strategy of company recruitment. Using this strategy, which is derided as "smokestack-chasing" by its critics, various units of state and local government have orchestrated literally thousands of inducement packages to lure established companies from one part of the country to another. Governments have competed shamelessly to craft combinations of tax abatements, subsidized training, and business-friendly labor laws. Some of the recent plant-siting competitions involving Japanese and German auto makers illustrate how fierce these contests can become. In addition, it is becoming increasingly clear that some states and communities have given away nearly as much as they have gained, and in the eyes of some observers the entire process has evolved into a zero-sum game with few real winners.

Within the last 10-20 years, however, government has gained more understanding and appreciation of the economic changes noted above. Many communities and states have abandoned or decreased industrial recruiting in favor of growing their own entrepreneurial technology-based economies (Kozmetsky, 1990). The 1992 Carnegie Commission on Science, Technology, and Government (Carnegie Commission, 1992) pointed out the necessity for state and interstate cooperation between government, industry, and science organizations. This challenge has been taken up by regional organizations as well. In the South, long the bastion of traditional industrial-development practice, the Southern Growth Policies Board and its Southern Technology Council have published sweeping agendas for change in how economic development is pursued in the region (Southern Growth Policies Board, 1988; Southern Technology Council, 1990), with major emphases on technology-linked entrepreneurialism. The Center for the New West has been a major advocate in the mountain and Pacific states for "high performance communities," with a policy mix of technology, entrepreneurial enterprise, greater attention to private-public partnerships, investment in human resources, and advanced telecommunications. Programs such as Enterprise Florida and the Kansas Technology Enterprise Corporation signal major policy shifts in state legislatures and significant public funds in support of new strategies.

The Role and Function of Technology Business Incubation

Within the economic and policy milieu of the past decade, there has been a parallel growth phenomenon—the rise of technology business incubation and incubators. This has been partly an outgrowth of the rapid and spontaneous burgeoning of technology-based start-up companies in general, but also a reaction to the types of entrepreneurs involved in them. Many of the new entrepreneurs have negligible experience in managing and growing a small enterprise. They are coming from a life of research in a university or laboratory, they may be independent inventors, or they may be middle managers from down-sized large corporations. All have ideas or technologies that potentially can be marketed as products or services. However, these entrepreneurs tend to lack certain key pieces of knowledge or experience.

The nature of those weaknesses can be seen, for example, by looking at "failure factors" of technology ventures. As described by Bruno, McQuarrie, and Torgrimson (1992), these tend to revolve around management and human resource issues, problems of capitalization, and issues of product development and marketing. Moreover, these issues tend to be acute in conjunction with certain milestones of growth—for example, the first sales, the first profit (or loss), a change in product technology, or emergence of a competitor. While all of these issues are critical to any new enterprise, they seem exacerbated in those that are based on new technology. In effect, business risk is compounded by the risk inherent in any new technology, and substantive expertise and experience is needed to surmount these obstacles.

As a result, the practices of technology business incubation—when properly conducted—tend to be assistance-intensive. The incubator that merely provides space and general support services is likely to be ineffective. As Udell (1990) points out in his critical analysis of incubator impacts, "Business incubators need to place much greater emphasis on providing financial, management, and technical assistance to clients." To summarize, a technology business incubator gives the inventor/entrepreneur the place and time to develop the product, as well as access to skills and tools needed to create a successful business. In the balance of this book we will describe those skills and tools.

RATIONALE AND OBJECTIVES FOR THE STUDY PROJECT

One clear programmatic implication of the intensive needs of technology entrepreneurs is that the country needs to develop its "maternal instincts" and become very good at nurturing new technology-based business enterprises by better understanding the policies, practices, and tools of **technology business incubation**, and applying them in quality program development. Significant work has already been accomplished, much of it by or through the National Business Incubation Association, to define useful approaches for *general* incubator programs. Most of this information has been developed in the form of guidebooks, training programs, case histories, and audiotapes. However, only a fraction of it has focused specifically on the technology-oriented business incubator.

However, new technology-based companies and organizations that assist them are involved in a more difficult challenge. In addition to the usual problems and challenges of business development, the entrepreneur and the service-provider by definition are also involved in the complex process of technological innovation. This process has a huge practice and research literature of its own (Tornatzky and Fleischer, 1990) that moves beyond the domain of business *qua* business.

A central premise for this project is the belief that it will be possible to define useful approaches to technology business incubation if a more deliberate and systematic **benchmarking** strategy is used. Following Spendolini (1992), we define benchmarking as follows:

> *Benchmarking: A continuous, systematic process for evaluating the products, services, and work processes of organizations that are recognized as representing best practices for the purposes of organizational improvement.*

From this perspective, a more fruitful approach to defining what works would be to gather detailed, operational information from a wide range of successful practitioners and organizations. Rather than drawing on a few analytic experts, the best-practice portrait should be a composite drawn by many artists. Many practitioners do a few things extremely well; few if any are best-in-class in every domain.

Moreover, the best-practice portrait also should be drawn at a fine level of resolution so others can replicate and utilize the information. In the language of patent examiners, it should be "enabling" so that a practitioner reasonably skilled in the art of incubation can follow the example. One of the criticisms of some guidebooks or lists of principles is that although they provide conceptual confirmation for those who already know what they are doing, they often fail to provide clear directions for those at an earlier stage of program development. Keeping these criticisms in mind, we have tried to give detailed descriptions of practices, given constraints of method and resources.

As noted in the above definition, the process of benchmarking works best in a context of **continuous improvement**. Therefore, the practice descriptions in this volume should be seen as works-in-progress. The array of practices will, we hope, be improved through incremental innovation and through the development of totally new approaches to various incubator services. If this volume has value, that value will be exceeded in future editions and supplements. One of the challenges confronting the field is how to facilitate that continuous improvement process.

Given the above, the objectives for the project were as follows:

1) To develop a peer group process, involving a national group of technology business incubator program managers, that would allow for the sharing of information and experiences;

2) To develop through peer process a shared vision of the benchmarking task, desired products and deliverables, and methods and procedures;

3) To catalog and develop through peer participation and review a documented set of best practices, strategies, and tools for technology business incubation; and

4) To disseminate the project results nationally to a diverse group of stakeholders engaged in the process of technology business incubation.

Methods and Procedures

Consistent with the above rationale and objectives, the following approaches were taken in regard to project execution.

Peer Group Process

This project was conceived and conducted as a collaborative effort involving the Southern Technology Council (STC), the National Business Incubation Association (NBIA), and the Institute for Local Government Administration and Rural Development (ILGARD) at Ohio University. The most important set of collaborators were the 50-plus technology business incubators from all over North America who actively participated throughout the project. Several steps were involved in making the peer group process work effectively.

In late 1993, the leadership of STC and NBIA led a series of discussions about the basic project idea of benchmarking best practices in technology business incubation. This led to a work and brainstorming session at the May 1994 meeting of NBIA. At that time, approximately 15 incubator managers reviewed the proposed methodology and deliverables. The group suggested changes to methods and procedures and identified an oversight committee of NBIA member incubators. At each step of the formal research process (e.g., questionnaire creation, review of draft practice descriptions), the project team solicited widespread involvement and criticism from incubator managers. Although this document has a nominal list of authors, it should be considered a group effort of the participating incubator managers.

Sample Selection

Given the objectives of a benchmarking study, the study group was not a true sample in the usual representative statistical sense. We were trying to identify those incubators that peers see as leading-edge or best-in-class. However, because no nationwide quantitative performance indicators exist to define exemplary programs, the process of defining the study sample was necessarily subjective. In effect, the approach was a reputational snowball. To nominate programs which should be included in the study sample, we started by asking a few informants who had national prominence and visibility in the incubator industry. This process built on itself and tended to be self-validating in that in time we received multiple nominations for many programs. Using this process, we identified 84 programs as candidates for data collection. Of these 12 could not be reached by telephone or unfortunately had ceased operations, another 13 declined to participate in the study, and five never returned questionnaires or declined interviews after they had originally indicated their willingness. Questionnaire data were gathered from 54 programs, and interviews were conducted with more than 50 incubators.

Survey Instrument

The research team developed a ten-page questionnaire to be used with all participating programs. The questionnaire was structured as a set of checklists, which were organized into the following "domains" of practices and services: 1) business planning; 2) finance and capitalization; 3) management development/selection; 4) research and technology; 5) markets and products; 6) legal; 7) monitoring and decision-making; 8) infrastructure; and 9) management. In each of these areas, incubator managers were asked to respond to a list of plausible activities and to indicate whether they provide each as a direct service, provide each activity by referral, or rarely or never provide it. The checklist included 68 potential practices or services. As a precursor or catalyst for subsequent interview data-gathering (see below), the questionnaire also asked respondents to "briefly describe a particularly novel or useful approach...that is used in your program" for each of the nine practice areas or domains. Most respondents jotted down a few notes on these items as reminders for the interview process.

Data Collection Approach

Consistent with a more comprehensive approach to benchmarking, the data collection approach was designed to yield both quantifiable information as well as rich and qualitative descriptions of best practices, strategies, and tools.

The actual data collection procedures were fairly straightforward. A member of the research team called each incubator manager and, during a brief conversation, described the approach and objectives of the study. Once incubators agreed to participate in the study, the interviewer made an appointment for an initial phone interview and express-mailed a copy of the questionnaire to be filled out prior to the interview.

The first telephone interview generally lasted 60-90 minutes. Each interview was recorded (with the knowledge and consent of the participants), and two to four members of the project team were involved in a group interview format. At the onset of the interview, participants were asked to provide the team with background information about the incubator (e.g., history, client mix). Then the general approach was to walk through each of the nine practice domains and to ask the incubator managers to describe strategies, practices, or tools that they were using which were seen as particularly useful, novel, or effective. At the close of the interview, the incubator manager was scheduled for a follow-up interview. The initial interview tapes were transcribed in a digested form and distributed to the project team. Practices that were either ambiguous, lacking in detail, or particularly interesting were addressed in the follow-up interviews. These taped interviews generally lasted 15-45 minutes, and the additional information was added to the composite transcript.

Data Analysis

Given the nature of the project, traditional approaches to data analysis played a minor role. We needed to develop summary statistics for the checklist data, as well as some limited comparative analyses of the same information (comparing urban vs. rural incubators, and those with close university affiliations vs. those without such affiliations). These are presented as a separate section in each of the chapters.

The magnitude of raw information provided by the incubators was significant, so the project team took several steps to identify and document key practices. First, the entire team reviewed the interview transcripts (individually, and as a group) to get consensus on which practices, strategies, and tools were the best choices to document as novel or best. The selected transcript materials were then drafted into standard prose descriptions of practices (or tools). These practice descriptions were then shared with the incubator managers from whence they came, via facsimile and/or mail. Most managers added detail, edited our write-ups, and clarified the descriptions.

These individual practice descriptions were then aggregated into categories and appropriate chapters, and edited again for clarity and transition. The draft set of practices in the form of a large manuscript was then shared with the 50+ incubator managers who were interviewed. They were asked to read the entire manuscript and note ambiguities and lack of detail about any or all of the practice descriptions.

Limitations of the Study

Despite the ambitious nature of the project, there were some built-in limitations to the approach. Most prominent was the simple limitation imposed by text descriptions for the best practices. Often, participants were reluctant to view their practices as novel because they engaged in them on a regular basis and were sure that others did as well. Moreover, it was difficult to get participants to describe every operational detail of a novel practice, strategy, or tool. Even if we had been successful in this type of detailed data collection, the resultant book would have been impossibly long. This problem may be resolved in the future with multimedia adjuncts to text descriptions of practices.

As described under **Data Collection Approach**, there was no attempt to gather validating data (e.g., outcome statistics) on the effectiveness of strategies, practices, and tools provided by incubator managers. Therefore, there is no way that the information provided can help the reader sort out in a more objective sense what is "best." If there were a standard set of outcomes or impact measures available for all programs, we could have examined the utility of different types or categories of practices. That was not the case, and this issue needs to be deferred to a future study.

There were also some limitations in how we drew the study sample. The weakness of our approach was that we had both a few "false positives" (organizations that were included, but which might have been inappropriate; for example, incubators that did not emphasize technology-based companies as much as expected), and an unknown number of "false negatives" (programs that we missed, but which should have been included). In our defense, we believe that the approach was self-correcting, or will be in the long run. For example, we tended not to get much in the way of best-practice descriptions from the false positives in the sample. In addition, if we view the benchmarking process as continuous and cumulative we can easily add missing false negatives in the future. Sample selection was also hampered by the general absence of standard (and available) performance benchmark measures.

Finally, it is not obvious from the results expressed in this book how the various discrete practices, strategies, and tools might be usefully combined in a super composite model of technology business incubation. At a practical level we expect that users of this book will see several good ideas among the documented practices and integrate them into their own programs. How these disparate program components will or should be pieced together remains a topic for another analysis.

Who Should Use This Book

This book is intended to benefit a variety of users. For one, we feel that the best practice descriptions will be of utility to managers of established programs who are interested in the continuous improvement of their services. We also expect that the descriptions herein will accelerate the program development process for newly established technology business incubators, or those in a planning stage. While the documentation is not sufficiently detailed to enable a "do-it-yourself" approach to program implementation, there are points of contact for additional information.

We also believe that this book should be of interest to economic development officials, particularly those exploring strategies to move beyond recruitment and into building and diversifying the existing economic base. We believe that the approaches described in this volume will be a useful adjunct to existing economic development strategies, particularly in areas that do not have a large base of technology industries.

In a like manner, because a majority of the incubators in the study sample were strongly affiliated with research universities, the book also should be of interest to university officials charged with intellectual property management and/or community outreach. While only a few of the examples are drawn from programs with linkages to federal labs, nonetheless the book also should be helpful to those involved in enhancing the technology transfer mission and performance of such facilities.

Finally, we feel that our results are of considerable relevance to political leadership at national, state, and local levels. In the long run, growing technology-based companies is too robust an economic development strategy to ignore. We are hopeful that there will be an increased degree of public investment and private-public partnerships in the technology business incubation programs and activities.

The following chapters cover each of eight practice domains. Each chapter begins with an introduction explaining the significance of the practice and summarizing the survey response and analysis. The "best practice" section of each chapter describes the various incubator programs and approaches.

Chapter 2

FINANCE AND CAPITALIZATION

Without adequate early-stage financing, even technology start-ups with the best ideas cannot transform themselves into successful businesses. Young companies need access to capital for research, prototype development, and testing. Companies can tap several types of financial resources, including private capital sources and networks, university-industry research partnerships, industry-government cooperative research and development, government-university collaborations, and state and federal programs to promote technology commercialization (Kearns, 1994).

Even with the variety of programs to finance technology commercialization, finding public or private investment willing to finance an "untested inventor" is no easy task. Private investors, or "angels," often provide the best source for early seed capital for emerging technology companies. These investors are more willing to take risks that other sources can't or won't take, and can make up their minds quickly (Ladin 1994).

Venture capitalists are another source of funding for technology companies, but are often out of reach for start-ups without a track record. Venture capitalists make highly selective investments in young companies with high growth potential. They usually become involved in the business at the early expansion stage and help finance production, marketing, and distribution, although sometimes they are willing to invest seed capital at an earlier stage (Eisinger, 1993). Venture sources are less likely to invest seed money now than they were in the 1980s, but they still play an important role in technology financing (Camp and Sexton, 1992).

In order to compete for business development activity, many states have developed venture capital pools to support small firms in research-oriented, innovative business sectors that have significant potential economic development payoffs (Eisinger, 1993). States that have venture capital pools will often invest seed capital at an earlier or riskier stage than private venture sources will (Ladin, 1994). States developed these pools on the theory that many companies cannot gain access to the market because they cannot raise the early equity capital. These state venture capital programs, which proliferated in the 1980s, are disappearing in the 1990s because of budget constraints, loss of political support, and inflexibility as compared to private venture funds (Eisinger, 1993).

Royalty financing is another financing method that is tailored to the needs of start-up businesses. In a royalty financing arrangement, capital is repaid from royalties on product sales. Companies get money early in the development process and do not have to begin paying it back until sales are generated. Royalty financing benefits include the fact that companies do not need to show assets for collateral, investors can achieve a return without huge amounts of sales growth, and the financing is "invisible"—no liability shows up on the balance sheet (Spragins, 1991).

The federal government has a variety of programs that aim to increase links between the public and private sector, facilitate technology commercialization, and increase global competitiveness. Federal programs that seek these goals include Small Business Innovation Research (SBIR) grants, the Technology Reinvestment Program (TRP), and the Advanced Technology Program (ATP). As this book is being written, some of these programs are under critical review because of congressional efforts to reduce overall federal spending. Nonetheless, it is likely that there will be a residue of federal funds which continue to be available for early-stage technology ventures.

Incubators play a major role in the acquisition of seed capital for early-stage technology companies. Essentially, all forms of business assistance provided by an incubator give start-ups an increased opportunity for capital acquisition. For instance, incubators help companies develop their management team and board of directors. Investors want to see a solid management team and believe that a weak one will mean business failure, even with the best technology (Ladin, 1994). Most incubators help companies develop their business plan and conduct market research, which is also crucial for financing. Through venture forums and with the help of financiers who often are on incubator boards, incubators give companies assistance in developing and practicing their finance presentations. Incubators also assist companies in obtaining SBIR support and applying for large federal grants. More directly, incubators operate seed capital pools and maintain formal or informal networks of angel investors and/or venture capitalists.

In the next section we will present descriptive statistics on the relative frequency and intensity of services provided by incubators in the area of finance and capitalization. As we will show, this is a major focus of most programs' activities.

OVERVIEW OF PRACTICES AND SERVICES: FINANCE AND CAPITALIZATION

We asked incubator managers to respond to a checklist of finance and capitalization practices and services provided to client companies. For each practice or service, managers were asked to indicate whether they provided the service or practice directly, brokered or referred the service or practice, did both, or did neither. The checklist had the effect of providing a scale of intensity for services and practices provided in the finance and capitalization area. The summary results are presented in Table 2.1 (next page).

The most common practices were providing access to seed capital, assisting in financial analysis, and gaining access to venture capital. Seed and venture capital are essential to starting and developing a business. Financial analysis is necessary for any early-stage business in order for it to plan its progress. The least common practice was arranging purchase order, or vendor, financing.[1] When provided, this service was usually provided by referral. The same is also true for royalty financing, which was also infrequently provided by incubators and even less often provided directly.

Summarizing these results, it would appear that incubators become involved in finance and capitalization practices that are more facilitative in nature and tend to avoid activities that are more techni-

Table 2.1: Finance and Capitalization Practices (valid percent responses)

	no, rarely/never	yes, by referral	yes, directly	both
provide access to seed capital	3.7	40.7	42.6	13.0
assist in financial analysis	5.5	21.8	56.4	16.4
help obtain venture capital financing	7.4	33.3	44.4	14.8
prepare financing proposals	7.4	31.5	42.6	18.5
obtain SBIR support	9.1	38.2	36.4	16.4
obtain bridge financing	13.2	64.2	22.6	0.0
facilitate corporate strategic partnering	15.1	24.1	44.4	16.7
provide assistance with large federal grants	15.1	49.1	26.4	9.4
assist in evaluation of tenant enterprises	21.6	35.3	33.3	9.8
organize joint ventures	27.8	29.6	33.3	9.3
obtain royalty financing	34.0	42.0	18.0	6.0
arrange purchase-order financing	43.1	41.2	15.7	0.0

cally complex or involve specialized knowledge. Purchase order financing and royalty financing are good examples of the latter.

We also conducted some comparative analyses among different categories of incubators. Table 2.2 (next page) compares services provided by university and non-university incubators.[2] We found none of the relationships between finance and capitalization practices and university affiliation to be statistically significant.[3]

Table 2.3 (next page) compares services provided by rural incubators with those in urban settings.[4] The relationship between urban location and assistance in obtaining venture capital financing was significant. This may be due to the greater availability of venture capital in urban areas. The relationship between urban location and assistance in obtaining bridge financing was also significant. This practice is usually referred by urban incubators, pointing to a greater availability of outside assistance in obtaining bridge financing. The relationship between location and assistance with large federal grants was significant. This service is both referred and provided in-house, pointing to greater expertise available in urban areas. Finally, we found a statistically significant relationship between urban location and assistance in evaluation of client businesses.

Data on the relationship between finance/capitalization services and urban/rural locations illustrate the fundamental problem for rural incubators. Small towns in rural areas are *not* centers of finance. Individuals who are knowledgeable about novel approaches to capitalizing technology ventures do not naturally migrate to these locations, and the resident banking and investment community tends to be conservative and careful.

In the next section, we will describe some of the more interesting and novel approaches to finance and capitalization. As we will show, these tend to reflect the trends described in the quantitative data.

Table 2.2: Finance and Capitalization Practices by Incubator University Affiliation (valid percent responses)

	no, rarely/never		yes, by referral		yes, directly		both	
	university	non	university	non	university	non	university	non
provide access to seed capital	3.2	5.6	41.9	33.3	38.7	50.0	16.1	11.1
assist in financial analysis	6.3	5.6	15.6	27.8	65.6	44.4	12.5	22.2
obtain SBIR support	6.3	16.7	37.5	38.9	40.6	33.3	15.6	11.1
help obtain venture capital financing	6.5	5.6	32.3	33.3	48.4	44.4	12.9	16.7
prepare financing proposals	9.7	5.6	35.5	22.2	38.7	55.6	16.1	16.7
provide assistance with large federal grants	12.9	23.5	41.9	47.1	38.7	11.8	6.5	17.6
obtain bridge financing	16.7	11.1	63.3	61.1	20.0	27.8	0.0	0.0
facilitate corporate strategic partnering	19.4	11.1	16.1	33.3	51.6	38.9	12.9	16.7
assist in evaluation of tenant enterprises	28.6	11.1	39.3	22.2	25.0	50.0	7.1	16.7
obtain royalty financing	32.1	35.3	42.9	41.2	21.4	11.8	3.6	11.8
organize joint ventures	32.3	22.2	29.0	27.8	35.5	33.3	3.2	16.7
arrange purchase order financing	41.4	41.2	44.8	47.1	13.8	11.8	0.0	0.0

Table 2.3: Finance and Capitalization Practices by Incubator Location (valid percent responses)

	no, rarely/never		yes, by referral		yes, directly		both	
	rural	urban	rural	urban	rural	urban	rural	urban
provide access to seed capital	7.1	2.5	57.1	35.0	28.6	47.5	7.1	15.0
assist in financial analysis	14.3	2.4	14.3	24.4	64.3	53.7	7.1	19.5
prepare financing proposals	14.3	5.0	50.0	25.0	28.6	47.5	7.1	22.5
obtain SBIR support	14.3	7.3	28.6	41.5	50.0	31.7	7.1	19.5
help obtain venture capital financing	21.4	2.5	57.1	25.0	14.3	55.0	7.1	17.5
obtain bridge financing	30.8	7.5	46.2	70.0	23.1	22.5	0.0	0.0
facilitate corporate strategic partnering	30.8	9.8	23.1	24.4	38.5	46.3	7.7	19.5
provide assistance with large federal grants	35.7	7.7	35.7	53.8	28.6	25.6	0.0	12.8
organize joint ventures	35.7	25.0	35.7	27.5	28.6	35.0	0.0	12.5
arrange purchase order financing	38.5	44.7	46.2	39.5	15.4	15.8	0.0	0.0
assist in evaluation of tenant enterprises	42.9	13.5	14.3	43.2	42.9	29.7	0.0	13.5
obtain royalty financing	46.2	29.7	30.8	45.9	23.1	16.2	0.0	8.1

Best Practices: Finance and Capitalization

Money (along with management and technology) is one of the prime foundations of a technology-based new company. The incubators in our study sample are involved in a wide variety of services, programs, and practices to serve their client companies in terms of finance and capitalization. Because many of the finance and capitalization approaches are combinations of grants, loans, and equity investment, and also run the gamut from very early to late stage finance, there was an overlapping of practices that did not lend themselves to discrete categorization. Nonetheless, the major categories of practices described include: 1) local seed funds; 2) tenancy-contingent funding; 3) university proof-of-concept funding; 4) state funds for advanced development; 5) venture funds; 6) loan programs; 7) an example of a foundation investment; and 8) conferences, presentations, and events.

Locally Organized Seed Funds

Several incubators have been involved in locally organized seed funds, with a significant portion of both capital and due diligence coming from local economic development agencies. Venture capital funds are in short supply, and often technology-based entrepreneurial companies have not reached a stage of development that can attract the interest of the typical venture funding. Very early stage or seed funding that accelerates technology development is a useful asset for an incubator. Moreover, geographically isolated incubators may have particular needs in this area. All the seed funds described in this section have some government money involved, and all have some focus on regional economic development.

The Evanston Business Investment Corporation (EBIC), located at the **Evanston Business and Technology Center (EBTC)**, Evanston, Illinois, is an early stage venture capital fund that makes equity investments in growth-oriented companies based in Evanston. Founded in 1986 as a nonprofit organization, EBIC has adopted a mission of encouraging entrepreneurship and new job creation in Evanston. EBIC initially raised $1 million from five institutions in Evanston: two local banks ($150,000 each), an insurance company and a local hospital ($200,000 each), and Northwestern University ($300,000). Each had different reasons for investing (CRA, charitable contributions, etc.). Founders of the fund initially set it up to be a revolving loan fund to help bolster the local economy by lending money to small businesses. The investments were limited to $50,000 and structured as 10-year notes. Because the fund's purpose was job creation and economic benefit to the community rather than financial return, the loans began to be structured as equity investments.

EBIC is currently forming a second fund that is structured more as a private fund but still is a component of the original fund and therefore is restricted to raising capital from Evanston companies. This fund is currently capitalized at $750,000 and is in the process of trying to raise up to another $1.5 million. EBIC has found that in trying to attract private investors who are interested in financial returns, rather than job creation, it is more difficult to raise the money in a community of Evanston's size.

EBIC invests only in potential high-growth ventures and structures its investments so as to provide the maximum potential for return. Matching investments from other sources are generally required, but the size of the match depends on the financial requirements of the applicant. Applicants must either be based in Evanston or make a commitment to relocate to Evanston within 90 days of EBIC's investment. As the fund has evolved, most of the investments have been in businesses located in the research park and the incubator.

In addition to a strong business plan and a capable management team, the principals of each applicant company must demonstrate that they have made a significant personal and financial commitment to the success of the business. The EBIC staff acts in an advisory capacity and generally requires representation on the boards of directors of each of the companies in its investment portfolio. EBIC has its own board of directors separate from the incubator. It also has an advisory board that includes representation from two established venture capital firms—one private, one public. This expands the exposure that businesses get when they apply for funding. As part of the EBTC network, EBIC is able to provide business planning assistance to incubator companies. EBIC has invested in 22 companies that have attracted an additional $29 million in capital.

The **State of Hawaii** established, through a one-time appropriation of $6.8 million, a seed fund that serves a resource for early-stage financing for incubator companies and small businesses. The purpose of the fund is to encourage economic development and diversification in Hawaii through investments organized in cooperation with private funding sources. The fund sought coinvestment with venture capital sources, managing to leverage the state's funding up to approximately $30 million.

One Hawaii-based venture capital limited partnership invests in start-up, emerging, and established companies located in the state of Hawaii, with an emphasis on high technology. The method of investing is through separate limited partnerships and closely held corporations. The venture capital fund will purchase up to a maximum of 50 percent of the limited partnership units while the other units are purchased by third parties who may not be directly involved with the company. The state's investments in businesses include an equity interest without a repurchase agreement for at least five years, royalties, a right or option to purchase equity interests, a debenture or loan whether or not convertible or having stock purchase rights, and limited partnership interests.

The **Technology Development Center** (TDC) of West Sacramento, California, a for-profit incubator, has established two seed funds to provide early-stage financing for incubator and other companies meeting its criteria. The TDC serves as the general partner in the fund, and other investors, most of whom have technology backgrounds, serve as limited partners in the funds. The funds serve as lead investor in the portfolio companies. The funds are currently $450,000 and $600,000, and investments typically range from $25,000 to $75,000. To protect investments, TDC incubates each company to increase the probability of success and lower the risk.

Start-up technology businesses located in Pennsylvania business incubators have access to royalty financing for product development and commercialization through the **Emerging Company Investment Fund**, administered by the four Ben Franklin Technology Centers.

The Emerging Company Investment Fund provides seed capital to companies with products that have demonstrated technical and market feasibility. Funds are to be used to commercialize and develop the product, through such activities as intellectual property protection, alpha or beta testing, third-party investments, and strategic alliances. Under royalty financing agreements, companies are expected to repay the investments based on their sales, beginning in the first quarter after funding. Repayment is three percent of sales per quarter, limited to three times the initial investment. Prepayment, or predetermining maximum repayment, may be arranged to limit the amount of repayment. Companies that do not have sales are not required to repay the investment until they do, which is one of characteristics of royalty finance.

Investments are awarded to companies with 100 or fewer employees and a new technology or a new application of existing technology. Generally investments are made for projects lasting one year; a maximum of three investments may be made in any one company. The application process is competitive, including a technical evaluation, and may include a commercial evaluation and a presentation to an advisory committee. These evaluations and other materials submitted by applicants are kept confidential. Cash or in kind matching funds—in a ratio of two to one—are required for each dollar requested of the Emerging Company Investment Fund. Investments range from $50,000 to $100,000; the average investment is $75,000.

Iowa State Innovation System (ISIS) helped to start and organize the **Ames Seed Capital Fund** in the early 1980s. The fund is now operated by the Ames Economic Development Commission. Thus far about $750,000 of investments have been made, with a large percentage going into incubator-affiliated companies. In order to facilitate the investments by the Ames Seed Capital Fund, the SBDC and ISIS together provide some degree of due diligence. This yields a fairly high hit rate for presentations to the fund. In addition, the mechanics of the Seed Fund work so that there is a five-to-one leverage of funds.

The **Wichita Technology Corporation (WTC)**, which operates somewhat like an "incubator without walls" as part of the Kansas Technology Enterprise Corporation (KTEC) system, has built-in access to capital resources. WTC is a not-for-profit corporation that is associated with a for-profit seed capital corporation, Wichita Holdings. This entity makes early-stage investments in new enterprises. When Wichita Technology Corporation (WTC) identifies a technology enterprise, it will pass it over to Wichita Holdings. However, WTC functions as the fund manager for Wichita Holdings, since the latter has no employees *per se*. WTC has a management contract with Wichita holdings to provide due diligence services for its portfolio of investments. The president of WTC is also the president of Wichita Holdings, although the companies are physically separated. The seed fund was originally capitalized with a combination of funds from KTEC and other local sources, such as a local economic development organization.

All of the seed funds described above have been successful by some measure. All have leveraged significant private investment monies, and all have built what appear to be promising portfolios. In each case the incubator has played a significant role in nurturing, managing, or brokering the fund. What remains to be seen is how many big winners emerge from these early investments.

Tenancy-Contingent Financing

One wrinkle on capitalization has been the bundling of capital availability into tenancy status. That is, once a company is admitted to the incubator, one of the "entitlements" it gains is access to finance, assuming that the company is on-track in its development.

The **Arizona Technology Incubator** formed a unique venture capital seed fund called the **Arizona Technology Venture Fund (ATVF)**. It is unique in that every company accepted into the incubator has access to an immediate $25,000 investment in return for ATVF taking equity in the company. The Arizona Technology Venture Fund is a for-profit limited partnership that is completely independent of the incubator. The incubator manager manages ATVF's funds but has a venture fund board that approves all investments.

Every company admitted to the incubator can access the $25,000 immediately, although some firms do not ask for the money. If the investment is made, ATVF enters into an agreement with the company regarding its value and the equity share ATVF receives for the $25,000 investment. A company can access a follow-up investment from ATVF if it has other backers who will put in three to five times as much as ATVF invests.

The ATVF does not normally restrict the usage of the investment, but may stipulate the use if a need is identified. For instance, if a company is in dire need of a prototype before any more progress can be made, ATVF may restrict the usage of the investment to prototype development only. Use of the funds for salaries is restricted.

Money to capitalize this fund was difficult to raise. Venture capitalists outside the area were initially willing to support the fund, but local venture capitalists were not, so the outside investors declined as well. The incubator then went to supporters such as local utilities and banks, as well as a venture capital firm from Utah and a family investment group from San Diego. Arizona state government also loaned money to ATI under the stipulation that it be placed in the investment fund, so ATI is the major holder in the fund (approximately 40 percent).

Although there is almost no stipulation on what the money can be used for, the companies use the investment for such crucial needs as market research, travel to customer facilities, and prototype development. This up-front investment can give companies the boost they need in order to be successful.

The **Massachusetts Biotechnology Research Institute (MBRI) Innovation Center** has developed an arrangement wherein MBRI gives companies financial support through a budget determined prior to acceptance into the Innovation Center, in exchange for an equity position in the company.

This arrangement allows the early-stage start-up companies access to the Innovation Center's services without the need to make cash payments. The budget provided also acts as an impetus to business planning by providing milestones for the company toward its development and eventual graduation from the Innovation Center.

The Center negotiates the amount of equity taken with each company upon entry, taking into account expenses such as equipment, lab supplies, utilities, space, and personnel, and such issues as whether or not to account for the depreciated value of equipment to be purchased. It also establishes milestones for the company's research and plans an "exit route" including timing, goals, and venture capital needed.

Funding of companies is provided by the MBRI's nonprofit venture capital company. If the venture capital company decides not to fund a company, other funding will be found by the Innovation Center. The Center only accepts companies for which funding can be found. MBRI tends to admit companies with a high likelihood of success and assured financial support, and provides intensive services in exchange for equity.

The **Metropolitan Center for High Technology (MCHT)** of Detroit, Michigan, takes a somewhat different approach to this issue. Its funds are all internal to the incubator organization and controlled by the board. Money comes from MCHT reserves, so the size of awards tends to be small. Money is primarily for the development of product prototypes. The awards are structured as loans, although the incubator will typically take a one to three percent royalty position on future sales as part of the deal.

University Proof-of-Concept Funding

University inventors may be a source of the core technology on which a new company might be based. However, in many cases this technology is in a very early stage, often literally or figuratively "wired together" in laboratory mockups. It is necessary to move to a working prototype, which will better demonstrate a proof-of-concept. Given the technical and business risk in such situations, private sources of capital are relatively rare, even from seed or angel investors.

Some university-based incubators have developed funding programs to address this very early stage of technology development. They typically involve significant government support. The **Advanced Technology Development Center (ATDC)** has the opportunity to use funds from the **Faculty Research Commercialization Program (FRCP)** of the Georgia Research Alliance. FRCP is currently funded at $500,000 annually from state funds administered by the Georgia Research Alliance. The awards are available to faculty at all universities that belong to the Georgia Research Alliance. (This includes Georgia Tech, the University of Georgia, Emory, the Medical College of Georgia, and Georgia State.) Individual awards are in the range of $20,000 to $100,000, and the work must be done in a 12-month period. Funding is explicitly targeted toward development, and the desired outcome or deliverable is a prototype or near-prototype that could become the basis for establishing a new company.

Annually in February a formal solicitation is issued and distributed to the member universities of the alliance. Preproposal conferences are held at the universities to discuss FRCP requirements. Faculty would-be entrepreneurs apply through their university, with ATDC playing a major role in organizing the proposal process and administering the review cycle. ATDC asks that proposals specify clear milestones, deliverables, and commercialization strategy. After an initial staff screening, the proposals are reviewed by *ad hoc* panels that are pulled together based on the content area addressed by the proposal. The review panels typically consist of three to five individuals drawn from big and small companies, and university and/or laboratory researchers. Selection criteria include scientific and technical innovativeness, market potential, qualifications of personnel, likely impact of an award, outside cofunding, relevance to the Georgia economy, and job creation potential.

Not all applicants have taken the steps to protect the intellectual property represented by their technology, but they are urged to do so. If prototype development projects are successful, they can lead either to direct licensing to an existing company or to a start-up (which might be based in the incubator). Therefore, emerging entrepreneurs from any of the universities may end up in the facility at Georgia Tech. If an award is made, funds are not given out in their entirety, but they are doled out as milestones are achieved. In addition, for larger awards (more than $50,000) there is a request for a corporate match.

Another example of funding for prototype development is found at **UBC Research Enterprises** at the University of British Columbia in Vancouver, Canada. UBC has established a prototype development group that is a for-profit subsidiary (albeit at "arms-length") of the university, set up to mature research-based technologies and develop prototypes. Money for the projects comes from the National Research Council (NRC) through its Industrial Research Assistance Program (IRAP) and from the university. Funds are routed through the prototype development group, which picks promising faculty technology. Awards are in the form of grants rather than loans or equity investments. Although the IRAP and the NRC are national programs, they are administered on a provincial (state-level) basis. This means that the service manager in British Columbia is relatively autonomous from Ottawa (as with block grants in the United States). If the staff at UBC Research Enterprises believes a prototype project has merit, they make a recommendation to IRAP, and decisions are made rapidly. This permits speed and flexibility in the processing of awards. Money can flow in as little as two to three weeks, and the prototype development can be done in university labs. The resulting prototype is not pre-production in its level of development, but a more rudimentary reduced-to-practice device, albeit suitable to present to potential licensees and/or investors. The development process is not just the creation of a physical prototype. It includes a market analysis conducted by office staff working with the inventor. In order to facilitate this process, the office offers grants of more than $20,000 to support marketing studies.

The **Center for Advanced Technology Development (CATD)** is a program operated out of the Department of Energy's Ames Laboratory, which in turn is managed by **Iowa State University**. The CATD has an annual budget of approximately $3 million (part U.S. Deparment of Commerce, part state money) that is dedicated to the support of projects intended to "de-risk" university technology. It holds an annual solicitation within the university, primarily focused on the physical sciences and engineering. Short (three to four page) proposals are requested for emerging technologies that seem to have some commercialization potential but still have some significant technical risks to surmount. *Ad hoc* review panels are convened, which include input from private sector people. Of 50 proposals, CATD typically funds about 10 one-year projects, each in the range of $50,000 to $400,000. Most projects are, in effect, prototype development efforts and/or reduction to practice. During their projects, the researchers work closely with the management of the ISIS incubator so that if they're successful, they can move quickly to a start-up situation.

All of the programs described above report significant downstream benefits that increase the likelihood that a viable company will result. For example, UBC spin-off companies have attracted $60 million in follow-on investment. ATDC reports that several recipients of Faculty Commercialization grants have gone on to establish companies, become tenants in the incubator, and ultimately graduate. The CATD at Iowa State reports similar results from its de-risking projects, with about 50 percent of the tenants in the ISIS incubator having gone through CATD funding.

State Funds for Advanced Development

In many states, the government has established or taken part in special programs to support applied research, product development, and other activities. These programs tend to have many of the features of seed funds or prototype development funds already described. However, state government tends to play more of a role and place fewer restrictions on how the money can be used. These programs are *not* targeted to incubators or their tenants, but incubators make extensive use of them, nonetheless.

The **GENESIS Technology Incubator (GTI)** at the University of Arkansas-Fayetteville was established by the university using a grant from the Arkansas Science and Technology Authority (ASTA). This state agency, which is independent of the university system, was organized to facilitate the development and dissemination of science and technology for economic development in Arkansas. The authority also offers various financial assistance programs to provide support for new technology-dependent businesses. Programs include funds for prototype development, acquisition of specialized scientific equipment, energy-related technologies, and bridge funding for SBIR grant recipients. The incubator's staff is knowledgeable about the application procedures, funding deadlines, and selection criteria, and helps companies prepare support applications.

The ASTA funds are capitalized by state appropriations, and awards are structured as grants or loans. Availability of funds depends upon annual state legislative action and payback from previously funded companies. Application procedures require a proposal using the authority's prescribed forms. These proposals are subject to competitive review on a recurring cycle. Support of proposals judged to have technical merit is dependent upon fund availability in each separate program category (prototype development, energy technologies, and bridge financing). Close working relationships between the incubator management and the staff of the ASTA allow incubator management to provide knowledge-able advice and assistance to tenant companies as they prepare proposals. Because the incubator sub-jects its tenant companies to careful scrutiny and evaluates their technical goals and objectives during admission and periodically thereafter, these companies tend to be at a competitive advantage, even without specific intercession on their behalf by incubator management or by the leadership of the University of Arkansas. This has resulted in an 80 percent approval rate for proposals from GTI ten-ant companies, which is high compared to the rate for all proposals.

Being able to compete successfully for state-sponsored funding gives tenant companies an impor-tant advantage in their efforts to prove technical concepts and develop prototypes, and, more general-ly, for financial and technical viability as commercial ventures.

Incutech Brunswick, Inc. utilizes the Atlantic Canada Opportunities Agency (ACOA) to help tenant firms obtain product development and bridge financing. ACOA is the regional agency respon-sible for leading economic development and job creation efforts in Atlantic Canada. ACOA's Business Development Program offers access to capital in the form of interest-free, unsecured loans. The maxi-mum level of assistance is 50 percent of the total cost for start-ups, expansions, modernizations, and related costs, such as equipment, leasehold improvements, working capital, and construction, and 75 percent of the total cost for operating costs such as studies, marketing, training, and quality assurance. Projects must demonstrate viability, economic benefit to an area or community, and the need for financial assistance. ACOA maintains offices in New Brunswick, Newfoundland, Nova Scotia, Prince Edward Island, and Cape Breton.

The North Carolina Technological Development Authority, Inc. (TDA), which manages the **First Flight Venture Center, Inc.**, draws upon the Innovation Research Fund (IRF), a seed investment fund that invests in high-growth businesses. IRF's mission is to serve the capital needs of high-growth start-up companies, including those in the First Flight Center. It also seeks to develop and commercialize technologies.

The IRF is state-funded and is currently capitalized at approximately $3 million. Investments range from $50,000 to $250,000 per company, usually in the form of equity or an instrument con-vertible to equity. Investments are usually staged based upon pre-determined milestones.

The IRF manager, located in the First Flight Venture Center, provides incubator tenants with assistance in qualifying for funds from the IRF. The IRF is interested in funding companies with strong management teams, quality products, and expanding markets. To apply for funding, a compa-ny submits a business plan that includes a description of the product, the market opportunity, the management team background, current and *pro forma* financial statements, and an explanation of how funding will be used.

Funded companies also receive monitoring assistance from the IRF management, including moni-toring of agreed-upon milestones. As most applicants for funding come from outside the incubator, the IRF serves as a source of new incubator companies.

The **Ben Franklin Partnership (BFP)** is an economic development program that was created by the Pennsylvania General Assembly in 1982. Focusing on the development and application of advanced technology, the mission of the Partnership is to support initiatives which will strengthen the state's economy. Investments made by the Partnership are intended to lead to job creation and retention, economic diversification, creation of new advanced technology enterprises, improvement in the competitive ability of technology-oriented companies with emphasis on young, small ventures, and development of a technologically skilled work force. Another goal of the program is to develop effective partnerships between universities and the private sector.

The partnership is managed by a 15-member board that approves funding for various programs and gives final approval for all individual initiatives that are supported with BFP dollars. The largest program administered by the board is the **Challenge Grant Program for Technological Innovation**.

The Challenge Grant program is highly decentralized. Four Ben Franklin Technology Centers (BFTCs) have been established through which BFP funds are used to support local initiatives. The BFTCs are independent nonprofit corporations, governed by boards made up of both private industry executives and university officials. These centers are responsible for identifying and generating technology innovation opportunities.

The Challenge Grant Program is normally funded at $20 million to $30 million on an annual basis. For 1995 to 1996, each BFTC will receive approximately $6.3 million. A portion of the funds (30 to 40 percent) is directed to entrepreneurs, start-up companies, and early-stage firms. The entity must be a product developer, manufacturer, or prospective manufacturer in Pennsylvania. Funds can be invested directly into the company to support product development efforts or allocated to universities which, in turn, provide technical support to the company. Some combination of the two funding schemes also can be allocated. The Challenge Grant Program for early-stage firms also is called the Innovation Program, the Seed Grant Program, Research and Development Funding, and Technology Development Funding. The different names pertain to the level of funding, the presence of university assistance, and whether or not the company is a first-time awardee. The general purpose of the funding is support of the company's product development efforts.

An early-stage firm requests funds by submitting a proposal and business plan to the BFTC that handles the region where the company is located. Typically, BFTCs can invest up to $100,000 per year for up to three years in early-stage companies.

Any early-stage firm in Pennsylvania that meets the BFP criteria can contact a BFTC to get proposal information. Business incubator centers in Pennsylvania can facilitate the process by helping their clients prepare viable proposals. Since funds are awarded on a competitive basis, the business incubator center can provide valuable input in preparation of a strong proposal.

Most of the Pennsylvania business incubator centers have strong linkages with the BFTCs. There is one unique situation in which the Northeast Tier (NET) BFTC manages its own technology incubator facility, located at Lehigh University in Bethlehem, Pennsylvania.

The **Technology Enterprise Center** of University of Maryland Baltimore County refers companies to the Maryland Challenge Investment Program (CIP), which provides funding of up to $50,000 to start-up technology companies in the state. The Challenge Investment Program provides early-stage technology companies with initial financing support for the commercialization of new technology-driven products and services. The funds are used to further develop the company's product or service and are not intended for basic research or to support existing products. The investment is designed to help offset the costs of final testing and market development. The program started out as a grant program in 1989, and is now an investment program, administered by the Department of Employment and Economic Development.

Challenge investment funding is available to Maryland-based companies having significant potential for growth. The companies may have no more than 25 employees and must have annual sales revenues of $1 million or less. To be eligible, applicants must have a comprehensive marketing and business plan, complete with executive summary and financial projections. Applicants go through a screening process using both internal state resources and outside experts. This highly competitive process may include oral presentations to a multidisciplined review panel. The state makes every effort to maintain the security of confidential information but does not accept responsibility or liability if such efforts fail.

The criteria for investment include the market potential for the technology, the ability of the company to attract private investment, the description of the product/service/ market, the impact of the product or service on the Maryland economy, and the credibility of the company's three-year financial projections.

The Challenge Investment Program targets the following industries: information technologies, electronics, precision manufacturing, environmental services/technology, life sciences, telecommunications, biotechnology, and health services.

Each challenge investment is $50,000. A CIP recipient must match the challenge investment with a private sector, third-party coinvestor match or commitment of $50,000. The term of the investment agreement is for a maximum of 10 years. Repayment terms are linked to the company's performance, and the challenge investments are recoverable if the venture is successful.

Two of the incubator companies in the Technology Enterprise Center have received challenge investments. The companies' location in the incubator and the incubator manager's recommendations were important factors in getting the funding. Direct equity investments enable the state to realize much greater returns on investments compared to grants and fixed returns from more traditional financing programs.

Venture Finance

As entrepreneurial companies mature both their technologies and their businesses, they become candidates for full-scale commercialization and venture levels of capitalization. Incubator programs themselves typically do not operate venture funds, but they can have direct or brokered access to such funds. One approach may be to develop brokering or networking programs that link to several potential sources of venture funds. Venture financing, particularly larger deals, will often signal the departure of the company from incubator tenancy.

The **Bio-Business Incubator of Michigan** is a subsidiary of the Michigan Biotechnology Institute (MBI), a major R&D facility. Another subsidiary of MBI is **Grand River Technologies (GRT)**, whose mission is to commercialize companies with "investment-grade" technologies, or those with a package of patents, technical know-how, documentation, and business opportunities. This is accomplished through joint ventures, outlicensing, and other arrangements. GRT has a separate board from MBI, and typically will take an equity share with companies in which it is involved. GRT works closely with the venture capital community, primarily through an arrangement with Seaflower Associates, a Boston-based venture development firm. GRT and Seaflower work with companies to prepare them for financing. This may involve working with and/or replacing management, intensive market planning, or developing funding presentations and prospectuses.

The **Rensselaer Polytechnic Institute (RPI) Incubator Center** has two venture capitalists on its advisory board who provide one-on-one consultations with tenant companies. Twice a year, RPI arranges private one-on-one sessions for tenant companies with leading venture capitalists. During these sessions, the venture capitalist spends three to five hours with each company and discusses its prospects from a venture capitalist's perspective.

Tenant companies are usually selected by the incubator manager based on the firm's financial needs, the industry sector of interest to the venture capitalist, and the likelihood that the firm will meet basic investment criteria of typical venture capitalists.

RPI also arranges formal, public presentations to venture capitalists. During the formal sessions, business plans are presented at a venture capital forum that includes local bankers. All sessions are provided as a service to the incubator, and there is no guarantee that a venture capitalist will provide funding to a tenant company.

While RPI does not provide capital to its tenants, the relationships they develop with venture capitalists can prove invaluable. Moreover, these sessions serve as reality checks for the entrepreneur. To date, incubator companies have received more than $500,000 in commercial financing based on these introductions. Two additional incubator firms are actively engaged in conversations with interested venture capitalists.

The **Office for the Advancement of Developing Industries (OADI)** incubator in Birmingham, Alabama, is one of a series of technology development and commercialization vehicles that the University of Alabama at Birmingham has established, either unilaterally or in cooperation with officials of the City of Birmingham and the State of Alabama. A venture capital fund is also part of this initiative. The fund has a target to raise and place approximately $30 million over the coming one-to-two-year period. Approximately one-third of that amount was raised prior to October 1994. Tenants and associates of the OADI incubator are welcome to seek financing from this source.

The fund is managed independently of the OADI incubator and the university. The fund manager is experienced in venture capital financing and in operating start-up technology-dependent ventures. The fund's degree of independence provides confidence to investors that the management will invest in ventures purely on the basis of their technical and business merit, rather than on other considerations. Incubator management does not make recommendations or specifically advocate financing for any tenant or associate. The incubator, however, facilitates introductions and provides assistance to tenants in preparing financial and technical plans for presentation to the venture capital fund management. These organizationally independent roles allow both the venture capital fund and the incubator to play their proper roles in this process. The incubator provides support services for the company, and the venture capital fund remains independent and free to make decisions on financial and conventional risk criteria.

The availability of locally managed venture capital, available to finance new ventures at seed and start-up levels, provides an advantage to firms starting out in the Birmingham area. It allows firms to remain and develop in Birmingham, rather than necessitating relocation or acquisition by a firm in a distant location with better access to financing. This provides a greater likelihood of success for ventures starting in the incubator.

The **Capital Network, Inc. (TCN)** is an Austin, Texas-based company that is one of the nation's largest seed and venture capital networks. TCN is a nonprofit economic development corporation that matches emerging companies with potential investors. These investors include individuals, venture capital firms, and corporate investors, although most are individuals. TCN also educates companies and investors on business financing issues and links emerging companies with professional business expertise.

TCN serves entrepreneurs that have the potential for significant growth. These entrepreneurs need earlier-stage financing or smaller amounts of financing than can typically be raised from more traditional or later-stage sources. TCN helps the entrepreneur bridge the gap between personal and family/friend money and later-stage capital. This capital gap continues to grow, as venture sources get into deals later to improve their averages, and other sources such as Small Business Administration (SBA) loans increase their qualifying requirements. A wide network of potential investors is needed to find links for companies.

TCN compiles a database of potential investors and available deals. Investors describe their over-all investment interests, and entrepreneurs describe the characteristics of their ventures. TCN deter-mines potential matches and sends the investor a summary profile of suitable ventures. Investors and entrepreneurs are matched based on six criteria: industry, size of venture, age of venture, amount of funding, location of venture, and type of investment. The matching process initially keeps both par-ties' identities confidential. After reviewing the summaries, investors decide if they would like to be introduced to any of the ventures listed. TCN facilitates the introduction but does not get involved in any potential deals. The fee for entrepreneurs to be listed with TCN is $450 for six months. Private investors pay $450 for a one-year registration, and institutional investors pay $950 for a one-year reg-istration.

TCN also coordinates support services for entrepreneurs. Topics include business plan develop-ment and deal structuring. TCN sponsors "venture fairs" featuring high-growth companies that make brief presentations to an audience of investors. TCN also maintains a nationwide reference list of individuals and firms that can assist growing companies with business development.

The **Austin Technology Incubator** (ATI) uses TCN for its tenant firms, which get a free listing because ATI and TCN are sister organizations. Although most incubator firms are not ready for ven-ture capital, some ATI companies have raised seed level money through TCN, and it has been a good resource for the incubator. The **Boulder Technology Incubator (BTI)** is working to create a regional investor network and plans to link with TCN to share investors. This arrangement advances TCN's mission to cooperate in efforts to facilitate new partnerships between entrepreneurial ventures and investors.

TCN is an important vehicle for companies who are ready for venture capital. It has assisted entrepreneurial ventures in raising almost $25 million since 1989. Investors in the network benefit from an increased flow of investment opportunities provided in a confidential and cost-effective man-ner. Entrepreneurs benefit from being reviewed by and receiving feedback from many potential investors, both in-state and out-of-state. One problem for incubator companies that utilize this sys-tem is that many incubator companies are not financially sophisticated enough to negotiate the deals once the match has been made, and there is no negotiator/facilitator in the TCN process.

The **Colorado Advanced Technology Enterprise** (CATE) is a statewide technology investment mechanism being formed by the Colorado Technology Leadership Group to create various methods for funding technology-based start-ups. The manager of the **Boulder Technology Incubator**, who represents Colorado incubators in the Leadership Group, is playing a leading role in the efforts to develop the funding sources. One of CATE's initiatives is to create a pool of investment capital from a variety of public and private sources, as well as a regional angel capital network that will link deals with investors by means of an electronic database. CATE is currently putting the angel network together, which is the key to this early-stage financing process. The incubator will have a network of its own and create alliances with other networks such as TCN to share investors and increase the pool. CATE's capital network will help bridge the early-stage capital funding gap, in which the entrepreneur has run out of personal and family/friend money, but is not ready for conventional debt financing.

CATE has an 11-member board of directors drawn from successful technology-based businesses in the area. There is also a state government representative on the board to keep a tie to state funding for operating expenses. CATE has gained acceptance from the state to begin funding efforts for the capital pool and hire a professional money manager. The board members are working to gain the interest of significant sources of capital such as pension funds. The capital raised by CATE for technology investment will be a blind pool of money, managed not by the board, but by a manager hired by the board, who will come out of a background such as venture capital or investment banking.

Another product of CATE, the venture capital network, will go beyond Colorado to access enough deals to keep private investors involved. In addition, CATE's capital network would involve many management advisory sources such as certified management consultants, venture fairs, and seminars for investors and entrepreneurs. Deals will be put into an electronic database, which will go out to representatives of private investors in order to get them to sign up as part of the investment network. Private investors that join will be listed in a database by areas of investment interest. The deal and the investor can then be linked electronically. For example, an investor interested in diagnostic medical devices would be shown several candidate companies in the electronic database. The database will include a one-page summary of the company and a contact number that the investor's representative can call. The network will probably not charge a fee initially but will begin charging when the system is fully active. Utilizing angel networks, venture capital, and national linkages, the Colorado Advanced Technology Enterprise will offer a comprehensive approach to helping start-up technology firms access capital.

Loan Programs

As entrepreneurial companies mature, they need to develop an ongoing relationship with sources of debt financing. However, initiating these relationships can be difficult for an enterprise with few if any customers, little capital, often unproven technology, and negligible collateral for loans. As a result, incubators have evolved some creative ways of brokering or facilitating loan arrangements.

The **Tri-Cities Enterprise Association (TEA)**, along with government and university partners, accessed $987,000 from the U.S. Dept. of Energy's 1993 Defense Authorization Act Defense Authorization grants for diversifying economic development. The funding helped establish the Entrepreneur Support Network, which 1) provides entrepreneur success training through the SBDC-sponsored Fast-Trac Program, 2) allows access to the Office Resource Center at the incubator, and 3) capitalizes a $600,000 equity investment fund.

The equity investment fund is broken into two loan funds. One fund, the Micro Equity Fund, was capitalized at $100,000 and makes loans of $15,000 to $30,000. The incubator manages this pool. The Micro Equity loans start as debt but can be converted to equity (TEA takes stock in the company and forgives a portion or all of the borrower's debt).

The other pool, the Capital Fund, was capitalized with $500,000 and makes larger loans. This pool is managed by the Benton-Franklin Regional Council. The Capital Fund allows for creative debt financing, such as interest forgiven the first year. These loans cannot be converted to equity, however.

The loan funds are attempting to leverage local matches with the $600,000 DOE money. TEA also has an additional $400,000 Microloan fund that high-tech and other companies can access for capital in amounts of up to $25,000.

Companies in the **Rutgers/CARR Business Innovation Center** (BIC) have access to a guaranteed small business loan pool set up by the City of New Brunswick and a consortium of local banks. While funds are available to any small business, incubator companies have an advantage in applying for the loan funds. The guaranteed loan pool allows small businesses to gain access to debt financing more easily than through the traditional commercial bank procedure.

The loan pool was set up by a consortium of local banks, each contributing $100,000. The City of New Brunswick provides a 50 percent loan guarantee from Urban Development Action Grant (UDAG) loan repayments. As of late 1994, the pool contained about $900,000. Loans average around $60,000 but may go as high as $150,000 to a single company. The funds may be used for any purpose, although funders prefer that the money not be used for working capital. The rate is prime plus two percent. While these loans are somewhat easier to obtain than debt financing from a bank, the process takes a long time. The loan decisions are made by bank representatives who look at both repayment potential and economic development criteria (such as job creation). These decisions tend to favor incubator tenants, which are more stable and likely to succeed. Since the pool was founded, two-thirds of the loans have gone to incubator tenants. It has been a useful funding source to incubator companies, but not the only source of financing they seek.

The **Idaho Innovation Center** has initiated a $1 million revolving loan fund that can be used to help companies purchase equipment or meet other needs. The fund provides needed financial resources for companies and does so without having to go outside the incubator. Funds are generally used for equipment purchases and to help meet the expense of modifying incubator facilities for new tenants, but they can also be used for working capital. The minimum loan amount is $1,000 and the maximum is $250,000. The rate/term for working capital is prime plus one to five percent for 60 days to five years; the rate/term for fixed assets is prime plus one to three percent for not more than 20 years or the useful life of the fixed asset. Some flexibility is allowed in rates and terms, depending on the borrower's needs. Interest rate subsidies or interest credits may be offered to businesses that hire and keep dislocated employees for at least one year.

Eligible borrowers include new and emerging high-tech businesses, businesses started by dislocated workers, and business start-ups or expansions that are committed to hiring dislocated workers. Businesses must be located in Bonneville County to access the fund. Selection criteria include a turn-down letter from a bank or private lender, and an emphasis on job-creating projects (at least one job must be created for every $50,000 of loan funds advanced). Loan funds cannot be used to finance existing debt.

The revolving loan fund is funded by the Economic Development Authority (EDA) along with county and state sources. Loan decisions are made by a board of directors, composed of loan committee members of the incubator's board of directors.

The **Metropolitan Center for High Technology (MCHT)** has developed a loan fund to address this need. The fund is administered by the MCHT staff, with decision-making input from members of the executive committee of the board. It consists of restricted money within the MCHT budget. The original financing for the fund came from a consortium of local bankers and the auto companies in Detroit but now is part of the MCHT operational budget. The work-up for a loan usually takes about two to three hours of staff time, and loans can be arranged in a matter of days. Loans are less than $20,000, with money being dedicated to specific product development or company development needs. Terms are typically less than six months, with various repayment schedules.

The **Montgomery County Technology Enterprise Center (MCTEC)** worked with local banks to create a loan pool for start-up technology business financing. The Suburban Maryland High Technology Council, MCTEC's managing organization, worked with eight to 10 local banks to capitalize a loan pool accessible to all small technology firms in the area, including incubator clients. Firms apply for loans through the Council. Loans can be used for working capital, equipment purchases, and other business development expenses, but they cannot be used for research and development. The Maryland Industrial Development Financing Authority has a loan guarantee program that guarantees 80 percent of the outstanding principal balance of each outstanding loan, so banks are only risking 20 percent of their investment, and that risk is spread throughout the pool.

Banks feel safer investing in small technology firms if they can share the loss and get loan guarantees. As part of the pool they will make loans that they would not make individually. Besides providing a source for immediate capital, the Suburban Maryland High Technology Council is also working to create a climate in which banks feel comfortable lending to technology companies. The loan pool is not designed to last forever, but it will get banks acclimated to lending to small technology firms. It is hoped that they will continue to do so on an individual basis after the loan pool is dissolved.

The **CYBER Center** (County of York Business and Entrepreneurial Resource Center), through its sponsor and owner, the York County Industrial Development Corporation (YCIDC), functions as the local administrator of a variety of small business loan funds. Financial backing for incubator companies can be provided by a variety of funding sources. Federal, state, and local government loan programs are used. When the local loan administrator is the incubator, tenants' financial needs can often be met through one source.

The Pennsylvania Department of Commerce has designated certain community economic development organizations to act as local administering entities for many of its loan programs. In York County, YCIDC and its sister organizations handle the economic development functions. The incubator manager works with a number of the sister organizations, as well as being a "loan broker" for the incubator. When an incubator client is in need of loan assistance a team approach can be brought to bear. CYBER administers all of the smaller loan programs, while a colleague at YCIDC administers the larger ones.

The Pennsylvania Capital Loan Fund (PCLF) is operated by the Center. The purpose of this fund is to foster the creation of long-term new employment opportunities through low-interest loans to businesses for capital development projects. This is the smallest dollar-amount loan fund provided by the state. Loan limits are set at $200,000 or 50 percent of the total project cost, whichever is less. Maximum loans for working capital are $100,000. Terms range from three years for working capital to 10 years for land and building acquisition. The rate is set at five percent per annum or three percent for apparel and agricultural processors. A private sector match is required. Fees include: a $500 nonrefundable application fee, a one percent commitment fee (minimum $500), and any out-of-pocket fees incurred in preparation of the loan package.

Manufacturing, industrial, and export services, and advanced technology and computer-related services are eligible, if they increase Pennsylvania's national or international market share. Loans are secured by lien positions on collateral, at the highest level of priority that can accommodate the borrower's ability to raise sufficient debt and equity match. All 20 percent-or-more owners of the company are required to personally guarantee the loan. Applicants must have 100 or fewer full-time equivalent employees. Export service companies must show that more than 51 percent of their sales are made outside Pennsylvania. Professionally prepared financial statements must be submitted. Phase I environmental audits must be conducted for all real-estate-related projects. Commitment letters must be obtained from all other sources of funding. In addition, the company must demonstrate that it will generate sufficient cash flow to service the debt. The terms also specify that for each $15,000 of PCLF funds one new full-time equivalent job must be created within three years of the disbursement of the loan.

CYBER also administers an in-house loan guaranty program called HELP (Headstart Entrepreneurial Loan Program). A loan guarantee, backed by the equity of YCIDC, is provided by the bank. The purpose of the loan guaranty is to provide small enterprises, particularly start-up and "near" start-up businesses, with funding for their initial growth phase. A maximum loan guarantee of $25,000, or 50 percent of the project amount per company, is available. Terms and interest rates are decided by the bank, but the maximum term of the guaranty is three years. Fees collected include a nonrefundable application fee of $250, and an annual fee of 1.5 percent of the guarantee amount that is payable on each anniversary date. Any out-of-pocket and legal fees incurred in approving or settling the guaranty agreement are the responsibility of the applicant.

Personal service and retail businesses are ineligible. Borrowers must have 10 or fewer full-time employees and annual sales of less than $500,000 at time of application. Real estate, machinery and equipment, leasehold improvements, and working capital are permitted uses for HELP-guaranteed funds. Applicants must create one full-time job within three years for every $5,000 guaranteed. A penalty of five percent of the guarantee amount will be imposed if the job creation standards are not met. Collateral and personal guarantees are required.

Finally, the Center acts as intermediary for the SBA Microloan Program. Loans are available to incubator tenants as well as to companies outside of the incubator facility. A volunteer loan committee reviews the loan application and makes approvals on funding. The committee is composed of members of the YCIDC board, small business owners, and local bankers. The incubator manager presents the loan packages to the committee and helps in preparing closing documentation. CYBER assigns a mentor to provide technical assistance to each approved borrower. Mentors are local volunteers, usually from the financial community. They meet with borrowers on a monthly basis to see how things are going and to address problems with the companies. Mentors report back monthly to CYBER concerning the progress of their protegés.

In a similar manner, the **Springfield Technology Center** functions as a "one-stop-shopping" broker of a variety of loan programs. It acts as administrator for the City of Springfield's revolving loan program, as well as the Clark County Development Corporation's SBA 504 program. In connection with the former, the City of Springfield received an EDA grant and a Community Development Block Grant (CDBG) to launch the revolving loan fund. Money is available for both established companies and start-ups, and can be used for any legitimate business expense. The revolving loan funds are typically leveraged by private sector participation, often a commercial bank. Terms range from three to 10 years, with interest rates usually lower than the prevailing prime rate. Origination and servicing fees and closing costs are usually less than $300. Loans can range from $10,000 to $450,000.

Foundation Investment

The University of Maryland, Baltimore County **Technology Enterprise Center** (TEC) brokered a "soft loan" for one of its tenant companies from a local foundation to develop educational software products for the local schools. TEC worked with the company and several teachers at a Baltimore City High School to arrange to develop and test educational software. Using the foundation grant, the company is developing software programs in biology, chemistry, and physics that will be free not only to the school but the whole school system. These will be marketable products that can be sold to other school systems. Any revenues will be used to repay the loan and will also be shared with the high school.

The tenant company, Password, Inc., is involved in computer-assisted education. The notion of cooperation with local high school teachers originated with the TEC director, who arranged for meetings between several teachers at Baltimore City's Western High School and the company to discuss the idea. The TEC director brokered the partnership between the tenant company and the high school. He then encouraged the company to apply for funding from the Abell Foundation, a sizable foundation that supports education and economic development in Baltimore. The TEC director has a good relationship with the foundation president and advocated strongly on behalf of the company. The Abell Foundation board approved making a small investment of endowment funds through a "soft loan" of $53,000 to the company. Generally, foundations are discouraged by their boards from making such investments. However, some foundations make program-related investments (PRIs) out of grant funds, and this was one.

The entire deal took nearly a year to work out, from the time of the initial discussions with the teachers. The software will be tested in one high school and will be available to all city high schools. If the products are commercialized and sold to other school districts, the Abell Foundation will be repaid out of revenue, and the high school will also get a stream of revenue as an in-kind investor. This arrangement gives the company control over its product instead of working for others under contract. The loan is repaid only if the products succeed.

The arrangement was successful in large part because of the reputation of the TEC director and his relationship with the foundation president. The Baltimore area is fortunate to have a sizable foundation that has as priorities education and economic development. The Abell Foundation makes grants to local companies and organizations, and has a particular interest in economic development.

Conferences, Presentations, and Events

Face-to-face interaction is often the factor that secures the financing and capitalization for new companies. However, newly minted companies are often naive or hesitant about approaching investors. Incubators are involved in a variety of activities to foster these relationships. For example, networking activities sponsored by incubators provide a valuable opportunity for tenant companies to interact with the business community and with other incubator companies. They assist companies' efforts to learn how to approach financial institutions and venture capitalists, to learn about sources of financing and technical assistance, and to exchange ideas on markets and products. Other services provided by incubators include preparation and training for interaction with funders.

Tenants of the **First Flight Venture Center** may participate in an Annual Venture Conference, held by the local Council for Entrepreneurial Development (CED), by applying to make a formal presentation. The conference allows venture capitalists from across the nation to view companies' presentations for venture financing. Tenant companies of the First Flight Venture Center are encouraged to participate if venture capital would be an appropriate financing mechanism.

CED management chooses approximately 15 companies to present at the annual conference. The selection process itself, conducted by a CED committee, is a useful training tool for start-up companies. They are required to submit a business plan and a two-page application for consideration. The committee focuses on companies with unique products and well-identified market opportunities, as well as a management team or a plan to complete such a team. A company needs to be ready for capital within 18 months if it is an existing venture, or be ready for rapid growth if it is a seed-stage company.

Once chosen to present, companies undergo more rigorous training sessions during which their formal presentations are rehearsed and fine-tuned, using as "coaches" CED members experienced in venture financing. Presenting companies will generally meet with their coaches two to three weeks before the conference and participate in a dress rehearsal the week of the presentation. Companies also print a three-page profile in a book available to conference attendees.

The North Carolina Technological Development Authority, Inc. (TDA), which manages the First Flight Venture Center, has been active in sponsoring and planning the annual venture conference, and in selecting and coaching companies chosen to present. Many of the companies funded by the TDA have presented at conferences and received funding either directly or indirectly as a result.

Incubators in the Baltimore area hold an annual **incubator fair** under the aegis of the Regional Incubator Board. The board was established by the Regional Technology Council of the Greater Baltimore Committee, the business association for the Baltimore region. The purpose is to publicize the incubator programs and expose the tenant companies to the business community and potential investors.

The Baltimore regional incubator fair is held each October in a downtown museum, as part of the Greater Baltimore Committee's "Technology Month." Participants include all of the tenants in Baltimore area incubators, as well as the College Park and Montgomery County incubators. The incubators display information about their programs and facilities. The tenant companies display their products and meet the business community. There is no fee for companies to display their products, and there is no admission fee for attendees. The modest cost of the fair is covered by sponsors in the Baltimore business community. In addition to the exhibits, the fair features a program with speakers and awards to companies.

The event is highly publicized by the Regional Incubator Board and the Greater Baltimore Committee. The publicity includes articles in local newspapers before and after the event. The fair is also mentioned in promotional material put out by the Greater Baltimore Committee, including the calendar for high-tech month. Invitations are sent to business people, elected and appointed officials, venture capitalists, and financial institutions.

The incubator fair is seen by the board as a very successful operation. All of the Baltimore area incubators have had good participation by their companies, and almost all of the **Technology Enterprise Center** (TEC) companies have taken part. One of the TEC companies was offered a venture capital investment as a result of the fair, but the company refused the deal. If other deals have resulted, they have not been publicized. Nevertheless, it has been a good networking opportunity for companies in the various incubators. It has raised the visibility of incubators in the region and publicized the need for such programs.

Through the incubator fair and other activities, the Regional Incubator Board has also helped to facilitate cooperation among incubators in the region. Through the Board, the incubators have done some joint marketing in the region. The Board has also proposed capital funding for incubators by the state. It has suggested a matching grant program that would be available for new incubators, as well as the expansion and enhancement of existing incubators. The Board is advocating this proposal because the existing Baltimore incubators are full. This effort has borne fruit because the Maryland Department of Employment and Economic Development has proposed a matching grant program for incubator construction for fiscal year 1995-96.

The **Southeastern Capital Connection** is a venture capital conference for investors and entrepreneurs from across the Southeast. For eight years, the conference has been sponsored by Enterprise Development, Inc. of South Carolina (EDI), the parent company of the **Center for Applied Technology (CAT)**. EDI is a private, nonprofit corporation responsible for identifying and delivering resources and programs to meet the needs of private sector business in South Carolina. EDI starts activities that are needed in the state and then spins them off as self-sufficient entities.

A two-day conference called "**Dare To Deal**" brings investors and entrepreneurs together in an informal environment. It is an opportunity for attendees to discuss deals and learn about new approaches and emerging companies. Sponsored by EDI and Clemson University, "Dare To Deal" has a wide variety of activities:

- Workshops for investors about current topics on equity financing;
- Showcase presentations of business plans;
- A nationally recognized luncheon speaker;
- Legislative and federal funding program updates;
- A networking reception; and
- A business expo—an opportunity for promising businesses to talk one-on-one with investors.

EDI solicits business plans to showcase through its newsletter and via a conference announcement, as does CAT. From the business plans received, EDI selects eight to 10 companies to make presentations and participate in the Expo. CAT staff perform an analysis of each business plan and an evaluation of each technology or product. The CAT prefers companies that fill a distinct market niche and are growing rapidly.

The conference is marketed mainly in North Carolina, South Carolina, Virginia, Georgia, and Tennessee, but it also has attracted venture capitalists from outside the South. The conference is held every in December at a resort location, with optional recreational activities. The registration fee is $295.

EDI has been responsible for planning the conference for eight years. Other sponsors provide financial support. Beginning in 1995, the College of Charleston assumed responsibility for sponsoring the Capital Conference.

The conference is now reasonably well-known within the multistate region. The benefit to the entrepreneurs depends on their ability to sell their products through their business plan presentation and one-on-one time around their product exhibit. The capital connection creates an environment where entrepreneurs and investors can structure new deals. To help make that interaction possible, the sponsors want to maintain attendance at approximately 200 participants.

The Dingman Center for Entrepreneurship at the University of Maryland operates the **Baltimore-Washington Venture Group**, which holds monthly or bi-monthly venture forums. Start-up businesses (including tenants of the University of Maryland **Technology Advancement Program**) present business plans to a panel, which analyzes them in an open forum. The audience includes entrepreneurs, professional service providers, and potential investors.

The **Arizona Technology Incubator (ATI)** participated in the formation of the Arizona Venture Capital Conference (AVCC), which occurs every year in December. Forty to 60 companies apply to present to a venture capital audience of up to 70 to100 potential investors. The 10 or 12 most promising applicant companies are picked by a selection committee to present at each conference.

This program is starting its fourth year and has raised well over $20 million for its participants. Four ATI companies have participated in the conference.

The **Austin Technology Incubator (ATI)** is a cosponsor of the American Electronics Association/Ernst & Young Fall Financial Conference for Emerging Growth Technology Companies. The conference offers growing high-tech companies the opportunity to meet a broad spectrum of investors providing all types of financing. During the two-day conference, held annually in Austin, Texas, a select group of participating companies make brief presentations to the general audience. Companies are then invited to make more detailed presentations to interested investors at private meetings.

More than 20 investment banks and venture capital firms, as well as individual investors, provide support to the conference. Each year, selected ATI tenant companies are invited to participate in the conference. These firms enjoy tremendous exposure to the financial investment community and gain invaluable experience in marketing themselves.

Through its close ties with the University of Texas (UT), the Austin Technology Incubator also provides valuable support to the International Moot Corp® Business Plan Competition, hosted by the UT Graduate School of Business. Moot Corp® is an international entrepreneurship and venture competition in which students from the leading business schools in the world are given the opportunity to develop a detailed, growth-oriented business plan and then match their efforts against their peers. This annual event has been described by *Business Week* as "the Super Bowl of world business plan competition." The 1994 and 1995 winners, from the University of Texas, found the ideas for their companies at ATI's affiliate organization, the Technology Marketing Group. Aside from providing the impetus for these winning plans, ATI helps turn these ideas into real business entities by awarding the winning team entry into the incubator at no cost until the team members graduate from school. After graduation they may continue in the incubator under the same terms as other tenant companies. This support lends credence to the competition and encourages entrepreneurial development in top business schools.

Twice annually, the Calgary Alberta **Technology Enterprise Centre** holds a **Mini-Trade Show** at which incubator companies are exposed to interested members of the community. The trade show allows the firms to display their products to potential financial sources, customers, and joint venture partners. The Mini-Trade Shows are held in the late Spring and in October, during national Small Business Week, sponsored by Chambers of Commerce across Canada. Many of the incubator's clients prepare exhibits for the event, held in the incubator's atrium. Each company is given a table and display space in which to show its product or service. Many companies make use of interactive technologies to show its products. The event is usually scheduled from 4 to 7 p.m. on a weekday, so that it is not very time-consuming. Attendees usually number about 250, including bankers, investors, and government, university, and research interests, as well as other technology businesses. The event is advertised in the Chamber of Commerce journal, local newspapers, and in the incubator newsletter.

The Mini-Trade Show has become a popular event; almost as much interaction goes on among attendees as with incubator companies. Several financing matches, especially involving venture capital, have arisen from the contacts that incubator companies have made at the event.

The **Ceramics Corridor Innovation Center** also uses a **group presentation** approach. All of the Center's businesses are centered around ceramics and various aspects of advanced materials, which tend to be slow-growth areas. As such, they tend not to attract high-flying venture capitalists, although they do attract some individual angel investors. The Center organizes group presentations, that may involve upwards of 10 people who can provide either capital or other kinds of resources. These will include both private and public sector investors, such as the state Department of Economic Development (as a potential source of training monies), the New York Job Development Authority, and several local bankers. Sessions usually last up to an hour, with participants receiving a copy of the business plan in advance. Sessions are held at the incubator, which makes the presentation more credible given that laboratory and other facilities are on view, as well as other, already established high-technology companies. The entrepreneur typically makes a short presentation, buttressed by comments and endorsement by the incubator manager, and "pre-deal" discussions are conducted. The group setting tends to instill a competitive spirit, particularly among the bankers in attendance. That is, funders see that others are interested and may be more inclined to participate in a deal. At the close of the meeting, the incubator manager tries to sum up the gist of the discussion and any action items. Subsequent to the meeting, two or more of the participating organizations will likely have discussions about how they parcel out the deal.

Tenants of the **Idaho Innovation Center** have access to training to prepare them to make presentations before venture capitalists and other funding sources. The incubator director and members of the Senior Corps of Retired Executives (SCORE), located in the Innovation Center, provide training to incubator companies by having them repeatedly rehearse a 20-minute presentation. The 20-minute format is commonly used by the local venture capital community. Using the "practice makes perfect" theory, entrepreneurs are prepared to make the best possible presentation, in addition to having a solid written commercialization plan. Faculty from Idaho State University and the local community college have also been used to provide training to incubator companies.

To assist clients with SBIR grants, the **Technology Ventures Incubator** utilizes the Washington Technology Liaison (WTL), sponsored by the New Jersey Commission on Science and Technology.
Through the liaison, individuals and small firms can receive assistance at no cost in technical marketing, customer development, proposal preparation, and strategic planning. For example, if an incubator company is working with alternate fuels, the incubator director can call the liaison and describe the company's technology idea. The liaison investigates and gives the company a contact name in a department that may be putting out an SBIR solicitation in that area. The liaison does not help write the proposal but facilitates the application process by reviewing a company's application to make sure it meets the standards. The liaison position is justified by the amount of SBIR funding brought into the state yearly, which has grown in recent years. The liaison conducts periodic workshops in New Jersey on SBIR and the federal marketing process. A major seminar is offered in the fall, and other workshops are conducted throughout the year. Although any New Jersey company can access the liaison officer, the incubator uses the service frequently for tenant firms. The liaison helps address applicants' questions about the agencies offering SBIRs.

As a general rule, technology incubators only accept technology companies. In certain situations, though, it makes sense to lease space to a non-technology company that can provide service to other tenants. As a prime example, the **Rensselaer Polytechnic Institute (RPI) Incubator Center** leases space to a consulting firm that assists tenants with SBIR proposals.

The firm, H&M Technology Acquisition, Inc. (H&MTA), specializes in writing SBIR proposals and also identifies specific and relevant R&D funding opportunities for client firms. Up-front dialogue results in a custom search template that completely details the client's specific needs, special attributes, and constraints. This data enables H&MTA to conduct informed searches that precisely identify targeted funding opportunities.

H&MTA prefers to work on an hourly fee basis, but it understands the cash flow constraints of start-ups. The firm is willing to work on a contingency fee basis, in which it will not be paid unless the tenant's proposal receives funding. RPI does not provide the consulting firm with any rent reduction, but it does provide a constant stream of referrals through its network of incubator clients, affiliates, and university alumni. The consulting firm and its services are frequently used in the RPI community.

H&MTA, RPI, and the Capital Region Technology Development Council also work collaboratively on a half-day workshop that outlines federal assistance programs for both tenants and nontenants. A 60-page handout is given to participants that discusses various programs and the agencies involved. H&MTA describes the government contracting environment and how to obtain a fair share of government R&D funds.

The R&D Funding Starter Kit is a fee-based service provided by the **Center for Applied Technology** (CAT) and the Technology and Business Information Center (TBIC). The service was recently introduced to help businesses apply effectively for SBIR, STTR, ATP, TRP, and other funding mechanisms. For a fee of $350, the company receives the following: registration to the national SBIR conference in Washington, D.C.; a copy of *Small Business Guide to Federal R&D Funding Opportunities*; a discount on federal R&D funding seminars offered by CAT; announcements and solicitations from all relevant mailing lists; introductions to agencies interested in a particular technology; a discount on database searches performed by TBIC; and a copy of *Writing SBIR Proposals*. In addition, subscribers are assured quick response to program questions and receive priority on proposal reviews and checklists for compliance.

The service is offered to both incubator tenants and nontenants. The fee covers the cost of materials and CAT's expenses. These consist primarily of staff time spent scheduling appointments, making calls, and helping identify the most relevant R&D funding alternatives for the business.

Tools

Capitol Capital: Government Resources for High-Technology Companies is a 214-page book that describes in a comprehensive, easy-to-read manner federal and state government programs that companies can access. These include funds for research and development (Chapter 1), tapping into federal laboratories (Chapter 2), defense conversion and dual-use programs (Chapter 3), manufacturing programs (Chapter 4), sources of domestic financing (Chapter 5), and international financing (Chapter 6). There is also a chapter of seven case studies describing success stories of companies that have accessed programs and services. The fully indexed book is well-organized; it defines key terms and lists numerous points of contact, including names, addresses, and phone numbers. The information is current as of 1994. The book is published by the American Electronics Association and costs $49.95 for nonmembers plus $5 shipping.

Contact:
AEA Customer Service Center
5201 Great America Parkway
P.O. Box 54990
Santa Clara, CA 95056-0990
Tel (800) 284-4232   Fax (408) 970-8565

Pratt's Guide to Venture Capital Sources has been widely hailed as the leading reference to the worldwide venture capital industry for entrepreneurs and growing companies. The 1995 edition contains investment, operating, and management data on more than 950 venture capital firms. Each listing includes contact name, phone and fax number, geographic and industry preferences, recent investment data, management rosters, and project preferences, including the roles played in financing, types of financing provided and preferred investment sizes. The book is indexed by company name, individual name, industry preference, and investment stage preference. Articles written by leading venture capitalists, attorneys, and successful entrepreneurs discuss how to structure a successful transaction, legal considerations, nontraditional financing sources, and more. The price is $249.

Contact:
David A. Fabel
Securities Data Publishing/Venture Economics
40 West 57th Street
11th Floor
New York, NY 10019
Tel (212) 333-9274   Fax (212) 765-6123

New Jersey Financing Resources Manual (1994), published by the South Jersey Entrepreneurs Network, provides new or growing businesses with a broad overview of the various aspects of business financing. The manual contains chapters on preparing a business plan, developing a relationship with a banker, lease financing, private investors and networking, later-stage financing, and federal/state financing sources. The contributing authors are experts in their respective fields, including corporate and securities attorneys, corporate executives, and commercial loan officers. Each chapter includes sources for additional information. The book explains each type of financing and includes sections detailing what to expect when approaching bankers, leasing companies, venture capitalists, or other financial sources. The cover price is $25.

Contact:
The South Jersey Entrepreneurs Network
Longwood Center, Suite D-2
600 Route 38 West
Cherry Hill, NJ 08002
Tel (609) 665-8855   Fax (609) 665-6767

Small business owners searching for ways to grow their business can access an on-line service developed by Coopers & Lybrand L.L.P., Dun & Bradstreet Information Services and the National Business Incubation Association to help them locate and evaluate potential strategic partners. The *Clearinghouse for Strategic Alliances, Trade and Equity Investment* provides a comprehensive database profiling incubator-related companies, midsized firms and large corporations that have interest in strategic partnering. The clearinghouse helps participants locate other companies specifically interested in technology licensing, research and development contracts, equity investment, design collaboration, joint production or contract manufacturing, joint selling or distribution arrangements, and marketing and promotional collaboration.

Each participant is enrolled in the clearinghouse through the addition of a company profile, specifying product and service capabilities and the types of alliances desired.   Access to the searchable database is provided through a secure on-line network. Clearinghouse subscribers pay $300 annually to obtain software that enables them to access the network. Among the participants in the clearinghouse are large corporations including Dow Chemical Company, Engelhard Corporation, Motorola, Bristol-Myers Squibb, Glaxo, Bic Corporation and Hoechst-Celanese, as well as many venture capital firms looking to identify investment opportunities. The Clearinghouse also includes entrepreneurial firms located in business incubators throughout the United States.

Contact:
   National Business Incubation Association
   20 East Circle Drive, Suite 190
   Athens, OH 45701
   Tel (614) 593-4331   Fax (614) 593-1996

Chapter 3

Research and Technology

Obviously science, technology, and related expertise are by definition at the core of any new technology enterprise. Often, however, not all of the requisite technical expertise to build a viable business has been incorporated or developed by the new enterprise. For example, in companies that are based on technologies derived from university research, there is often a need to mature or "harden" the technology through the development of scaled-up designs, prototypes, or alpha and beta test versions. The facilities and/or expertise to get to this level of development may be beyond the capacities of the entrepreneurial firm itself.

As a result, much of what incubators do in the domain of research and technology involves the identification and brokering of expertise. This may involve searching out individual experts, as well as arranging cooperative research relationships with large R&D organizations. As the quantitative data show, this may involve organizing a role for loaned faculty or graduate students, or accessing various databases of researchers and technologies. One of the novel aspects of these types of services or practices is how they are financed. Some involve interesting cost-sharing agreements, while others feature a prominent role played by state government.

As the best practices section below illustrates, incubators can also play a role that is, in effect, pre-enterprise. This is to identify early-stage research and technology that has a dimly seen or acknowledged commercial potential, and then to breathe life into the potential enterprise and stoke the animal spirits of entrepreneurialism in the researcher or inventor. We have labeled this "technology ferreting" and discuss it below.

One of the sets of practices that has been described in more detail below is not really a practice in the usual sense of the term. It has to do with the structural relationship that many incubators have with major science and technology organizations, typically universities. Thus the access to science and technology, expertise, and facilities is built in as part of a more comprehensive, interorganizational relationship. Obviously, incubators that are isolated have difficulty in fostering these kinds of structural relationship, as the analyses below indicate.

Overview of Practices and Services: Research and Technology

We asked incubator managers to respond to a checklist of likely research and technology services and practices provided to client companies. For each practice or service, managers were asked to indicate whether they provided the service or practice directly, brokered or referred the service or practice, did both, or did neither. The checklist had the effect of providing a scale of intensity for services and practices provided in the research and technology area. The summary results are presented in Table 3.1 below.

Table 3.1: Research and Technology Practices (valid percent responses)

	no, rarely/never	yes, by referral	yes, directly	both
access to external technical facilities	3.8	13.5	65.4	17.3
loaned/consulting university faculty/students	5.7	28.3	52.8	13.2
location/identification of key technical staff	5.8	42.3	30.8	21.2
databases of researchers and technologies	7.8	33.3	47.1	11.8
research and development financing	23.1	44.2	28.8	3.8
technical review board	33.3	21.6	39.2	5.9
design/initiation of research/technical project	34.0	32.1	28.3	5.7
development of CRADAs or their equivalent	38.3	38.3	17.0	6.4
alpha and beta testing	59.6	26.9	11.5	1.9

The most common services were providing access to university faculty and graduate students, whether "on loan" or on a consulting basis, and providing access to technical facilities outside of the incubator, including university, industry, and federal laboratories. Special technical facilities and expertise in the technology area are essential for developing a commercializable technology. Often these services are provided on a loan or short-term basis, so the new company need not bear the financial burden of permanently supporting technical staff or facilities.[5]

Very few incubators are directly involved in alpha and beta testing. While some incubators do provide this service, it is generally by referral. Alpha and beta testing require expertise that most incubators may not be able to provide.

In a survey of the provision of these services by incubator type, a few trends become particularly evident, as seen in Table 3.2 (next page). Every university-affiliated incubator has some arrangement for the use of faculty and graduate students by client companies. Not surprisingly, the practice of using university faculty and students had a high correlation to university affiliation of the incubator. Two other research and technology practices were found to have a statistically significant correlation to university affiliation. University-affiliated incubators were also more likely to provide access to external technical facilities and use of databases of researchers and technology.

Comparing incubators in rural areas with those in urban areas, we found that differences in services were significant only in one case. The practice of using university faculty and graduate students as consultants was found to be significantly related to location, with all urban incubators and 83 percent of rural incubators providing this service. This seems to indicate a closer relationship with universities among urban incubators. Table 3.3 shows the frequency of research and technology services provided by rural and urban incubators.

Table 3.2: Research and Technology Practices by Incubator University Affiliation (valid percent responses)

	no, rarely/never		yes, by referral		yes, directly		both	
	university	non	university	non	university	non	university	non
loaned/consulting university faculty/students .	0.0	11.1	16.7	50.0	73.3	22.2	10.0	16.7
access to external technical facilities	0.0	11.1	6.9	27.8	79.3	44.4	13.8	16.7
location/identification of key technical staff .	3.4	11.1	37.9	44.4	34.5	22.2	24.1	22.2
use databases of researchers and technologies .	3.4	17.6	24.1	47.1	62.1	23.5	10.3	11.8
research and development financing	27.6	16.7	37.9	55.6	31.0	22.2	3.4	5.6
technical review board	31.0	33.3	17.2	33.3	51.7	22.2	0.0	11.1
design/initiation of research/technical project.	33.3	33.3	30.0	33.3	33.3	22.2	3.3	11.1
development of CRADAs or their equivalent	40.7	46.7	33.3	26.7	22.2	13.3	3.7	13.3
alpha and beta testing	65.5	50.0	24.1	33.3	10.3	11.1	0.0	5.6

Table 3.3: Research and Technology Practices by Incubator Location (valid percent responses)

	no, rarely/never		yes, by referral		yes, directly		both	
	rural	urban	rural	urban	rural	urban	rural	urban
access to external technical facilities	7.7	2.6	15.4	12.8	76.9	61.5	0.0	23.1
location/identification of key technical staff .	8.3	5.0	25.0	47.5	58.3	22.5	8.3	25.0
use databases of researchers and technologies .	8.3	7.7	33.3	33.3	58.3	43.6	0.0	15.4
loaned/consulting university faculty/students	23.1	0.0	15.4	32.5	61.5	50.0	0.0	17.5
development of CRADAs or their equivalent	27.3	41.7	54.5	33.3	18.2	16.7	0.0	8.3
research and development financing	30.8	20.5	53.8	41.0	15.4	33.3	0.0	5.1
design/initiation of research/technical project.	30.8	35.0	38.5	30.0	30.8	27.5	0.0	7.5
technical review board	38.5	30.8	23.1	20.5	38.5	41.0	0.0	7.7
alpha and beta testing	69.2	56.4	23.1	28.2	7.7	12.8	0.0	2.6

BEST PRACTICES: RESEARCH AND TECHNOLOGY

One of the more important sets of practices and services conducted by incubators lies in this area. In this chapter we will concentrate on the "soft" side of research and technology, such as structural relationships and access to people. Access to laboratories and equipment and related practices are addressed in the physical infrastructure chapter (Chapter 7). For purposes of presentation, we have grouped best practices into three categories: 1) structural integration of incubators and colocated universities; 2) technology ferreting and outreach (by incubator management); 3) brokering access to research and technology expertise; and 4) tools.

Structural Integration of the University and Small Business Incubation

All technology business incubators have ties to "technology source" organizations, whether those organizations are major corporations, federal laboratories, universities, or informal combinations of all of the above. However, some incubators are much more closely coupled to sources of technology, and therefore to emerging inventions and budding entrepreneurs. In effect, they are *integrated* into one functional unit, which shares staffing, mission, and resources.

Sometimes technology source organizations particularly ones that are publicly funded, such as state universities, may wish to maximize the local or regional "capture ratio" as they license out their technologies or innovations. In effect, this ensures that commercialization and value-added economic activity will remain within their region. This objective influences them to steer their licensing activity more toward local start-up enterprises and away from licensing to national firms that have no obvious regional interest. In the absence of a rich regional network or infrastructure that supports technology ventures (as in rural areas), the technology source organization may take a proactive role in aligning with incubation programs or services. Participating programs in the study provide several cases.

As one cautionary note, there also may be *too much* integration of the incubation function and the university, if the culture and organizational practices of the latter impede the former. The manager of one incubator in the study which was tied to the university business school complained that he had to go through two or three levels of approval to do anything.

UBC Research Enterprises at the University of British Columbia is a good example of a positive organizational arrangement. This office deals with all aspects of the university's portfolio of sponsored research with industry, as well as all aspects of intellectual property management, patenting, and licensing. In addition, it takes on the task of functioning as an incubator without walls. There is no physical facility, or tenants as such, but the office is willing to assist faculty inventors as they work through the entrepreneurial process. In contrast with many university technology offices, which tend to focus exclusively on licensing to already established companies, UBC Research Enterprises routinely provides (or brokers) many of the services that traditional incubators offer.

The **Ceramics Corridor Innovation Center** offers another variation on this theme. It involves a close partnership not only with Alfred University and two incubator facilities, but also with a *Fortune 200* corporation, Corning, and local economic development organizations. Alfred had long been a preeminent institution in research and training in ceramics, but outside of Corning there were few employment possibilities in the rural area. Corning, in turn, had gone through some downsizing and restructuring in the 1980s and was looking for ways to maintain regional employment for its high-skilled former employees and also to nurture technology that was "orphaned" in the corporation. Both of these goals were shared by two county economic development organizations.

A corporation was charted with membership from Alfred University, Corning, and the two county organizations. The New York Science and Technology Foundation provided $10 million (part grant and part loan) to construct two incubator facilities, and money from the Appalachian Regional Commission kickstarted program staffing.

Two factors are pervasive throughout the program. One is the presence and role of Alfred University ceramics engineering graduates, as tenants as well as supporters. Second is the importance of the shared regional vision of the program. That is, the center has been focused on developing an industrial corridor or sub-region and anchoring high-skill jobs and high-technology companies therein. The long-term goal is to create a ceramics version of Silicon Valley that is self-reinforcing, synergistic, and collaborative. These ideas have been incorporated into a vision statement that has circulated widely among stakeholders throughout the immediate region, at the university, at Corning, and among the "extended family" of Alfred alumni. Relations between the incubator and the university are extensive and pervasive. The incubator manager sits *ex officio* on various decision groups at Alfred, while university officials play a similar role in the incubator. The vision itself is used as a tool to push cooperation, teaming, and larger initiatives.

Another example of a close integration between a university and a colocated incubator is found at the **BioBusiness Incubator of Michigan.** The incubator is owned by and located in the Michigan Biotechnology Institute (MBI), a state-funded, nonprofit R&D organization located adjacent to Michigan State University. MBI was established in the early 1980s as an initiative of the Michigan Strategic Foundation. The purpose was to create research faculty and programs that were colocated with major universities in the state and intended to bridge the gap between academics, research and industry. MBI itself has a 120,000-square-foot research facility and a mission to commercialize biotechnology in the state. The incubator that is within MBI is a logical extension of the MBI mission. The incubator manager is employed by MSU as director of venture development, and the president and vice president for research of MSU sit on the board of MBI. MBI may acquire technologies (faculty inventions) from the university, mature them, and spin them off into new companies which may end up in the incubator.

The **University of Iowa Technology Innovation Center** is a part of the university and closely allied with its intellectual property/licensing function (UI Research Foundation), as well as with the university research park. In fact, the director of the Innovation Center (incubator) is also director of the UI Research Foundation. The incubator and the research park are both seen as integral parts of the overall research mission of the university and are incorporated into its written strategic plan, as is the importance of start-up companies. As noted in its 1991 strategic plan, a major strategy of the university is to "establish licensure to start-up firms as a priority of University of Iowa intellectual property management." In addition, one of the selection criteria for tenants who are not faculty inventors is the extent to which their company's technology complements the core research competencies of the university. With start-ups based on faculty inventions, the UI Research Foundation may take an equity share in the company as part of the licensing arrangement. The close connection between the incubator and the licensing office makes the start-up option more visible and viable when a faculty inventor is planning a commercialization path. About 20 percent of university licenses are issued to start-up companies, many of them based in the incubator, and since 1991 there have been 12 start-up companies based on technology or intellectual property developed at the University of Iowa.

The mission of the **Manoa Innovation Center** is to facilitate technology transfer from the University of Hawaii. The incubator is located adjacent to the main campus of the university, and the university office of technology transfer is an anchor tenant of the incubator. The industry and technical foci of the incubator reflect strengths in the university, particularly in the areas of digital media and biotechnology, though not all tenants are university spin-offs. Half of the costs for the lab space are paid by the university office of technology transfer, which also co-manages that space. Lab revenues are shared, and royalty positions may be negotiated on products developed, particularly in the area of multimedia training products. In effect, the laboratory is operated as a joint investment of the incubator and the university technology transfer office, which tends to reinforce the larger working relationship.

The **Ohio University Innovation Center** in Athens, Ohio is part of the organizational structure of the university, not a separate corporation. It was established by the university board of trustees and reports to an authority board consisting of three university deans and three individuals from the external corporate community, with the president of the university acting as an *ex officio* member and chairman. All members of the board are nominated by the president, approved by the board of trustees, and serve for five years. The innovation center is a key element in the university's economic development strategy. Ohio University is relatively isolated in a poor rural area. There are few modern manufacturing companies, much less technology-based companies in the area. The university felt a need to carefully nurture its small technology portfolio, through more proactive and deliberate technology transfer, by getting involved in start-ups. The director of the innovation center incubator is also head of the technology transfer office. Faculty inventions are evaluated on a case-by-case basis for their potential for either licensing or commercialization through a business start-up.

There is a seamless relationship between these two commercialization paths, through the program's common management. The technology transfer office director will handle the intellectual property aspects of a deal and then pass it over to the innovation center (also himself) to perform the incubation tasks and services. Part of this arrangement may be reflected in the actual licensing agreement with the company and investors. For example, the Ohio University Foundation may be an investor and equity shareholder in a start-up. When and if the initial round of financing is cashed out via an initial public offering, the foundation proceeds will be reinvested back in the academic department of origin. In addition, some of the milestones and benchmarks that need to be realized in the incubation process may be reflected in the licensing agreement (e.g., getting a business plan by a certain date, getting a full-time manager).

Being a "program" in the university has had other implications for the incubator program as well. The budget for the incubator is separated from the rent revenues derived from the tenants. This provides a more stable budget for operations and services, albeit less secure control of space. As a program within the university, it is also much easier for the incubator to broker assets, facilities, and partnerships. One key component of the innovation center program is the involvement of students. During academic sessions, between 10 to 15 students work on technology commercialization projects.

The **Office for the Advancement of Developing Industries (OADI)** in Birmingham, Alabama is structurally part of the research and technology development administration of the University of

Alabama at Birmingham (UAB) and is viewed as an integral part of the university's service mission. Although the university technology development office is organizationally and physically separate from OADI, both the head of the licensing office and the head of OADI report to the same university vice president. As an integral part of the university, OADI is able to broker access to university services for tenant and associate companies on the same basis as other university departments and organizations. If charges are not normally assessed, OADI tenants and associates are not charged. If charges would normally be passed back to users, tenant and associate companies are expected to pay. This organizational and financial structure allows OADI to offer a broad array of services at a lower cost to tenant and associate companies.

The **GENESIS Technology Incubator** at the University of Arkansas-Fayetteville is a function of the university's Engineering Research Center and is considered an integral element of the school of engineering's outreach and extension program. The incubator's management committee is composed of the dean of the school of engineering and a number of university administrators. As an integral part of the university, the incubator can access a broad range of university services for its tenants, and tenants are considered "regular customers," as are students and faculty.

The **North Central Idaho Business Technology Incubator**, owned by the University of Idaho, has as an anchor tenant the university's technology transfer arm, the Idaho Research Foundation. The Idaho Research Foundation needed to be located where it could be easily accessible to both industry clients and university researchers. The incubator, located at the edge of campus, provides a perfect location. In addition, the foundation's location in the incubator helps the incubator attract university spin-out or licensed companies.

Incubator tenants are selected in part based on their relationship to the University of Idaho; many are faculty, former faculty, or alumni. Holders of university intellectual property licenses are also in the incubator.

The Idaho Research Foundation commercializes university research and manages its intellectual property. An independent, nonprofit corporation, this perpetual tenant has provided some assistance to incubator companies on legal issues, such as recommending patent attorneys. In addition, it can potentially provide several research and technology-related support services, such as assistance in acquiring commercial rights to university technology and developing research contracts with the university. Currently, the foundation provides information of a general nature to other incubator tenants on issues of technology licensing, intellectual property protection, and management.

The **Wichita Technology Corporation** is one of three nonprofit "commercialization corporations" established by the Kansas Technology Enterprise Corporation (KTEC), each of which is colocated with a state research university. Structurally, the commercialization corporations are independent not-for-profits. However, they are programmatically linked with the university to perform an adjunct commercialization function. That is, the commercialization center will review technologies emerging from the university and attempt to identify those that have the potential to form the basis for a significant business. The role that the Wichita Technology Corporation plays is one of putting together the business—which might imply pulling in other technologies—identifying other business partners, securing capitalization, and so on. Since, the parent organization, KTEC, also invests heavily in university-based research centers of excellence, the commercialization corporation has ready access to university technologies.

The **Alpha Center** is a biotech incubator managed by the Dome Corporation, a wholly owned subsidiary of Johns Hopkins University and Health Center. The Dome Corporation manages the properties of the Bayview Campus of Johns Hopkins University. The Bayview campus is a biomedical-oriented campus, occupied by Johns Hopkins institutions and teaching hospital, federal labs, and research facilities. Dome renovated one of the vacant buildings on the campus for a start-up company. When that company moved elsewhere within the research park, Dome turned the lab and office space into the Alpha Center, hired a manager, put together an incubator program, and developed a marketing strategy. It is gradually working toward break-even on the project. As its tenant companies have matured, the center has eliminated the full-time manager. The priority of the Alpha Center is to transfer technology out of Johns Hopkins University.

The Alpha Center is now managed part-time by a property manager of Dome Corporation. This individual, who is responsible for working with tenants, consults with business people within Dome Corporation to review the business plans of incubator tenants, as well as with Johns Hopkins faculty and staff on more technical aspects of the business. The manager also refers tenants to a list of vendors and consultants that have offered to provide business services at a discount.

Dome staff also work with public sector agencies on various working capital loan programs and work to facilitate those transactions for tenants. Dome set up a seed fund several years ago and spun it off as a subsidiary organization. It is now totally independent.

Dome has also worked to connect the incubator companies to Johns Hopkins as a purchaser of their products and services. Johns Hopkins is the largest private employer in Maryland through the hospital and the university and is a huge customer for biotech products and services. Dome tries to help its incubator companies enter into procurement relationships with the university. Because it is a part of the university, Dome is able to help these companies get an entree.

Most of the academic institutions that are closely integrated with a local incubator report an increased rate of commercialization via start-ups, as well as a greater utilization of university graduates. This is reflected in the percentage of total license deals that take this route, as well as the vitality and number of the resultant start-ups.

Technology Ferreting and Outreach

Some incubator programs have developed fairly aggressive programs to discover technologies with commercial potential and budding entrepreneurs from the research community. In many cases this involves consciousness-raising interactions with basic scientists and academic researchers.

Researchers who are involved in fundamental or curiosity-driven research frequently do not focus on the commercial or product implications of their work. Most have little or no business background and are unschooled in the processes of product and enterprise development. However, they may be quite entrepreneurial in basic orientation, often behaving aggressively in staking out their research area, securing funding, and building a research organization. The working assumption of any technology ferreting program is that with appropriate inducement, and with a little help from an external change agent, some research scientists will become interested in technology commercialization and entrepreneurship.

Several kinds of results from these activities are possible. In some cases an immediate "a-ha" will occur during a meeting, in which the product potential of a body of research results becomes obvious. Sometimes the effect will be to motivate the faculty member to act on the product idea she already had, for example, by filing an invention disclosure. Of course, in many cases, nothing will result.

The **Advanced Technology Development Center** (**ATDC**) at Georgia Institute of Technology has been involved in such an activity. Benefiting from its structural relationship with the university (ATDC is a part of Georgia Tech's Economic Development Institute), ATDC has worked with the technology licensing office and has had the blessings of senior administration (VP level) and deans in the appropriate schools. The basic approach is to ask college and departmental administrators to identify faculty members who have healthy portfolios of externally funded research, some of which may have commercial value. The ferret will then set up a series of informal one–on–one meetings with the targeted faculty. The ferret will learn about the various research projects in process; the faculty member will learn about the various processes involved in technology commercialization, as well as the services provided by the incubator.

At **Michigan State University** this function has been formalized somewhat in the form of a position called a director of venture development (the current incumbent in the position also manages a colocated incubator). The director of venture development has a "hunting license," so to speak, for faculty in various colleges, to determine whether their research has commercial potential and whether they have entrepreneurial inclinations. The director of venture development has had meetings with more than 120 faculty members, with suggestions for candidates provided by deans and department chairs. If there is potential (which is true in about 10 percent of cases), the venture development person will act as "unpaid staff" for the faculty inventor and work with him or her to establish a company. This may mean acting as a *de facto* chief financial officer during the process of incorporation and early capitalization. Some of those new companies end up in the incubator. Michigan State reports the establishment of eight new companies in the past six months, with 12 to 15 waiting in the wings.

The **Carleton Technology Innovation Center** (**CTIC**) is conscious of the need to inspire and create spin-off companies in the region. The center finds and publicizes the need for more technology-based companies. Its outreach is done more by general advocacy and education than by one-on-one meetings with potential entrepreneurs. This outreach may include seminars for potential entrepreneurs, as well as working with major companies to encourage spin-off or spin-out options for technologies that are not in the mainstream of a current product portfolio.

The **Boulder Technology Incubator** (**BTI**) has an active technology matching component as part of its strategy. The incubator works with various entities in the area, such as the universities and federal laboratory facilities, to identify technologies with commercial potential. The incubator then helps pull together the management talent needed to launch these technologies as businesses.

The incubator's advisory board helps identify technologies with commercial potential and find resources that would bring a business or technology transfer to fruition. Sometimes the incubator works with a corporate strategic partner in a spin-on arrangement in which the corporation provides the management, capital, and sometimes the facilities. The incubator also works with corporations that are willing to match management to commercializable technology and spin the match out into the incubator, with the incubator functioning as a "skunk works" facility.

BTI sometimes helps find financing for a technology even before it is matched to a business. Utilizing a combination of incubator advisory committee meetings and review boards, the incubator can move a technology through its seven-step Entrepreneur Success Model, at least informally, in order to rate the technology even before a corporate partner or management team is developed. The inventor may play a secondary role as the incubator matches the management team and resources with the technology.

The **Center for Applied Technology** (CAT) maintains a fax and e-mail distribution list of about 200 businesses, researchers, and media in South Carolina that serves to raise the awareness of faculty members and other researchers to entrepreneurial opportunities. The center notifies university researchers and others throughout the state of federal funding sources such as the Small Business Innovation Research (SBIR) program, Small Business Technology Transfer (STTR) program, Advanced Technology Program (ATP), and Technology Reinvestment Project (TRP). The service also provides information on conferences and meetings that can help entrepreneurs identify opportunities for their technology.

CAT developed the list by targeting businesses and researchers in South Carolina that were seeking R&D funding. They used university directories to identify department heads and professors, primarily in engineering and science fields. Anytime someone makes an inquiry based on the newsletter, CAT offers to put them on the fax/e-mail list as well.

Whenever CAT receives new information about any federal programs for R&D, it sends a one-page summary by fax or e-mail to everyone on the list. There is no cost to recipients, and it is relatively inexpensive to send a one-page fax with computer fax management software. About 130 are e-mailed, and 70 are faxed.

The fax memo has been a tremendous lead generator for the incubator. The recipients are now fully aware of all the small business initiatives being offered at the center. It does a lot for outreach, in terms of getting people introduced to SBIR and other federal programs. CAT also uses the memos to point out opportunities for example, federal funding for research is going down, but opportunities such as SBIR are increasing. This approach is also a way to let recipients know that the center is there to help them, and has ultimately resulted in more technology being commercialized via start-ups and spin-offs.

CAT's experience is that its information dissemination activities, if done periodically, increase the flow of technology deals.

Access to Research and Technology Expertise

Despite the fact that most technology-based start-up companies will have leadership with technical skills, that in-house expertise will be thin in many areas. Frequently the company will need to access niche expertise that complements or supplements staff abilities. Incubators themselves typically do not have resident technical expertise. The solution to this problem is to broker company relationships with external expertise, often through a contract or grant, and often on a significantly subsidized basis.

Tenants of the **Business Technology Center** of Columbus, Ohio, and of three other incubators funded by Ohio's Thomas Edison Partnership Program, have access to the state-funded Ohio Edison Centers of Excellence as though they were member companies of the centers. This arrangement gives the incubator companies sophisticated technical assistance and services at a reasonable cost.

Incubator companies have access to up to eight free hours (exclusive of travel time) of technical consultation annually, from each of the seven Edison centers. The Edison centers provide contract research and development in diverse technology areas, for member companies paying an annual fee. For technical services, such as research and product testing, as well as facilities and equipment provided by the Edison center, incubator companies are charged at the "best member rate" for one year, without paying the membership fee. The incubator director makes referrals to the appropriate Edison center. These referrals are then subject to the approval of Edison center staff. Edison center staff may also answer brief questions over the telephone. This arrangement between the Edison centers and the Edison incubators was initiated in July 1994. The centers and incubators are also working together to develop spin-off companies from the centers.

Incutech Brunswick tenant firms utilize the services of the Research and Productivity Council, a provincial organization, for prototype development and testing. The Research and Productivity Council conducts research, product development, and specialized machining, particularly for the nuclear industry but for other industries as well. The Council can assist firms in materials analysis and in building and testing prototypes.

The Research and Productivity Council has a staff of more than 100 people and a budget of $40 million per year. The Council does most of its work with large companies on a fee-for-service basis; it was not set up to assist small firms who do not have the financial capacity to pay for the services. In order to lend support to small technology firms and keep them from being "left out" of the high technology industry, the council provides services to **Incutech** tenants at no cost.

The **Montgomery County Technology Enterprise Center** (**MCTEC**) utilizes the Maryland Industrial Partnerships (MIPS) program at the University of Maryland to link tenant firms with faculty for research and testing. Maryland Industrial Partnerships is a state-funded program administered by the University of Maryland as part of its Engineering Research Center. Its goal is to facilitate university/industry cooperation that leads to commercialized technologies. The program provides matching funds for faculty at the University of Maryland to assist firms in research and testing products in university lab facilities.

The University of Maryland's Engineering Research Center helps match companies with faculty researchers. A technical board reviews proposals for assistance from the MIPS. The proposals are written by the company's principal(s) in cooperation with the faculty partner. Projects are selected based on potential economic benefit and technical soundness. The four major eligibility requirements are: 1) the company must have operations in Maryland; 2) the research must be in the areas of engineering, computer technology, or physical or life sciences; 3) the proposal must be coauthored by a University of Maryland researcher; and 4) the participating company must provide a match in cash and in-kind contributions.

The program provides grant money for the joint research. The start-up company matches that amount with 10 percent in cash or an in-kind contribution of employee project involvement, equipment, or an investment commitment from an outside source. The maximum grant for any single project is $50,000 for start-up firms.

Technology incubator tenants in Pennsylvania have access to the **Ben Franklin Partnership's Applied Research and Development Fund**, administered through the four Ben Franklin Technology centers. Companies can request direct funding from this program, or they can ask that the money go to a university of their choice that will assist them with product development. The funds can also be split between the company and the partnering university.

The program awards financing to nonprofit research institutions for projects done in coordination with Pennsylvania-based companies with no more than 100 employees; however, preference is given to companies with no more than 50 employees. These joint projects must have a near-term to midterm commercial outcome, with financing available for up to three years. Investments range from $25,000 to $100,000. The average amount is $60,000.

These awards are structured as *royalty financing*, and companies are expected to repay the investments based on their sales, beginning in the first quarter after funding. Repayment is three percent of sales per quarter, limited to 1.5 times the investment. Prepayment or predetermining a maximum repayment may be arranged to limit the amount of repayment. Companies that do not have sales are not required to repay the investment.

Both original funding and annual renewals are subject to a competitive process, including a comprehensive technical evaluation. Companies may be subject to commercial evaluation and presentation to an advisory committee. Companies requesting renewal funding must submit financial statements. Information from the application process is kept confidential. All applicants are required to commit nonstate resources as matching funds. These matching funds may come from a number of sources and may include in-kind support.

The **University City Science Center** supports on-site the Ben Franklin Business Information Center (BIC), whose goal is to improve business decision-making by providing market, industry and competitive information that is normally too difficult or costly for a small business to acquire on its own. BIC accesses over 4,000 databases containing information from journals, newspapers, newswires, government publications, trade and industry newsletters, corporate financial reports, and scientific research papers. Companies use this information to assemble market research and gather competitive intelligence; analyze market, industry and economic trends; identify government regulations and industry experts; and find distributors, potential manufacturers, venture partners and technical problems. Search fees include an hourly charge for staff time and on-line expense. A typical search ranges in cost from $150 to $500.

START Technology Partnership is an independent consortium supported by the **University City Science Center** to augment the commercialization activities of universities, research institutions, and incubator companies in the Philadelphia area. In partnership with The British Technology Group USA, START offers the following services: evaluation of commercial potential of new inventions; business, market, and technical information; patent management and assessment; funding the early development of technology; seeking and negotiating license opportunities; and marketing research strengths and technologies to corporations worldwide.

The **Long Island High Technology Incubator,** through its relationships with adjacent universities, makes available to its tenants a faculty profile database. This is accessible on-line, or searches can be requested and delivered in hard copy. Information is organized by faculty members' fields of expertise, and users can conduct a key word search. Contact information is also provided, and tenant companies are then free to work out their own arrangements with potential partners or consultants.

The **Center for Health Technologies** (CHT) has adopted this approach to work with the Southern Technology Applications Center (STAC), which is one of several National Aeronautics and Space Administration (NASA) regional centers. CHT has a blanket contract with STAC to provide certain services for its affiliate entrepreneurs. This includes assistance in SBIR and STTR; access to the STAC databases of federal technologies and laboratory capacities; and, more recently, help in cooperative research and development agreements (CRADAs) with federal partners. STAC provides these services (up to a limit) at no visible cost to the companies, although CHT needs to negotiate the aggregate scope of services in any program year. Any costs over the initial help are the responsibility of the affiliate and may evolve into an ongoing partnership relationship with STAC.

As part of a CRADA with the federal Idaho National Engineering Lab (INEL), tenants of the **Idaho Innovation Center** have access to free technical assistance from INEL. The hope is that eventually some of these small businesses will develop individual CRADAs or other joint efforts with INEL, which will bring in revenue.

The INEL CRADA—which includes all small businesses in the states of Idaho, Utah, and Wyoming—entitles each small business to up to 40 hours of technical assistance and evaluation from INEL. Requests for assistance go through the SBDC, which is located in the incubator. The SBDC determines if the requested resources are available and are an appropriate use of resources; if so, it makes the connection to the lab staff. This screening prevents businesses from using the technical assistance if the assistance is available from other sources. Thus, INEL staff is used where it can provide unique knowledge and technical skills, for example, in engineering and water-quality management. If a business requires more than 40 hours of assistance, arrangements may be made for a fee or *pro bono* service. The CRADA has been in place since the Spring of 1994.

Since the Idaho Innovation Center adjoins INEL, its tenants are especially well-positioned to take advantage of this arrangement. However, because many of the innovation center tenants are current or former INEL employees, they can also use informal means to gain access to INEL expertise, rather than strictly following the terms of the CRADA. The CRADA has, therefore, been of benefit to other small businesses in the region.

Tenants of the **Rutgers/CARR Business Innovation Center** and other New Jersey incubators may become associate members of the New Jersey Advanced Technology Centers and use this relationship to gain access to research and technology support. This access is especially important due to the inability of small companies to provide full cost support for graduate student research, which is a component of center services.

The 13 New Jersey Advanced Technology Centers serve as basic and contract research facilities for their commercial members. Large businesses may pay annual membership fees as high as $40,000, but small companies can become associate members for about $5,000 per year. As members, companies can arrange to obtain services on a cooperative or a negotiated fee basis.

The **University of Maryland Baltimore County Technology Enterprise Center** also brokers technical services with faculty in the university. Once companies are in the incubator, they may enter into cooperative research with faculty. In one of the companies, the principal was given an adjunct professorship after coming into the incubator. A number of SBIR proposals have been developed using UMBC faculty. The incubator is also able to broker connections to the University of Maryland at Baltimore Medical School.

The **Technology Ventures Incubator** at Stevens Institute of Technology puts a strong emphasis on entrepreneur-faculty interaction and technical assistance. Faculty members either donate their expertise to companies or are hired on a consultant basis. The incubator director matches the faculty members to companies through past experience and informal networking. The director reports to the dean of research at the university, who often can assist in the matching process. The incubator seeks faculty partners who have not only the appropriate expertise but also an interest in becoming involved with the start-up company.

The contractual arrangement often depends upon how the academic department perceives the value of what the start-up is doing, so it is important to have faculty who champion the cause of the start-up. One method for increasing the visibility of entrepreneurial companies is a lunch hosted at least once a year by the provost. The department heads, administrators and the president of Stevens are invited, and each client company makes a brief presentation. This is an opportunity to inform faculty members and department heads about the incubator. The lunch has led to a better image of the incubator, with additional collaboration between the incubator and university faculty.

In a collaborative effort, the **NET Ben Franklin Technology Center**, working with Lehigh University, has established the University Corporate Liaison Program, which provides access to university facilities and equipment.

Six departments at Lehigh University participate in the program. These departments include the Center for Molecular Bioscience and Biotechnology, the Materials Research Center, the Institute for Biomedical Engineering, the Building and Architectural Technology Institute, the Mechanical Engineering Department, and the Department of Computer Science and Electrical Engineering.

The program was originally developed for large companies to perform consulting and small-scale research. Its purpose was to help establish a relationship with industry and possibly bring more money into the university through partnerships to obtain federal research dollars. Each department creates its own fee structure, which is negotiable. Membership fees range from $5,000 to $15,000 for local companies. Program components include access to facilities, equipment, faculty consulting days, and networking opportunities with the university and any other affiliated companies.

Companies within the incubator also utilize the program, and the cost for their membership is subsidized by the state's Ben Franklin funds. For example, one tenant of the NET Ben Franklin Technology Center rents office space from the center, but uses the university's bioprocessing facility to perform all of the technical and testing work needed to develop its proprietary process.

The **Business Technology Incubator** of Peoria, Illinois, has an excellent working relationship with Bradley University. The incubator utilizes the technology center of the university to link with the college of engineering and technology for product design, prototype development, testing, and faculty expertise. In order to ensure efficient utilization of important university resources, the Business Technology Incubator tenants must show some direct need for university resources to gain admission to the incubator. The technology center program was state-funded until 1991 and is now funded by tenants, government grants, and other sources.

Linkages between the incubator and the technology center take several forms. Faculty are sometimes called upon to help screen particular technologies prior to firm admission to the incubator. Faculty and students affiliated with the technology center also work on projects with incubator tenant firms. The incubator keeps a database of all faculty, categorized by expertise and willingness to work on projects. Tenant firms working with the Technology Center can utilize university lab space as well as prototyping and testing facilities. Students also help tenant firms with market research. A few incubator clients are Bradley professors, who work on projects through the technology center and use the incubator for office space.

The Business Technology Incubator also houses offices for a manufacturing consortium of several colleges and universities. Funded by the National Institute of Standards and Technology (NIST), the Central Illinois Manufacturing Innovation Consortium (CIMIC) identifies manufacturing technology needs and assists in meeting those needs by providing faculty/outside consultants, funding projects, and other related services.

Tools

In addition to the various services described above, there recently has emerged a number of commercial "tools" to help companies identify external technology and/or expertise. Usually, these are in the form of databases or data services, including:

Community of Science, sponsored by the **University City Science Center**, is a global registry designed to help identify and locate researchers' interests and expertise. It provides rapid, easy-to-use information about scientists and the funding of science; it contains an on-line inventory of researchers, inventions, and facilities at leading U.S. and Canadian universities and other R&D organizations. The *Community of Science* contains over 40,000 first-person expertise records, 5,000 inventions records, and 2,000 facilities records. Companies and corporations access this database when they are seeking collaborators or organizations funding scientific research.

Contact:
Community of Science
1615 Thames Street
Baltimore, MD 21231
Tel (410) 563-5380   Fax (410) 563-5389
hw3@bestpl.hef.jhu.edu

Gateway is a free service that helps business and industry callers access technology, research-in-progress, expertise, and unique facilities at more than 700 federal laboratories, as well as federally funded research conducted at universities. It is operated by the National Technology Transfer Center (NTTC) based in Wheeling, West Virginia. *Gateway* is easily accessible by calling 1-800-678-6882. Customer service representatives handle information requests, which are assigned to technology access agents.

International Technology & Business Opportunities Database (ITBO), a product of Klenner International, is a database service available worldwide. Klenner International (formerly Dr. Dvorkovitz & Associates) pioneered on-line search-and-retrieval and has been involved in the licensing of more than 1,000 products and processes throughout the world. Sources of new technology and business opportunities may be listed in the ITBO database at no charge. The organization offers a number of standard subscription services to organizations that are looking for new technologies from outside sources. Klenner also offers a full database of technologies in software format to organizations around the world for exclusive use. Costs range from $200 for single searches to annual retainers of up to $2,000 for specific categories. A standard subscription service that allows searches for up to 10 categories of technology is available for $1,000 per year and $50 per abstract. The company also serves government agencies, universities, research institutions, and small companies by finding licensees for their developments.

Contact:
Klenner International
P.O. Box 1748
Ormond Beach, FL 32175
Tel (904) 673-4339   Fax (904) 673-5911

Knowledge Express is an on-line database service that provides information about licensing opportunities, collaborative ventures, and corporate, university, and federal technology transfer opportunities. The service, a product of Knowledge Express Data Systems, offers access to more than 20 databases, including federal technologies and inventions (for example, EPA, NIST, USDA/ARS and DOE), *Comtex Business News*, Corptech, PHS Technologies, *Technology Access Report*, *NASA Tech Briefs*, Bioscan, and technologies and inventions from more than 100 universities. *Knowledge Express* is available for an initial fee of $250, with an annual renewal fee of $100. There is a $2-per-minute usage charge and a fee that ranges from $1.25 to $9.25 for each report generated. Pricing options may allow a client unlimited use of a particular database for a separate annual fee and per-hour usage charge.

Contact:
  Knowledge Express Data Systems
  1235 Westlakes Drive, Suite 210
  Berwyn, PA 19312
  Tel (800) 529-5337   Fax (610) 251-8001

MicroPatent provides patent research tools and services to the public and private sector and offers a number of patent-related services and products. *PatentSearch* is a series of comprehensive CD-ROMs that provide detailed information regarding U.S. and European patents. Patent information is updated monthly. MicroPatent also offers customized CD-ROMs to meet specific search criteria, such as patents in a narrow field of research or information about a competitor's patents. *PatentQuery Bulletin* is a monthly floppy disc that allows searches of all patents in the subscriber's industry from United States, European, and world patent offices. The bulletin offers patents categorized and summarized by patent number, assignee or applicant, inventor, title, and abstract. The information is fully searchable on any or all of these fields, including key words in the title and abstract. On-demand search queries by telephone are also available. MicroPatent creates a search strategy, executes the search, discusses the results by phone, and faxes or mails the results to the customer. The PatentSearch CD-ROMs are available for $1,400 per year including monthly updates. The price of customized CD-ROMs varies. The *PatentQuery Bulletin* is available for $60 per year. The price of telephone searches varies depending on search complexity.

Contact:
  MicroPatent
  250 Dodge Avenue
  East Haven, CT 06512-3358
  Tel (800) 984-9800   Fax (203) 466-5054

CHAPTER 4 # MANAGEMENT

Entrepreneurs who start enterprises based on their technologies suddenly find themselves dealing with the many responsibilities involved in managing a business. Once the business grows to more than one employee, management issues such as employee selection, professional development, and organizational design become relevant. Until the company grows large enough to bring on an administrative staff, the entrepreneur must deal with basic administrative functions such as payroll and financial reporting. In order for a start-up to grow into a successful technology business, management development, networking, strategic partnering, and strategic planning must all become areas of focus, along with the development of the technology.

Before resources are available to staff a management team, the entrepreneur needs to know some basic principles of business management. With zero funds for management training, it is important for new businesses to utilize available resources in the community. These resources may include universities, community colleges, and government business development offices that provide training at little or no cost. Often the biggest problem feared by owners of start-up technology businesses is finding the time to access the services available. It is important for entrepreneurs to see the need for management development, then take advantage of the resources available.

Start-up businesses can often get tremendous help from community members with business management expertise who are willing to help small firms. Business leaders will often become advisory board members for new companies and offer their assistance on various management issues. Mentoring programs developed by incubators or business development offices are good ways of linking start-ups to resource people in the community.

Strategic partnering also can benefit small companies that lack resources or expertise in areas such as marketing or manufacturing. Small companies often join with other businesses that complement their strengths. A technically innovative company can combine with one experienced in manufacturing, for instance. Skills and experience lacking in a business can be added by the strategic partner (Stevens, 1992).

Start-up businesses can be so overwhelmed with day-to-day business operations that strategic planning is put aside for another day. However, identifying short- and long-term goals and objectives may be especially important for the smallest companies. A million-dollar mistake is going to hurt a small business much more than it will a large one. Michel Robert, strategic planning author and trainer, says that without strategic planning, businesses are practicing "the Christopher Columbus School of Management."

"When [Columbus] left, he didn't know where he was going. When he got there, he didn't know where he was. And, when he got back, he couldn't tell where he had been" (Kinni, 1994). Start-up businesses are constantly making decisions that affect future opportunities and can often benefit from a structured decision-making process. With strategic planning, decisions can be based on where the business wants to go in the future, not merely on where it is today (Buss, 1995).

Incubators offer a wide range of management assistance, including access to management training, management team and board selection, administrative support services, and strategic planning. Incubator managers, who often have daily interactions with tenant companies, can reinforce the need for management skills development. Incubators are great network builders for start-ups, accessing community members with skills in various management areas who are interested in mentoring new businesses. Often members of the incubator's advisory board assist tenant firms. Working one-on-one with companies, incubator managers know the issues that each company is facing, and they can provide a link with service providers to meet those needs. Many incubators have formal or informal monitoring of companies in order to identify areas that need strengthening and broker resources for start-up success.

In the next section, we will provide some descriptive statistics on the range and frequency of management-related services and practices. As in the previous chapters, this will be followed by a description of practices that are seen by incubator managers as particularly novel, useful, or productive.

Overview of Practices and Services: Management

We asked incubator managers to respond to a checklist of likely management support and development services or practices provided to client companies. For each practice or service, managers were asked to indicate whether they provided the service or practice directly, brokered or referred the service or practice, did both, or did neither. The checklist had the effect of providing a scale of intensity for services and practices provided in the management area. The summary results are presented in Table 4.1 (next page).

By far the most common practice is organizing tenant networking and peer technical assistance. This practice is an integral part of an incubator's functions. Other types of networking, such as forming mentoring relationships with business executives and university faculty, are also provided by most incubators.

Less than half the incubators provide temporary management services and use project management tools, such as decision rules, to decide whether or not an R&D effort should be continued. Likewise, incubators are not often involved in organizational design and structuring.

We conducted comparative analysis of different incubator types. The analysis of incubators by university affiliation is found in Table 4.2 (page 55). Three of the management practices show statistically significant relationships based on university affiliation. Non-university affiliated incubators were more likely to provide assistance with organizational design and restructuring, the provision of temporary management service, and the use of project management tools. However, if one scans Table 4.2 and examines what different types of incubators don't do (or do rarely), it shows some interesting hints of relationships. For example, university-affiliated incubators tend to avoid locating managerial staff, conducting formal technical reviews, and monitoring financials.

When we compared incubators in rural areas with those in urban areas, we found that in almost all areas, more services were provided by urban incubators, as shown in Table 4.3 (page 56). Assis-

Table 4.1: Management Practices (valid percent responses)

	no, rarely/never	yes, by referral	yes, directly	both
organize tenant networking/peer technical assistance	3.9	7.8	78.4	9.8
develop business executives/faculty mentoring	10.9	12.7	60.0	16.4
monitor enterprise financials	12.0	8.0	74.0	6.0
provide temporary staff	13.0	25.9	55.6	5.6
conduct management training for tech businesses	13.2	41.5	30.2	15.1
conduct exit interviews and exit assistance	13.7	2.0	82.4	2.0
facilitate strategic partnerships	18.2	27.3	41.8	12.7
locate/identify key management staff	20.0	29.1	34.5	16.4
conduct strategic planning sessions	23.6	21.8	43.6	10.9
build management team	26.4	37.7	28.3	7.5
conduct formal technical reviews	32.0	16.0	46.0	6.0
select and assess employees	41.5	24.5	24.5	9.4
use formal project selection tools/instruments	46.0	14.0	38.0	2.0
introduce advanced management practices	44.4	44.4	11.1	0.0
use organizational design and structuring	47.2	24.5	24.5	3.8
use project management tools	56.3	16.7	25.0	2.1
provide temporary management services	52.8	22.6	20.8	3.8

tance in developing the management team, through approaches such as venture teaming, was found to be significantly related to incubator location, with urban incubators more likely to provide this service. This relationship suggests that outside management professionals are more common in urban areas. Both provision of temporary management services and organizing tenant networking and tenant peer learning were significantly more likely in an urban area. Provision of temporary management services may be more feasible in an urban area where there is a greater supply of available management professionals. It is unclear why there is also such a strong relationship between urban location and promotion of tenant networking, other than simple density issues.

In the next section, we will present the best practice descriptions that our sample of incubators provided. As in previous chapters, they correspond with the checklist data just described.

BEST PRACTICES: MANAGEMENT

Reflecting the crucial importance of management in the success of a technology-based venture, the range of practices and services provided by incubators is comprehensive, as illustrated by the checklist just reported. The variety of best practices (those seen as useful, novel, and particularly effective) that were discussed by incubator managers in the interviews tended to be narrower than the vari-

Table 4.2: Management Practices by Incubator University Affiliation (valid percent responses)

	no, rarely/never		yes, by referral		yes, directly		both	
	university	non	university	non	university	non	university	non
organize tenant networking/ peer technical assistance	3.6	5.6	10.7	0.0	78.6	83.3	7.1	11.1
conduct exit interviews and exit assistance	10.7	22.2	0.0	5.6	89.3	66.7	0.0	5.6
develop business executives/faculty mentoring	12.5	11.1	18.8	0.0	59.4	66.7	9.4	22.2
provide temporary staff	12.5	17.6	25.0	29.4	59.4	47.1	3.1	5.9
conduct management training for tech businesses	13.3	11.1	50.0	33.3	26.7	38.9	10.0	16.7
monitor enterprise financials	17.9	5.9	14.3	0.0	60.7	88.2	7.1	5.9
facilitate strategic partnerships	18.8	22.2	28.1	27.8	46.9	33.3	6.3	16.7
locate/identify key management staff	25.0	5.6	28.1	33.3	28.1	50.0	18.8	11.1
conduct strategic planning sessions	28.1	16.7	21.9	16.7	40.6	55.6	9.4	11.1
build management teams	30.0	22.2	40.0	38.9	26.7	27.8	3.3	11.1
introduce advanced management practices	32.3	55.6	51.6	38.9	16.1	5.6	0.0	0.0
conduct formal technical reviews	40.7	16.7	11.1	22.2	48.1	44.4	0.0	16.7
select and assess employees	48.4	29.4	19.4	29.4	25.8	23.5	6.5	17.6
develop organizational design and structuring	51.6	38.9	32.3	11.1	16.1	38.9	0.0	11.1
use formal project selection tools/instruments	60.7	23.5	10.7	23.5	28.6	47.1	0.0	5.9
provide temporary management services	63.3	27.8	20.0	33.3	16.7	27.8	0.0	11.1
use project management tools	73.1	35.3	7.7	35.3	19.2	23.5	0.0	5.9

ety of practice use suggested by the checklist.

The best practices described in this section have been grouped into the following major categories: 1) direct administrative support services provided by the incubator; 2) consultant services; 3) management training; 4) mentoring; 5) advisory boards; and 6) exit assistance. In addition, we have described one comprehensive approach, as well as several management tools.

Direct Administrative Support Services

In addition to the strategic and leadership aspects of management, principals of ventures usually are not prepared to cope with the involved processes and routine record-keeping requirements of simply running a business. At the early stages of a company's development, there may be only one or two employees in addition to the principal. Start-up companies find it useful to have access to business support functions without having to take on administrative support staff. To allow tenant companies to focus their attention on business development, some incubators provide such direct administrative support services to tenant companies. These services vary depending on the stage of development of the company and may be provided directly though onsite contract services or though referral to other

Table 4.3: Management Practices by Incubator Location (valid percent responses)

	no, rarely/never		yes, by referral		yes, directly		both	
	rural	urban	rural	urban	rural	urban	rural	urban
organize tenant networking/ peer technical assistance	16.7	0.0	16.7	5.1	66.7	82.1	0.0	12.8
develop business executives/faculty mentoring	21.4	7.3	21.4	9.8	50.0	63.4	7.1	19.5
provide temporary staff	21.4	10.0	14.3	30.0	64.3	52.5	0.0	7.5
conduct management training for tech businesses	21.4	10.3	35.7	43.6	28.6	30.8	14.3	15.4
monitor enterprise financials	23.1	8.1	0.0	10.8	69.2	75.7	7.7	5.4
conduct exit interviews and exit assistance	33.3	7.7	0.0	2.6	66.7	87.2	0.0	2.6
use formal project selection tools/instruments	33.3	50.0	16.7	13.2	50.0	34.2	0.0	2.6
facilitate strategic partnerships	35.7	12.2	35.7	24.4	28.6	46.3	0.0	17.1
locate/identify key management staff	35.7	14.6	35.7	26.8	21.4	39.0	7.1	19.5
conduct strategic planning sessions	42.9	17.1	28.6	19.5	28.6	48.8	0.0	14.6
select and assess employees	42.9	41.0	21.4	25.6	35.7	20.5	0.0	12.8
introduce advanced management practices	42.9	45.0	50.0	42.5	7.1	12.5	0.0	0.0
use project management tools	46.2	60.0	23.1	14.3	30.8	22.9	0.0	2.9
conduct formal technical reviews	50.0	26.3	0.0	21.1	50.0	44.7	0.0	7.9
build management team	57.1	15.4	21.4	43.6	21.4	30.8	0.0	10.3
use organizational design and structuring	64.3	41.0	14.3	28.2	21.4	25.6	0.0	5.1
provide temporary management services	92.9	38.5	7.1	28.2	0.0	28.2	0.0	5.1

service providers. Assistance with employment processing and payroll, accounting, bookkeeping, word processing, and general clerical support are examples of commonly provided services.

The **GENESIS Business Incubator (GBI)** at the University of Arkansas-Fayetteville is an activity of the University and is organized within its formal structure. The incubator offers payroll services on a limited basis to tenant companies. For tenant companies at the earliest stage of development, GBI arranges for the company personnel to be hired as temporary employees of the University of Arkansas-Fayetteville. Employees are entitled to a limited package of benefits and may be employed for up to 1,500 hours in any year. The university payroll office arranges withholding of state and federal income taxes, social security taxes, and whatever costs are appropriate for benefits to which temporary employees are entitled. The companies are assessed the out-of-pocket costs for wages and benefits, and the university calculates withholding and makes payments to the proper government agency at no additional charge. This service is obviously suitable for the first few months of a company's operation but is limited by the 1,500-hour ceiling. The incubator management is extremely diligent in collecting the funds required to underwrite salaries and withholding and does not allow companies to fall behind in payments. If the funds are not collected on a current basis, the service is withdrawn.

Once companies are moving along well enough to be able to handle their own payroll, the GBI staff puts them in touch with a commercial payroll preparation company, which has an arrangement with the National Business Incubation Association and provides its services to tenants of member incubators at very favorable rates. This progression of services allows tenant companies to change their services to meet their own individual needs and growth patterns.

As another example of payroll services, **Laboratory Associated Businesses, Ltd.** is a for-profit corporation that provides laboratory space to emerging biotechnology and medical testing companies. The corporation provides management functions for the tenant companies, such as payroll, taxes, and accounting service. The service is provided by a contractor who does automated payroll, withholding taxes, and all required reporting. In addition, the corporation has a group health plan that provides health insurance for employees of all 10 tenant companies.

The **First Flight Venture Center** has an anchor tenant that provides business administration support services to entrepreneurial companies. This company, Entrepreneurial Assistance, Inc. (EAI), provides services to tenant companies, as well as to non-tenant companies, on a fee basis. EAI provides such business support services as accounting, bookkeeping, payroll, word processing, and general clerical and secretarial services. These services are listed in the First Flight Venture Center service menu. The arrangement evolved from discussions initiated by the management of EAI, who saw in the incubator an opportunity to expand its existing business, which focuses on providing services to small and medium-sized firms, with an emphasis on entrepreneurial businesses. While discounted rates to tenant companies are not required by the incubator, a special arrangement does exist with the incubator management.

Approximately 80 percent of First Flight companies use some EAI services, as does the incubator management itself. One benefit of this arrangement is that it gives EAI flexibility to tailor services specifically to the greatest needs of each tenant company. As these needs grow, EAI can increase each service provided until it is more cost-effective for the company to internalize the service. A further benefit of this arrangement is the level of professionalism provided by the company, which specializes in business support services and is generally better equipped than the incubator staff to provide these services. This permits the incubator staff to focus on other issues, such as facility management, funding, publicity needs, and providing other client services. The arrangement also benefits the incubator by lowering overhead and administrative costs.

Consultant Services

Management is one of the key components of a successful enterprise. This includes expertise in all of the key functions of a company, perhaps embodied in one or two individuals. Technology-based start-ups in particular have needs for more specialized expertise and consulting assistance than does the average start-up enterprise. One way of brokering this type of help is to bring specialized service providers to the companies in the incubator facility. Incubators do this through shared service programs, providing access to free or low-cost consulting, brokering consultant services, and making other arrangements to provide access to management services. Start-up companies usually cannot afford high-quality consulting in the areas of marketing and finance, though these are critical for survival and success. One of the most valuable services of any incubator is bringing in experts at no additional cost to tenant firms. No incubator has sufficient staff talent to meet all the needs of managers of new enterprises. The solution in most cases is to *broker* or facilitate the use of outside consultants.

The **Long Island High Technology Incubator** has a service program that includes a venture capital firm, two patent firms, two major accounting firms (Peat Marwick and Price-Waterhouse), and two general legal firms. These service companies share a work space in the incubator (a 1,000-square-foot office) and meet with entrepreneurial companies there. Each of these service providers pays the incubator an annual fee of $4,000, which is in the form of a license agreement for the use of the space. The amount of time that each service provider spends on the grounds varies widely, but the point of contact for each is well known to tenant companies in the incubator. Companies may either make appointments with one of the service providers or meet on a walk-in basis during general office hours. The first meeting between the company and the service provider is usually on a *pro bono* or reduced-rate basis, with terms and conditions specified thereafter. Several of the tenant companies have established ongoing relationships with one or more of the service providers. However, if tenant companies want to access other consultants for more specialized assistance, the incubator management will also make those referrals. In addition to the participants in the service program, there are other resident companies in the incubator who are involved in related services (e.g., market research), and tenants frequently work with them as well.

The **Iowa State Innovation Center (ISIC)** takes a somewhat novel approach to brokering consulting services. The incubator is located in a rural area that does not have a large supply of experienced managers, and most of the entrepreneurs are current or former academics. As a result, ISIC organizes consulting assistance in much more of a teaching or "modeling" approach. Most consultants are under contract jointly to the Small Business Development Center (SBDC) and ISIC, and their client relations are carefully monitored. In effect, the relationship between the consultants and the SBDC takes a case management form. Payment for consulting help is part of the client company's contract with the incubator, although direct payment by the company develops later on. Consultants are selected not only for their expertise, but also for their ability to teach and model appropriate behavior. Consultants report to the SBDC in writing about their progress with the client, and these reports become part of the case file.

The **Metropolitan Center for High Technology (MCHT)** operates two physical facilities and an incubator-without-walls program to serve a five-county metropolitan area. To meet businesses' needs, they have developed throughout the region a network of consultants that they liken to a "circuit rider" program. These individuals are on retainer, at a *per diem* rate or through an annual umbrella contract. They tend to complement the skills of the resident staff in areas such as manufacturing, engineering, and legal assistance. Each week the vice president of technology development (who coordinates services for the entrepreneurs) sets out a program of visits and consultations. He writes a report on the results and expectations of the meetings, and it is maintained in the entrepreneur's file. Between the staff and the circuit riders, a "virtual management team" is established for each company. For example, staff and consultants may accompany the entrepreneur to meetings or interviews. All of these services are free to the tenant company and are paid for out of the corporate budget, which is largely supported (70 percent) by state funds.

MCHT also uses another, less formal approach to brokering assistance that directly involves its board members. An insert in the "board book" briefly describes the current needs of companies in the incubator. After the quarterly board meeting, one or two entrepreneurs may meet with members of the board and informally discuss their needs and pressing business issues. Often the board member may be able to match up the entrepreneur with someone from his or her network of business associates. This is a form of networking and mentoring (discussed later).

The **Idaho State University Business and Technology Center (BTC)** offers a creative method of obtaining and monitoring free services provided by local consultants to tenant companies. BTC developed the "50 Hour Club" to provide consulting services to incubator tenants free of charge. University faculty, private business owners, accountants, and attorneys are asked to volunteer 50 *pro bono* hours each. This time is placed into a "bank" which tenants can utilize for consulting services. Each tenant is given an account with 50 hours of credit. This free time can be spread over a range of business needs.

The program was established with a clear set of written guidelines for both providers and consumers of the services. The guidelines state the following: only BTC tenant companies are eligible; consultants will not do for tenants what they can and ought to do for themselves; consultants are not to be held liable by the tenants for their volunteer services and counseling to tenants; tenants will be required to sign a statement to this effect prior to accepting consulting services; tenants' requests for service will be made through the BTC manager; the manager will screen all requests and refer to appropriate consultants; requests shall not place unreasonable time commitment upon consultants; and services, unless other arrangements are made, shall be provided during normal, working hours. Moreover, the manager reserves the right to deny service requests deemed inappropriate or excessive.

The tenant completes a one-page request-for-services. The tenant's name, company, telephone number, and date are recorded on the top of the form. The form requires tenants to describe the urgency of the request for services, identify the nature of services needed, describe the problem area, and determine the amount of time necessary to arrive at a solution for the problem. Tenants also indicate their preference for meeting times. Tenants must sign and date the form before submission to the incubator manager. An application process was instituted to assist the incubator manager in weeding out problems that should be solved by the tenant. For example, tenants cannot use the time for tax preparation. In addition, screening promotes the best use of the consultant's time.

The application is also reviewed by the incubator manager and the tenant to determine the appropriate amount of time. For example, a tenant can ask the manager for help in setting up a computerized accounting system. The manager may determine that five hours is needed to complete this process. The manager then reviews the consultants on file and finds one with relevant expertise. Both the tenant and the consultant's time are debited five hours. Theoretically, the team can continue the process until the 50 hours are used up. Currently, the accounts are kept in a ledger and monitored by the incubator manager. Times are recorded on the application sheets and placed in the file. The system will be computerized when use of the program increases. The program has been seen as positive by those companies who make use of it, although overall usage has been somewhat lower than expected.

Companies in the **Rutgers/CARR Business Innovation Center** have access to the New Jersey small business voucher program, which provides matching grants to assist small businesses in obtaining professional services. Funded by the New Jersey Commission on Science and Technology, the small business voucher program allocates vouchers of up to $10,000 in value to small businesses. Funding from the business voucher program helps small companies pay for needed assistance through service providers enrolled in the program. Companies can use vouchers to pay for services from the state's incubators and 13 Advanced Technology Centers (located at various universities in the state). These service providers are then reimbursed by state funds. Service providers may subcontract for specialized services to a small business, such as accounting or marketing firms. Vouchers may also be used for incubator rent. The grants require a two-to-one match from the company, so in effect the state pays one-third of the cost of the services. Any small, New Jersey-based technology company is qualified to apply for these funds.

The application process is relatively simple. Small businesses apply for the vouchers through a letter proposal. The vouchers are distributed on a rolling basis; worthy proposals are funded as long as funds are available. The program has continued to be funded by the state legislature. There is currently no limit on the number of times a company may apply for a voucher, but the program is intended to be used infrequently.

The voucher program has proven very helpful to start-up companies in paying for services, especially for one-time-only projects, such as establishing a chart of accounts. One problem for service providers is that the reimbursement process is slow.

The **Technology Development Center** (TDC) of West Sacramento, California has cultivated an associates program of local retired executives and active consultants who provide *pro bono* advice to incubator companies on a regular basis. Through the associates program, incubator companies gain access to experts in specialized management fields. The relationships can be full-time or on an as-needed basis. Consulting associates join the program in order to gain exposure to growing companies, which they may join as management team members or take on as paying clients for special projects.

Associates, including attorneys, accountants, marketing specialists, investors, and business people act as volunteer consultants to incubator companies. There are currently nine associates who volunteer an average of two to three hours per week. They also participate in business plan reviews, company assessments, and monthly social events held for incubator companies, among other TDC activities.

Professionals who approach TDC about joining the associates program are interviewed by TDC management and are asked to become associates if they possess expertise useful to the incubator companies. On a trial basis, they may also be asked to participate in a company assessment to see how they perform. Once associates join, they are asked to sign an understanding of expectations and confidentiality agreement. They are provided with office space and access to office equipment.

By mutual agreement, an associate may join the management team of an incubator company, usually as CEO or CFO. TDC has available a boilerplate form for these agreements. Alternatively, associates may be paid by the company for any long-term consulting on special projects, either on a cash or noncash basis. TDC may also pay these consulting fees, to be reimbursed by the incubator company. Usually a reduced rate for consulting is charged to incubator companies. If a consulting fee is charged, TDC receives 20 percent of the gross fees from the associate.

The TDC CEO serves as a liaison between associates and companies. The CEO is responsible for interviewing potential associates, coordinating assessments, and matching companies and associates; these activities take up about 15 percent of the CEO's time. If the matching results in the employment of an associate with a company, the TDC may receive a finder's fee.

The **St. Louis Technology Center** has spearheaded the creation of a resource directory and referral system in order to help entrepreneurs more easily sort out the services they may need. As in most metropolitan counties, the St. Louis metropolitan area has numerous economic development programs run by a variety of agencies and governmental jurisdictions. Entrepreneurs may waste time visiting several offices and still never identify the programs that can help their particular situation.

In order to facilitate better coordination of services to businesses, the center sponsored a workshop that brought together the economic development providers in the county. One outcome of this workshop was an omnibus resource directory with characteristics of all the economic development offices that participated. From that point, the Metropolitan Business Assistance Program was formed, made up of the five principal organizations in the county that provide support services to businesses. The organizations in the Metropolitan Business Assistance Program include the SBDC, the St. Louis Technology Center, and the University of Missouri Continuing Education Department. This program helps coordinate a package of services for clients; the participating service provider organizations agree to stick to their own areas of expertise and to refer clients to other programs as appropriate.

When a client makes an initial inquiry to an economic development program, he or she is referred to the Business Information Center, an intake and referral service staffed by SCORE volunteers who have a good overview of programs available in the metropolitan area. The Business Information Center is open during regular business hours. The St. Louis Technology Incubator directs inquiries from potential clients to the Business Information Center first, and it is working to encourage the other organizations in the area to refer clients to the central location. The CEOs of all the involved economic development organizations meet monthly to keep the process going and deal with any ongoing implementation issues.

Comprehensive Management Assistance Models

Incubators face the difficult task of providing assistance in multiple areas to companies at different stages of development. The **Boulder Technology Incubator (BTI)** has developed a comprehensive model for technology business assistance, utilizing a seven-step process from initial screening of potential incubator tenants through the preparation of a presentation to investors. The Entrepreneur Success Model is a comprehensive, flexible approach to business assistance, providing marketing, product development, organization, and financing assistance in a customized format that can be used for companies at any early stage of development, regardless of the entrepreneur's experience.   The process utilizes six committees, with members tailored to the individual company, and who move with that company through the stages of the model. These customized committees serve as an ongoing advisory board for the company. The steps are as follows:

Stage 1: Initial Screening—When a company expresses an interest in entering the incubator, the executive director conducts an initial screening. If the executive director deems the company a suitable match for the incubator, the company then enters the committee process.

Stage 2: Admissions Committee—This committee screens companies for entrance into the incubator. The chair of this committee is elected yearly. The other committee members are chosen based on the technology and the executive director's preliminary screening concerning the needs of the company. If the company is admitted, these customized committees become a company's board of advisors, and stay with it throughout the Entrepreneurial Success Model process. This involves the development/improvement of the business plan and its presentation through the next four stages.

Stage 3: Product Development Committee—This committee works with the company on technology, product, or service needs, concentrating on what is critical to create a real product/service or business.

Stage 4: Market Development Committee—During this stage, the company needs to demonstrate that it knows enough about the market and a specific market strategy for the company to progress through the remainder of the process.

Stage 5: Organizational Development Committee—This stage includes further development of the management team, the corporate structure, and board of advisors, including incubator committee members.

Stage 6: Financial Development Committee—At this stage, committee members examine all financial statements including cash flows, *pro formas*, and financial assumptions.

After six stages are complete, the company progresses to the funding or capitalization stage.

Stage 7: Client Funding Committee—This committee determines if the company is ready for initial capital investment. It consists of experienced investors who prepare the company for the due diligence and investment processes.

Members of the six committees are business leaders in the community who volunteer their time. The executive director of the incubator recruits these volunteers through board member networking and referral. A committee member may be working with two or three companies at one time. The advisory board meets often; the frequency depends on the company's need and its stage in the process. Meetings are more frequent at the beginning and the end. Committee members serve with enlightened self-interest, meeting potential clients and investment opportunities while doing a service for the community.

The process is customized depending on the stage of the company entering the incubator. If the entrepreneur has been successful previously in a related area, he or she may skip a stage. The advisors are experienced in similar enterprises and know when a company is proficient in an area and can bypass that stage. The average time a company spends completing the seven-stage process is six months. Depending on the company, the process may take as long as one year.

The Entrepreneur Success Model works as an integral part of BTI's method of getting the best possible prospects into the incubator and providing them with the most effective services. These components include a mentor/advisor network to supplement the skills of the entrepreneur, a capital network to help the firm reach the appropriate funding stage, and the Entrepreneur Success Model itself.

The Entrepreneur Success Model can be used with incubator clients at any stage of development. Companies are told about the model at the beginning and know what to expect throughout their stay in the incubator. Upon completing the process, the company will have an improved management team, a board of advisors, a business plan, and a well-developed financial/investor presentation. The model also keeps business leaders in the community affiliated with and supportive of the incubator.

The **Tri-Cities Enterprise Association (TEA)**, along with government and university partners, accessed $987,000 from the U.S. Department of Energy's 1993 Defense Authorization Act Defense Authorization grants for diversifying economic development. The funding helped establish the Entrepreneur Support Network, which 1) provides entrepreneur success training through the SBDC-sponsored Fast Track Program; 2) allows access to the Office Resource Center at the incubator; and 3) capitalizes a $600,000 equity investment fund.

The equity investment fund is broken into two loan funds. One fund, the Micro Equity Fund, was capitalized at $100,000 and makes loans of $15,000 to $30,000. The incubator manages this pool. The Micro Equity loans start as a debt but can be converted to equity (TEA takes stock in the company and forgives a portion or all of the borrower's debt).

The other pool, the Capital Fund, was capitalized with $500,000 and makes larger loans. This pool is managed by the Benton-Franklin Regional Council. The Capital Fund allows for creative debt financing, such as interest forgiven the first year. These loans cannot be converted to equity, however.

The loan funds are attempting to leverage local matches with the $600,000 DOE money. TEA also has an additional $400,000 Microloan fund that high-tech and other companies can access for capital in amounts of up to $25,000.

Management Training

Despite their technical knowledge, many entrepreneurs are relatively ignorant of management concepts, and management training is a definite need. Technology business incubators use a variety of approaches to provide or broker management training and to motivate tenants to participate.

The continuing education division of the University of Maryland Baltimore County (UMBC), in combination with the Michael Dingman Center for Entrepreneurship at the University of Maryland College Park, runs entrepreneur roundtables several times a year which are open to incubator companies as well as non-incubator companies. Roundtables typically have two or three speakers from some area of expertise—such as venture capital, tax law, or accounting. They also run several short courses that deal with subjects such as the preparation of business plans, how to raise capital, management organization and other business management subjects. To encourage participation in such training programs, the **Technology Enterprise Center** (TEC) of the UMBC provides a rebate of a portion of the tuition through a rent credit. For example, if a Dingman Center seminar costs $75, the incubator will be charged $50, and the incubator will rebate $25 to the company by reducing its next month's rent.

In addition to these carrots, there are also sticks to encourage participation in training. TEC companies enter into a license agreement to use the incubator space, which is essentially a lease agreement. The license agreement specifies that the company must attend at least one training course during the year. Failure to participate in training programs can be a factor in the incubator refusing to extend the company's lease for a third year or deciding to terminate its lease.

There are numerous and varied opportunities for companies to participate in training programs. The Dingman Center programs—either seminar, roundtable, or workshop courses—are held almost once a month. In addition, the Regional Incubator Board puts on two or three programs a year of a similar nature. The TEC also sponsors tenant breakfasts with guest speakers on finance, marketing strategies, market research, and other topics. The breakfasts are held about once a month and are free to tenants. The incubator pays for the food.

To monitor participation, the incubator manager and director attend almost all of these events themselves so they know who is there. They have a very good idea of who participates and who doesn't. Notices of these workshops, seminars, and roundtables are included with the tenants' mail and posted on the incubator bulletin board.

The TEC approach to management training provides maximum flexibility for the client in choosing which training programs to attend, while also encouraging maximum participation through both monitoring and incentives.

The **Technology Enterprise Centre** in Calgary, Alberta, is working with a local community college to provide on-site workshops to its tenants on strategic planning, business planning, and sales and marketing skills. Participants pay about two-thirds of the costs of these workshops, generally about $100 to $125 per person. The incubator absorbs the balance of the costs. On-site workshops provide useful information to incubator companies, and the convenience of location on-site ensures that they are better attended than off-site workshops.

The **Business Technology Center** of Columbus, Ohio, provides management training seminars and workshops to its tenant companies through several means. The incubator has provided seminars and information sessions in conjunction with local organizations, hosted on-site sessions run by for-profit training organizations, and developed specialized seminars with state agencies. Sessions focus on basic business training for the start-up companies, as well as specialized needs of technology companies.

The Center hosts quarterly seminars that are held by for-profit organizations and open to all interested businesses. These sessions, on such topics as business structure, accounting, and human resource issues, are held with the provision that "scholarships" will be given to all interested incubator companies. Thus far, the Business Technology Center has been approached by several organizations offering this service. The center has also developed specialized seminars of interest to its tenants. These have included a seminar on SBIR run by staff from the State of Ohio. All seminar topics are determined by tenant input and include such subjects as capital formation, sales, taxes, bookkeeping and computerized management systems, and government contracts and grants.

Seminars on "the basics" have been found to be the most useful, but there is an audience for virtually every topic. Because of its newly expanded facilities, the Business Technology Center has been able to provide more programs run by outside organizations. By determining seminar topics based on tenant input, the Business Technology Center can be sure it is meeting its tenants' needs.

The **Austin Technology Incubator (ATI)** hosts a series of seminars on various business management issues. The content tends to be driven by customer demand; the incubator first solicits topics of interest from member companies, then engages speakers with expertise in those areas. Topics range from business plan writing and basic accounting practices to human resources issues. Seminars are scheduled as demand dictates. ATI secures speakers from law firms, banks, accounting firms, and more. Not only do member companies and other entrepreneurs in the community receive valuable business assistance, but ATI also increases its exposure in the community.

To assist companies with goal-setting and follow-up, the **Arizona Technology Incubator** utilizes the Management Action Programs, Inc. (MAP). The incubator sends all the CEO/presidents of the tenant companies to a two-and-one-half day workshop conducted by MAP which focuses on issues such as self-appraisal, growth goals, growth strategies, action steps, progress, and corrective strategies. The workshops are run by highly trained instructors, and there is substantial follow-up by the incubator manager to ensure that companies are following their plans.

This program takes a long-term approach to management skills development, goal-setting, and controls. The incubator manager is heavily involved in the process and supplies MAP with an overview of each firm and what the incubator management sees as the firm's strengths and weaknesses. So that the incubator manager can monitor the progress, MAP sends him or her the plan developed by each company during the workshop. MAP supplies this service free to incubator firms in the hope that companies will purchase the services when they become successful.

Mentoring Programs

Companies need a variety of mechanisms to address questions and receive advice during critical growth stages. Mentorship always has been valued as a way to learn how to grow and succeed, and as a way to give start-up companies access to professional services and advice at no or little cost. Entrepreneurs at early stages of business formation especially need advice from someone who has been through the start-up process or has experience in business. They may not need or be able to afford intensive consulting services, but by having access to free advice, they can get answers to questions and get pointed in the right direction. Many incubators set up mentoring programs that link the CEO of an incubator firm with retired executives or with someone in the community who is interested in a particular start-up company and/or supportive of business incubation. Using members of an advisory board as mentors provides a high level of advice to new and growing companies who are tenants of the incubator. At the same time, board members remain involved in the operation of the incubator and the success of companies served.

A major benefit of mentorship is the chance for start-up companies to interact with others in similar circumstances and/or those that have already achieved success. Many incubators have programs that link tenants with successful entrepreneurs in the community, including incubator graduates who have succeeded. The tenants get to see the successes that result from good business practices and can use the successful companies as models.

Because of the one-on-one component of a mentorship program, mentors can become more familiar with a company than company advisory committees and often can offer a different perspective on issues than the incubator management might provide.

Companies affiliated with the University of Maryland's **Technology Advancement Program (TAP)** at College Park have access to the Dingman Center for Entrepreneurship's New Venture Mentoring and Management Counseling Program. TAP subsidizes the program fee for its companies. The program has more than 100 volunteer mentors, including faculty members, entrepreneurs, and professionals in accounting, compensation/staffing, financing/financial planning, government contracting, international business, joint venturing, law, marketing/sales, and strategic planning. The mentors also have experience in diverse technical fields at professional and management levels. Mentors may provide introductions to business contacts, give advice, and focus start-up businesses on key problems they are facing. Companies are charged $25 per hour for the mentoring service, but TAP pays for 80 percent of this rate for the first 30 hours, 50 percent for the next 20 hours, and 20 percent for the following 400 hours. Generally a mentor will meet with a company once a month for a few hours and will maintain regular telephone contact with the company. If a match is determined to be unsuitable after the first meeting, the company is not charged for that meeting.

Companies must submit a one-page application and a business plan executive summary so that mentors and companies can be properly matched. The application asks for a description of the business, year founded, number of employees, revenues, type of mentor services requested, and estimated duration of mentor need. Companies must be able to demonstrate that they have prospects for significant revenue growth and job creation.

In order to avoid real or perceived conflicts of interest, mentors may not receive payment from nor hold equity positions in the company while volunteering for the program. Additionally, they are subject to university and state conflict-of-interest policies; participating companies also must obtain approval and conflict-of-interest guidance prior to entering into any relationship with a mentor outside of the program.

The **Center for Innovation and Business Development** (CIBD) at the University of North Dakota has developed a network of executives to provide mentoring services to its client businesses. CIBD created one part of the network by tapping into its entrepreneurial alumni base. The mentors are recruited mainly through personal contact, and CIBD staff attend alumni events, exchange business cards, and ask alumni if they can call on them for their knowledge and expertise.

CIBD also facilitates one-on-one relationships between retired executives and entrepreneurs. They make the introduction and then see if the personal chemistry works. This network is similar to the SCORE model in that when successful it results in a mentoring relationship. As one example, a retired patent attorney has been extremely valuable to several of the center's clients.

To cultivate the network, CIBD keeps a database of the people it has contacted and who have offered to help out and sends them information quarterly about the Center. In addition, the 3-M

Executive-on-Loan program provides the Center ready access to methods and techniques of commercializing new products. Semi-retired or retired executives visit the campus to meet with clients and speak to classes. The network has been an effective way to expand the information network of the center and to help clients with specific problems. The volunteers have been very generous with their time and talents and helpful in making key contacts.

The **GENESIS Technology Incubator** at the University of Arkansas-Fayetteville has established a practice of having members of its Business Advisory Board serve as mentors to client companies. This practice exposes leadership of the client company to business leaders and provides them with a steady source of advice, guidance, and successful role models.

The GENESIS Technology Incubator has a fairly large advisory board, composed of business leaders from throughout the state of Arkansas. Members are drawn from the banking and finance community, manufacturing concerns, and retail and wholesale sales and distribution firms located in the state. The board is not required to play any supervisory or managerial role in the operation of the incubator, and meetings are limited to once or twice yearly. The sole continuing responsibility of board members is to serve as mentors to one or more of the incubator's client companies. The mentorship requires no specific responsibility, and the mentor-company relationship is generally determined by the interaction between the board member and the principals of the company, as driven by the needs of the venture. New clients are asked to provide the incubator management with three preferences for mentors from the list of board members. The incubator management then tries to match interests and needs as closely as possible without overloading members with a number of companies. Incubator managers take care to avoid potential or perceived conflicts of interest, while still maximizing the possibility that the mentorship relationship can help the company grow and flourish.

The mentorship program gives board members a significant investment in the success of incubator client companies. At the same time it provides companies access to individuals with substantial business experience, whose knowledge and contacts can help the company maximize its chances of success.

Incutech Brunswick Inc. also uses incubator board members to mentor each client firm. Each company in the incubator is assigned at least one mentor. Most firms have a three-person mentor committee, made up of a primary mentor with expertise most needed by the company, a second mentor with expertise that matches a secondary need of the firm, and the incubator manager, who serves on all the mentor committees. Mentors are assigned based on expertise. For example, computer software experts on the board work with the software companies, business professors on the board work with firms who need entrepreneurship training, and so on. The incubator manager sees the entrepreneurs daily and acts as a full-time mentor. Clients can see the manager at any time to address problems, and the manager continually inquires about issues. There are nine members on the incubator board, and each agrees, when appointed, to be a mentor. Each board member mentors a maximum of two companies—one as a primary mentor and one as a secondary mentor.

Similarly, the **Arizona Technology Incubator** has a mentoring program that links the CEO of each incubator firm with either someone on the incubator board or another community member with business expertise. The incubator requests that mentor meetings occur at least monthly so that the CEO can receive ongoing advice independent of the incubator. In some cases, the incubator manager must oversee the scheduling of the monthly appointments to ensure they take place. The assigned mentor provides an additional source of technical support by meeting regularly with the CEO of the new company and lending experience and insight on various issues.

The board of trustees of the **Business Technology Center** of Columbus, Ohio, also is actively involved with incubator clients. The 17-member board of trustees has a seven-member client committee that meets monthly. The client committee of the board serves as a pool of mentors for incubator companies and provides incubator companies with access to the expertise of interested professionals, including successful entrepreneurs. The business development specialist on staff determines the mentoring needs of clients and presents these to the client committee. Members of the committee then volunteer to serve as mentors to a particular company. This assistance is coordinated by the business development specialist. As many as two or three committee members may volunteer to help a single company with multiple mentoring needs. Many trustees are themselves entrepreneurs, and some are interested in client start-ups from a business perspective. Trustees may spend extra time with companies and some have taken a financial position in a company. The active role of the trustees attracts entrepreneurs and other individuals, such as a representative of Coopers & Lybrand, to serve on the Business Technology Center board of trustees. Currently, four client companies are being mentored.

Another example of a mentoring program is the CEO Strategic Forum at **Boulder Technology Incubator** and **Arizona Technology Incubator**. The CEO Strategic Forum is a monthly meeting that brings together CEOs from tenant firms, graduates, and other companies in the area. Each meeting focuses on a single tenant company and gives the entrepreneur an opportunity to discuss issues and get advice from CEOs who have had similar experiences. The monthly conference is a management support mechanism based on modeling successful incubator graduates and other entrepreneurs. It provides an additional avenue for advice to CEOs of incubator companies.

The conferences are scheduled monthly at each incubator and limited to CEOs of companies in the incubator, graduate tenants, and other CEOs by invitation. Outside participation is limited because the discussion is often proprietary. The conferences usually involve 20 or fewer CEOs. The CEO of the company being highlighted that month is asked to prepare a presentation one month in advance. At the meeting, the CEO of the highlighted company goes through the strategic process and the critical success factors driving the business. These issues are discussed at length. The conference usually lasts two-and-one-half to three hours. With 20 CEOs in one room, it is likely that at least a few companies have already been through most of the strategic problems presented.

Entrepreneurs are often more willing to take advice from those they know have been in similar circumstances. This program allows the incubator to increase its management support capacity by accessing the expertise of successful businesses to address almost any strategic issue that may arise from its tenant firms.

Management Recruitment

As a company grows, so does its need for qualified employees. Aside from normal networking and referral functions, helping to identify management staff is a common role of incubator managers. Many new business owners do not have the time to locate and interview every potential applicant. Therefore, it is helpful to have someone wade through the employment pool and select the best candidates to interview. While most incubators are limited by time constraints to merely maintaining a resumé file, some incubators will actively help companies locate skilled managers.

The inventor or faculty member in technology businesses based on intellectual property will usually have little or no business management skills. To ensure survival of the enterprise, the company must be supplemented with an experienced manager. In some areas, this is a matter of building a network of potential managers and referring entrepreneurs to the network. In some rural areas, where there is not a large supply of individuals with managerial skills, incubators devise a more aggressive recruiting approach.

The **University of Iowa Technology Innovation Center** makes a special effort to work with its client firms to find experienced managers. Incubator staff work with placement firms, sit in on interviews, and help develop managerial job descriptions and roles. To go the extra mile, they also will assist with spousal placement (either in the university or the community) and help get adjunct appointments in a relevant academic department for candidates' spouses. The center will aid a candidate with housing and relocation information, including a recruitment packet describing the advantages of Iowa City.

The **Rensselaer Polytechnic Institute (RPI) Incubator Center** links its tenants to the Career Development Center (CDC) at the university to assist with the selection of potential employees. The CDC acts as an executive recruiter for many tenants. It places not only current graduates but also alumni who wish to make a career change. CDC services include arranging on-campus recruiting schedules, matching students and alumni with companies for hire, listing information on co-ops and internships, and providing career-specific salary information. Services are free to tenant companies and any firm that recruits university graduates.

Tenant companies discuss personnel needs with the incubator director. The two parties then develop a job description as a result of that conversation, or prior to it. The incubator director then contacts the career development center, which identifies several potential applicants. The Center forwards a number of resumés to the incubator manager for use by the tenant company. For example, a tenant company looking for a mechanical engineer was specifically looking for someone who both had a theoretical background and wanted to "roll up their sleeves and do some work." Together the company and the incubator director developed a job description and sent it to the career center. The CDC had 200 engineers on file and selected 25 resumés that met the tenant company's criteria. Supplied with the 25 resumés, the tenant company was able to make a selection.

More frequently, tenant companies use the open job listing at the center. This listing is for companies that have an immediate opening and do not wish to spend time in a formal recruitment process. Companies can submit a job description at any time, and students have access to immediate positions. Information in the database is generally removed after each academic semester.

RPI also maintains an internal resumé database of students, alumni, and individuals from the surrounding community who have an interest in working for young companies. RPI selectively distributes the resumés among tenants based on the company's needs and the qualifications of the potential applicant. Some resumés may overlap with what is available at the career development center, but many will not. The incubator director receives three to four resumés a week, which are kept in a central file in the incubator. The director will review the resumés, consider the best possible match, and make notes concerning distribution. The secretary will copy and distribute them to the appropriate companies. Screenings usually take 20 minutes a week. The incubator director is generally not involved in the actual interview unless he or she knows the candidate well.

Employee selection is a time-consuming process. By utilizing the career development center, tenant companies have immediate access to a qualified pool of applicants. Tenants may call upon the center two to three times a month for services. The combination of this service with the resumé database provided by RPI provides tenant companies with effective tools for employee selection.

Using another approach, the **Colorado Bio/Medical Venture Center** board includes an executive recruiter who also is fairly active in the incubator's informal network. That individual helps in management development and selection by running executive searches for client companies and recommending team members.

Networking

High Technology of Rochester holds monthly tenant meetings that serve to inform participants about program developments as well as to provide an opportunity to network with other tenants. Each meeting usually has one or more outside speakers who give presentations on subjects of interest. The incubator management provides information about any incubator program updates, funding sources, and resources available to tenants. The setting is social, and the incubator management tries to keep the meeting from being a gripe session by having a firm agenda and maintaining an informational focus. Problem solving is deferred to separate sessions. The meeting also gives tenants the opportunity to talk with each other in a more relaxed setting. To avoid "crunch times," the meetings are generally held in the late afternoon, mid-week and mid-month. Avoiding the busiest times for tenants, such as Mondays, Fridays, and times of month-end shipments, helps ensure that the sessions are well attended.

High Technology of Rochester has also held incubator open house sessions and tours to which community leaders are invited. These sessions are useful in marketing both the incubator and its client companies. High Technology of Rochester developed a community open house at the initiation of its incubator program and plans to have annual open houses in the future. Invitations were sent to leaders in the community in business, government, and academia, as well as to prospective tenants. The event was open to all members of the community. A community open house is useful to attract broad attention to the incubator itself and to its tenants.

The **Idaho Innovation Center** holds meetings to encourage networking between tenants and give them exposure to outside professionals. The session also serves as a time when the incubator management can talk with the tenants collectively. The sessions give tenants the opportunity to discuss their problems, solutions, and contacts made with each other. It also gives the incubator management a forum to discuss issues of common interest and to introduce new tenants. Speakers from outside the incubator may be invited, such as attorneys and accountants. This forum provides information to incubator tenants and may lead to relationships between the outside service providers and the incubator tenants. While they are useful, it is often difficult to regularly schedule such meetings, since many incubator tenants have other jobs.

As part of the general management support provided to technology companies, the **Ottawa-Carleton Research Institute (OCRI)** hosts monthly Technology Executive Breakfasts (TEBs). The TEBs bring together seasoned executives from new and existing businesses. TEBs are held once a month for 10 months at a local restaurant. Attendees are charged $15. Usually 100 to 200 executives attend the breakfasts. Participants find these breakfasts useful as a means of networking and having an honest exchange of experiences.

The **Office for the Advancement of Developing Industries (OADI)** incubator in Birmingham annually stages an open house event that attracts service providers (such as attorneys and accountants) from the community as well as incubator tenants. The open house allows those people interested in small businesses and small business development to meet tenants and hear about their businesses. The latest open house attracted 400 guests. The event provides an effective way for the incubator to promote its program to prospective new ventures and for current incubator tenants and associates to showcase their businesses and accomplishments before a broad segment of the interested Birmingham community.

This event buttresses other public relations efforts on behalf of both the incubator and its tenants. The OADI incubator staff, in cooperation with supporting university offices, plans and publicizes the open house and coordinates it with tenant organizations. The small business open house demonstrates the OADI commitment to small business development, provides positive publicity for tenant and associate companies, and offers networking opportunity for potential buyers, suppliers, and service providers.

Trilogy Systems, Inc., a for-profit incubator located in Mountain View, California hosts evening meetings once a month for community members to visit the facility and hear about what the incubator has to offer. With the goals of helping to develop commercializable technologies, increasing economic development in the area, and making a profit, Trilogy Systems tries hard to find entrepreneurs with the potential for high profits. Since the incubator operates on an equity-based arrangement and does not charge rent, it can take earlier-stage start-ups that may not be seeking facilities or know of the opportunity to access Trilogy's services. It has open meetings as a vehicle for identifying business opportunities.

One Wednesday evening per month, Trilogy Systems, Inc. hosts a brainstorming session that is free and open to the public. Because of the nature of the business environment in Silicon Valley, if an entrepreneur is visiting the incubator and has a question about a possible product, there is usually someone in the meeting (either incubator affiliate or visitor) who has market expertise regarding that product. Because a number of "outsiders" with expertise in different areas attend, the meetings are helpful in corroborating the feasibility of a commercial opportunity in a technical market that may be unfamiliar to incubator personnel.

Most incubators have developed or used some version of a venture forum. Most of these are aimed at obtaining capital for new firms and are discussed in the section on financing. **The Advanced Technology Development Center (ATDC)** of Atlanta runs a quarterly venture forum to enable entrepreneurs to get a concentrated dose of review from peers and/or experts. Much of business success involves craft knowledge rather than formula or science. As a result, the accumulated experience and wisdom of successful entrepreneurs is useful and can be critical at certain decision crossroads. At the forum, each company makes a presentation (less than 20 minutes), which is followed by a 30-minute critique by the panelists. The balance of time (up to one hour) is devoted to questions and answers from the audience. The audiences are a mix of entrepreneurs, service providers, and others.

The **Port of Benton** incubator, located in Richland, Washington, also has tenants make formal presentations before the Port's governing board at each of its meetings. The Port of Benton incubator program is overseen by the Port district's board of commissioners, who are elected officials. The special district was created by local taxpayers, with the aim of business and industrial development in the area, and the district's activities, including incubator rents, are tax-subsidized. The three-member

Commission not only serves as the incubator board of directors but also oversees the Port's five industrial sites which include two airports. Tenant Highlight presentations let the Port Commission know what is happening in the incubators and gives the companies valuable public exposure and practice in making presentations. Members of the public are present as well as Commissioners. The presentation may include a tour of the company's operations.

The **Rensselaer Polytechnic Institute (RPI) Incubator Center**, in collaboration with the university, has established a venture affiliates program. Under the leadership of the university president, Rensselaer broke new ground in late 1988 by founding the Center for Entrepreneurship of New Technological Ventures. The center acts as a bridge between Rensselaer's School of Management and the incubator program. In recognition of this growing infrastructure for new and young technological ventures, Rensselaer established the Venture Affiliates of RPI (VARPI) in March of 1989. The program was designed to provide participating companies with a formal link to RPI and access to the resources of the expanding infrastructure.

This organization has two kinds of meetings: general membership meetings and workshops. Both focus on networking and education. The general membership breakfast meetings are held four times a year. Meetings begin with the introduction of members and any relevant announcements. Successful entrepreneurs, venture capitalists, or other individuals involved in new venture developments make short presentations followed by a question and answer period. Plenty of time is allotted for networking both before and after the presentation. The cost associated with organizing and conducting these meetings is covered by the annual membership dues.

Although networking among participants naturally takes place, the focus of the workshops is on knowledge and skill development. In most cases, outside experts are brought in to address, in detail, issues of interest to members. These workshops are held periodically in response to the needs of members. Each workshop carries a nominal fee to cover costs. At a recent VARPI workshop on R&D funding opportunities, participants were given an overview of major government R&D funding programs, and information on how to write winning proposals. The session was free to members of VARPI, Technology Development Council guests, and others with reservations.

Incubator tenants are automatically members of VARPI. Non-incubator companies can make a "financial investment" in the program for $200 per year. If a member is unable to attend, a replacement from the company is accepted. Members may also bring guests.

Typically, about 75 executives from local companies attend. Sharing experiences with other entrepreneurs and discussing fresh ideas with noted leaders in the field of venture development can be beneficial. Moreover, membership status facilitates access for non-incubator companies to additional resources available through Rensselaer.

Strategic partnerships are useful to many start-up technology businesses, especially those in the software field. Companies that enter into partnerships are able to move more easily to the next stage of development. The **University City Science Center** encourages such partnerships and facilitates them through the Application Development Center (ADC) annual partnering event for software companies. The University City Science Center hosts the event which brings together large, mid-size, and small software companies interested in developing strategic partnerships.

The ADC is a membership organization and resource center with members within the Science Center and throughout the Delaware Valley. The ADC functions in some ways like an incubator without walls because it provides support services and networking opportunities to software companies. The annual partnering event brings together between 40 and 50 large and mid-size companies, including DEC, Novell, Martin-Marietta, and Microsoft, to meet with ADC members. The larger companies are interested in obtaining application software and services, and the local entrepreneurs seek markets for their software. The base for invitations comes from the ADC's mailing list, which currently includes about 1,000 software companies in the region.

Each business attending the partnering event submits a questionnaire about what it is looking for in a partner. Once the ADC receives the questionnaires, it matches up companies seeking compatible marketing agreements, strategic alliances, or other relationships. During the event, the companies meet briefly on a one-on-one basis. If the initial contact is favorable, follow-up meetings are scheduled by the companies.

The charge for the event is $50 for ADC members and $195 for nonmembers, which includes a one-year membership in the ADC. The cost includes introduction to 10 possible partner companies, as well as a continental breakfast and a box lunch. The event this year will be held at the Valley Forge Convention Center.

The pre-event questionnaire and the event format allow companies to make contact with a number of prescreened potential partners in a short period of time. Thus, more useful partnerships are likely to be initiated through this program. These partnerships can be critical to the success of start-up software companies and benefit the local software industry as a whole.

The **Montgomery County Technology Enterprise Center (MCTEC)** is managed by the Suburban Maryland High Technology Council, which has established a network of professional support services for tenant firms. The Council has approximately 450 members, many of which are technical service providers. The incubator utilizes approximately 60 of these member firms, which have volunteered to provide technical assistance to incubator tenants. The member firms are asked to renew annually as volunteers.

If a tenant firm has a particular need that can be filled by a Technology Council member, the incubator manager makes the initial contact and sets up the first meeting. It is then up to the tenant firm and service provider to make arrangements for assistance. The member companies provide services at substantial discounts and sometimes free of charge, although the incubator management sees merit in a nominal fee arrangement in order for the companies to appreciate and fully utilize the service.

While much of the assistance provided by Technology Council members is to tenant firms, some members assist companies that are applying for admission to MCTEC and need to improve sections of their business plan. This arrangement is also brokered by the incubator manager after initial contact with the potential applicant and discussion about business planning needs.

Although the volunteer network includes approximately 60 firms, MCTEC may only utilize the assistance of a portion of that number in a given year, depending on the needs of the companies. Many of the service providers specialize in more advanced business assistance practices that are not suitable for start-up firms. Nonetheless, this arrangement not only provides high-quality assistance to incubator tenants at low cost but also keeps the members of the Technology Council interested in and supportive of the efforts of MCTEC.

With relatively tight cash flow, start-up businesses are usually not in a position to pay dues to business or professional organizations, such as the chamber of commerce. However, membership can provide many networking and technical assistance opportunities. **The Idaho State University Business and Technology Center (BTC)** pays for the first year chamber of commerce membership dues for its tenants. The BTC contacted the director of the Greater Pocatello Chamber of Commerce in 1992 to discuss the development of a program to increase the number of incubator tenant members. Membership provides tenants with unlimited assess to workshops, leadership programs, the chamber after-hours program and committee assignments. Based on this conversation, the chamber granted a fee waiver for membership dues for the first year. Subsequent years' membership dues are the tenant company's responsibility.

Initially, the chamber subsidized the costs for the program out of its dues revenue. However, the Idaho State University Business and Technology Center felt it was valuable enough to assume the cost for dues. This is considered an operating expense for the incubator and debited accordingly.

Since its inception, several tenants have taken advantage of this service, and the chamber has increased its membership. The potential for contact with mature businesses is beneficial in fostering mentoring relationships. It also may serve as a tool for keeping graduates in the local community.

The **Colorado Bio/Medical Venture Center** (CBVC) provides access to a broad network, since it is a regional affiliate of the Health Industry Manufacturers Association (HIMA) and the Biotechnology Industries Organization (BIO). These national organizations provide useful information on health care issues, regulations, legislative analyses, and programs that affect the biotech industry. Through its affiliation with these organizations, CBVC is able to pass along information to Colorado biomedical companies and its Bio/Medical Friends. It also gives HIMA and BIO a better mechanism for keeping informed about what is happening in the industry in Colorado.

The CBVC's role in this effort is to disseminate information through its monthly newsletter in the form of alerts about legislation, conferences, and regulatory changes. Issues of recent concern include medical device user fees and pharmaceutical price controls. In order to inform the national agenda, CBVC also collects information on regional trends and issues, which it passes along to BIO and HIMA.

Some forms of networking are designed around fun rather than business. In a large research park, such as the **University City Science Center**, there is great potential for both formal and informal relationships between companies, which can greatly benefit start-ups. Among other activities, the University City Science Center has a softball league with 20 teams. The softball games may be the key to making introductions among the start-up and established companies in the park and to creating relationships between companies. Among other opportunities for interactions between companies, the University City Science Center also is home to an art gallery that holds monthly opening receptions. Annual trade shows are also held at the Science Center. Strategic partnerships and other business relationships often arise out of these informal occasions.

The **Evanston Business Technology Center** has created a physical and organizational environment designed to provide a free flow of information among companies and between incubator management and the companies. The incubator interior is designed to have as much glass as possible. There are few places in the building where you can close a door and not be seen. It is a four-story building, with discrete areas for each company, but there is some shared space on each floor. The incubator offices are not in front, however, so the manager does have to seek out the companies.

Talking to the companies regularly and finding out what they need is a priority for incubator management. This is done in several informal ways. By creating a cordial environment, management encourages the exchange of ideas and information. If a company has a problem, the entrepreneur feels more comfortable telling the incubator manager. The management makes special efforts to facilitate interaction through social and networking functions. There are periodic social events such as holiday parties, incubator picnics, and impromptu mid-week dinners. In addition, the incubator manager occasionally will take tenants to lunch at a university facility and invite faculty along. Management also tries to hold once-a-month lunches where one of the companies provides a topic for discussion and lunch is provided by the incubator.

The key is the nature of the environment—the "ecology" of the incubator. One of the biggest reasons that the incubator is successful is this open flow of information. This is notable more as an outcome than as a practice. Because of this environment, connections between companies have been made that would not have been made otherwise, and the current tenants go out of their way to help other companies.

Networking and referral of outside resources with specific expertise are among the most valuable business assistance provisions of any incubator. The staff at **Trilogy Systems, Inc.** maintains a "Golden Rolodex" of experts in specific technologies, management, marketing, supply channels and other critical factors. When a company enters the Trilogy Systems, Inc. incubator, the incubator management and the entrepreneur jointly prepare a shopping list of services needed. The incubator maintains a database of approximately 500 people who have responded to incubator publicity and indicated that they would be willing to work with a company in a certain area for an equity position. The incubator uses the names in the Golden Rolodex to complete the assistance that the incubator cannot provide with in-house staff. All of the incubator firms continually contribute names for the database, providing cross-introductions and referrals.

The Golden Rolodex is large enough to handle most areas of need and continues to grow as more people hear about the incubator and tenant firms add names. Potential assistance providers contact the incubator readily because of the opportunity to gain equity in a promising company.

To facilitate internal networking, Trilogy Systems, Inc. uses a large white board to display the names of the incubator firms and their progress based on benchmarks. Many of Trilogy's start-ups are preseed, prebusiness plan, "straight off the kitchen table" entrepreneurs who may be in and out of the facility around the clock, so it is difficult for incubator firms to keep up with other firms' progress and needs.

Trilogy posts the board with each company name, a brief description, and the contact name. On the right is a numbered legend of benchmarks in areas such as cash, prototype development, patents, FDA approvals, and cash flow. The firms accumulate the corresponding numbers under their heading as they reach the benchmarks. The board is updated monthly and displayed in a common area of the incubator.

The open display of each company's benchmarks and progress keeps everyone informed of the status and unmet needs of companies for potential networking and referral. It also allows for competitive communication among unrelated business efforts.

An emerging trend with a few U.S. incubators, and perhaps more incubators in other countries, is *Global Networked Entrepreneurship*. Start-up companies are often linked through incubators in other countries with entrepreneurs, university faculty and students, and know-how networks, to explore global alliance and market opportunities. The objective is to let entrepreneurial, fast-growth companies take advantage of global market opportunities to spur growth. Often a small technology-based company will be able to develop a strong market niche in a developing country, while competition "at home" stifles the start-up's growth.

At the **IC²** (Innovation, Creativity, and Capital) **Institute, The University of Texas at Austin**, The Austin Technology Incubator (ATI) has formed a global network of alliances with incubators in China, Russia, Ukraine, Brazil, and Portugal. Students, faculty, and entrepreneurs travel among these sites and keep in frequent communication through e-mail. For the future, two-way video links are planned to facilitate education, research, and speedy business transactions. POLO Software (a consortium of software companies based in Curitiba, Brazil) has a full-time marketing representative assigned to ATI to facilitate the product development and marketing of Brazilian software products in the United States, and to facilitate the product development and marketing of Austin-developed software (primarily companies in ATI) in South America. IC² Institute sponsors a China Industry and Management of Technology Training (CIMTT) Program. It sends graduate students from a range of disciplines to China, for eight weeks in the summer to assist small and emerging Chinese technology companies (often spin-outs from universities and research institutes) with business plans, financing alliance building, and global marketing. During their residence in China, these same students build local networks and act as marketing representatives or liaisons for ATI companies.

Finally, the **Center for Applied Technology** produces a quarterly newsletter to provide information about the incubator to its tenants and the university community. The newsletter is a way to market the incubator and recruit entrepreneurial prospects. Started in Spring 1994, the newsletter is sent to all three major technology universities in the state—Clemson University, the University of South Carolina, and the Medical University of South Carolina. The mailing list consists of approximately 3,000 names in those universities and also in high-tech businesses throughout the state. The three-page newsletter includes information about the incubator staff and programs, profiles of tenant companies, information on graduate companies and sometimes a response card. The publication has increased the level of awareness about the incubator and its services. It has also increased the number of inquiries from the universities.

Advisory Boards

Most early-stage companies do not have their own active or effective board of directors in place. Early in its history, a new enterprise needs an advisory body equivalent to a board of directors. Many incubators have set up such temporary advisory structures, typically made up of volunteers, to help provide input on business planning and management support to tenant firms. Advisory boards may also be used in a more formal monitoring or review capacity. Because of the diverse nature of tenant companies, and the great variety of incubator operations and services, the composition of advisory boards will vary widely.

An example is the approach taken at the **Ceramics Corridor Innovation Center**. It has offered to each resident business the use of advisory boards, composed of faculty from the Alfred University College of Business, members of the private-sector business-services community (accountants, lawyers), and local entrepreneurs. Each company has a different advisory board that meets quarterly with the company leadership. The incubator asks for a three-year commitment from advisory board members to work with a company, all on a *pro bono* basis. The board tries to establish milestones for the company, as well as facilitate networking with resources. Not all companies in the incubator have used the advisory board service because it is not mandatory.

The **Ohio University Innovation Center**, given its close university linkages and its commitment to "place-based" economic development, takes a novel approach to structuring an advisory function for a tenant company. Since many of the companies in the incubator are based on university technologies, a common stipulation in the licensing agreement is that Ohio University Foundation members sit on the board. Since Ohio law disallows university employees from holding such positions, board members are drawn from the ranks of Ohio University alumni who may be investment bankers, attorneys, or business managers. They look out for the interests of the university and reinforce the strategy of regionally focused economic development, as well as provide valuable advice for the entrepreneur. Advantages include the close linkage to the university. Disadvantages include the fact that alumni are often spread out across the country, making personal communication difficult. Those who wish to pursue this approach should be cautioned that it is not always easy for these board members to serve two masters—the university's interests and the responsibilities of a company board member.

A select group of tenants at the **Rensselaer Polytechnic Institute (RPI) Incubator Center** meets monthly with members of the incubator advisory board, which serves as each tenant's board of directors. This board is composed of the incubator director, a volunteer faculty member, two volunteers from Coopers & Lybrand, and a volunteer from the local business community.

In the past, the incubator director selected companies that needed the most help. Now companies are chosen because they can benefit the most from assistance and are more likely to implement suggestions of the advisory board.

Prior to the first meeting, a team of accounting students is assigned to help a company set up its accounting system and financial statements. The process usually takes one semester, and students receive academic credit for their work. Once the company is set up to produce these statements, the incubator director convenes the first meeting of the advisory board. The board uses the meeting to review the financial statements. The meeting also serves as a springboard for more business and strategic advice for companies. Companies participate for nine months with one meeting per month. Meetings are then scaled back to once a quarter, and a new set of companies starts the process. Meetings last approximately an hour-and-a-half for each company. At the bare minimum, tenants are expected to arrive at each meeting with an updated monthly financial statement. In addition, they should be prepared to discuss the challenges they are facing and have relevant questions to ask the advisory board. The outcome of these sessions is informal advice and some specific suggestions. However, the overarching goal is to educate entrepreneurs so they will begin to think critically about their company. Approximately eight companies have used this service.

The **Technology Ventures Incubator** at Stevens Institute of Technology requires the CEO of each tenant firm to attend a semi-annual, structured meeting with the incubator advisory board to review the progress of the firm's business plan. The advisory board then makes recommendations to the entrepreneur based on the review.

The incubator advisory board is made up of senior industry representatives with backgrounds in areas such as product design and manufacturing, accounting, banking, and patent law. Upon joining, members of the advisory board agree to attend regular meetings with each company in the incubator. The incubator firms also agree to participate in the meetings as a requirement for entry.

The structure is that of a formal, "suits around a table" meeting. The chair of the advisory board sets the agenda for the meeting with input from the incubator director. The incubator director attends the meetings but does not participate in the review process in order to ensure that the company receives objective information and feedback from the advisory board.

The company leaves the meeting with specific recommendations from the board. The board keeps a list of the recommendations for review at the next meeting. The board is technically just "suggesting approaches" rather than "offering advice to be followed."

These formal meetings are supplemented by informal meetings that occur between advisory board members and entrepreneurs. The incubator also encourages informal mentoring on a one-on-one basis.

Trilogy Systems, Inc. has equity arrangements with tenant firms, so the incubator monitors the companies as a stockholder as well as an assistance provider. When a company first enters the for-profit incubator, the staff meets with the principals at least once a week in order to monitor progress and provide assistance and referral. After six months, meetings drop to every two weeks. After the first year, meetings are monthly. Continual contact with firms at the beginning allows for timely technical assistance and referral to keep companies on track.

The **Arizona Technology Incubator** uses an advisory board and a financing committee made up of volunteers who are willing to meet regularly and answer questions from incubator companies. The 25-member advisory board is a group hand-picked by the incubator management and made up of corporate attorneys, engineers, entrepreneurs, bankers, corporate managers, and the like. These experts advise companies on their strategic direction, much as a public board of directors might. On average, 15 board members attend meetings. The financing committee is also selected by the incubator manager and is made up of venture capitalists, members of investment banking firms, state officials, private investors, and brokers. There is no time limit for serving on the advisory board or financing committee, but committee members resign if they have other commitments or feel they are no longer useful on the committee.

Companies must apply in order to present to one of the committees. Only one firm presents per meeting of either committee. The incubator manager stresses the value of these committees to the firms and helps them take full advantage by assisting in the development of the presentation and key issues to be addressed. The incubator manager coaches each firm to present a few key issues in one area, such as marketing. The committee members receive a packet that describes the company and articulates the two or three key issues confronting the firm. These are distributed approximately one week before each meeting.

The advisory board and financing committee are very popular services among tenant companies, and firms often must schedule a meeting with one of the committees five to six months in advance. The advisory board currently meets once a month; the incubator is considering splitting the board in order to assist more companies per month.

Scheduled meetings with an advisory board encourage the entrepreneur to think about what he or she needs in the area of business assistance and encourage discipline with regard to the business plan. These advisory board arrangements often lead to individual committee members contracting services to an incubator firm for free or reduced rates, because individuals on the committees develop a particular interest in a company. In two cases, members of the committees have invested in a company and become its CEO/president.

Exit Assistance and Follow-up

One obvious indicator of a program's success is when an entrepreneur leaves the incubator facilities, no longer needs the assistance and support services, and is launched as a free-standing business. The process of exiting has received much attention from incubator programs, and several have developed practices and strategies to anticipate and meet the needs of graduating companies. In addition, a number of incubators have taken a longer-term perspective on exiting and conducted follow-up services or activities, both to ease the transition of the company and/or to better learn about the strengths and weaknesses of their programs. The consensus of many technology incubator managers interviewed is that technology companies may have longer incubation periods than general business incubator tenants. Many have modified exit policies to reflect the unique needs and tone of technology companies in getting a product to market.

The **CYBER Center** anticipates its tenants' graduation needs by performing an incubator tenant review well in advance of the target date. With a maximum tenancy period of five years, CYBER increases the frequency of questions it asks about future plans around the beginning of the third year or when the tenant requests more space (which may or may not be available). Year three is targeted for this process because the center needs to plan well in advance for exit and organize appropriate resources from the state and the community. A formal two-page survey is disseminated annually to tenants. The survey requests information about current sales, projected sales, percentage of sales in-state and out-of-state, current number of employees, and annual payroll. Tenants are also asked if they have updated their business plan and if they need help with an update. Graduation is discussed in terms of time frame and what resources will be required. Tenants are required to record the percentage of inventory/materials purchased from the state and county.

In addition, the survey functions as a tool for evaluation of incubator services. For example, questions are asked about which services the companies use and what other services are needed. Tenants may also list suggestions for improvement in incubator operations.

As a result of this survey, both parties have documentation of client needs. It forces the tenant to be mindful of graduation, as well as outlines ways the manager can assist the tenant in a smooth transition from the facility. Both the incubator manager and the principal meet to discuss the survey and are required to sign the form as part of the agreement. This meeting is conducted by the program manager. If a tenant company has several principals, then they decide if all should attend. If during the tenant review a principal requests services that CYBER cannot provide, the program manager will search for another provider or suggest alternatives.

The **Office for the Advancement of Developing Industries (OADI)** incubator in Birmingham conducts a formal annual survey of tenant and associate companies in order to evaluate the quality and impact of services offered and to determine the changing needs of the tenant and associate organizations. The tenant survey helps OADI incubator management to assess and manage the services provided, both in terms of their quality and in terms of their value and responsiveness to tenant and associate company needs. The survey offers tenant organizations an opportunity to comment on the quality and level of services provided and the cost involved, as well as the presence of potential unmet needs.

The incubator management prepares the survey instrument, distributes it to the tenant and associate companies, follows up to ensure as complete a response as possible, and conducts a general analysis of the results. Survey results can assist incubator management in a meaningful way to correct problem areas, reevaluate cost structures and increase levels of service where appropriate, or to initiate new services to cover unmet needs. For example, adding the data safe service for tenants and associates (see Chapter 7 on infrastructure) resulted from comments in the last annual survey. The survey mechanism complements a close relationship among incubator management, the tenant, and associate companies provided by repeated meetings between the incubator director and the CEOs of the tenant and associate companies.

The **Arizona Technology Incubator** (ATI) has found that its graduates prefer to maintain an ongoing relationship with ATI after graduation. ATI has an Affiliates Program for non-tenant clients, which includes all services except tenancy for a fixed monthly fee. All of ATI's graduates have chosen to continue as ATI affiliates.

Graduates of the **Idaho Innovation Center** may choose to retain their affiliation with the Center by joining the associates program and paying a monthly fee. The associates program allows a company to continue incubator services after it graduates. A company may also retain affiliation if it can benefit other incubator tenants. Associates may participate in monthly meetings, workshops, and other incubator events. Some will retain office space in the incubator. About half of the incubator graduates become associates.

The **Technology Advancement Program** (TAP) at the University of Maryland, College Park, schedules post-incubator interviews with companies six months to one year after they have graduated from the incubator. Interviewing companies several months after graduation allows the TAP to ask companies now in the "real world" if the program has been useful.

The time away from the incubator gives the company perspective on how helpful the incubator has been to its survival. Interviews are informal and are generally held over lunch. They are not conducted by the incubator director but by someone outside of the incubator staff, so that evaluation of the incubator program may be as open as possible. The TAP has found that the evaluations by program graduates are very useful in determining what the incubator does well and what changes need to be made in its programs.

The **Center for Innovation and Business Development** (CIBD) at the University of North Dakota has developed a formal evaluation questionnaire for its clients. Each year, CIBD provides business and technical support services to hundreds of individuals and businesses who have product ideas. They send out an evaluation at three months and at one year after the initial contact. The questionnaire provides feedback on the services provided as well as an evaluation of the success and progress of the company. CIBD includes in the evaluation some of the entrepreneurs who did not receive services.

The **Metropolitan Center for High Technology** has developed a process to involve graduates of the program in the annual meeting. Graduate companies are invited to set up table-top exhibits or product displays, and this provides a good venue for peer-to-peer interaction. As many as 300 people attend these events. In addition, the incubator staff maintains contact with the graduate companies and tries to track their sales and growth. At the annual meeting, one of the graduate companies and one of the current tenant companies are featured.

Incutech Brunswick Inc. helps firms decide on a graduation date based on net profits, which is seen as a better indicator for readiness to exit the facility than length of residency. The manager sets a target graduation date, which gives firms a goal to work for. It does not lock them into a rigid time limit for tenancy, and management exercises considerable flexibility. Semi-annual review meetings help determine progress toward the target date and the need for possible business plan and graduation date revisions. Most of the tenants do not stay in the incubator longer than five years.

Regarding relocation outside the incubator facility, the **University of Iowa Technology Innovation Center** explores several opportunities for its graduates. Given its working relationship with the university research park, it will assist some companies in placement in the park. In addition, the incubator is highly networked to economic development organizations all over the state. Many of these organizations are interested in recruiting companies to their area, and the incubator management will help set up interviews between the graduating tenant company and these recruiters. To a significant degree, public incentives are involved (e.g., tax breaks, training arrangements), and these become part of a recruiting package for the company. All of this is consistent with the university's mission of anchoring technology-based companies in the state.

The **Port of Benton**, Washington, focuses its incubator activities on companies that eventually will purchase facilities developed by the Port. Located in a rural area, the Port of Benton seeks to develop the area through industrial parks. This goal derives from the function of port districts to stimulate business and industrial development. The development policy allows the Port of Benton to create incentives that will keep incubator companies on site, even after they begin to grow.

Once a company is large enough to grow significantly, the Port will sell it the land and the building it occupies. This sale does not displace any other companies because by the time the company is ready to purchase the facility, it has already "taken over the building." The profit from sale of facilities is used for improvements to Port facilities and for new buildings. The Port continually purchases undeveloped land in order to continue developing the largely rural, 540-square-mile port district. The Port of Benton currently has five industrial sites, with incubator facilities at four of the sites. The Port facilities are both general use and specialized, including a shared kitchen/food processing facility. Tenants are both high-tech and general industrial. Reflecting the agriculture industry in the area, they include food-processing businesses.

Incubator companies must be new businesses and not compete with current businesses in the area. They also need to have a reasonable chance of success to be admitted to the incubator program. While the tax-subsidized rents are tied to the companies' income, tenants are not forced to leave the incubator after a set period of time. Rather, the Port wants companies to stay on-site and purchase the land and facility. In essence, the companies do not graduate. Because they can stay where they are, growing companies are not hindered by having to find a new location and can focus on managing their growth rather than on relocation.

Three buildings have been sold to incubated companies since the incubator program was started in 1978. The strategy of developing new industrial parks, and incubating businesses to grow into them, stems from the Port's mission of business and industrial development and is related to its other activities, including industrial recruitment. The end result is an area with more developed land and more businesses owning industrial facilities on the tax rolls.

As part of a collaborative effort, **NET Ben Franklin Technology Center** has joined forces with three other local economic development groups to fund a post-incubator facility. Technology companies always have the need for good lab space. In Bethlehem, Pennsylvania, it is hard to find. Moreover, it can be expensive to fit a lab with the right equipment. The facility provides the right financial incentive for small business owners.

The Bethlehem Technology Center is a 44,000-square-foot post-incubator facility on grounds formerly owned by the Bethlehem Steel Corporation. Since Bethlehem Steel no longer needed the land, an agreement was reached with the city to develop the center. The building was created with the hope of helping small companies continue to grow. It is also in close proximity to Lehigh University to ensure that companies can continue to utilize the school. The facility is subcontracted with a property management group.

This facility provides a smooth transition from the incubator. It is a standard commercial facility, but the lease rates are well below average cost because of the subsidies provided by EDA, Northampton Development Corporation, Lehigh Valley Industrial Development Parks Inc., and Bethlehem Economic Development Corporation. No additional services are provided to tenants of the post-incubator facility because companies are expected to be viable businesses once they have graduated from the incubator.

Finally, graduation from an incubator can be a time of joy and pride. That is why the **Idaho State University Business and Technology Center (BTC)** maintains a "Wall of Fame" for its graduating companies. The idea is to recognize and reward tenants for hard work and business success upon graduation. It reminds tenants and visitors that the purpose of the incubator is to create self-sufficient, successful businesses.

The growth of a tenant company dictates its exit from BTC, which is cause for celebration. As the graduation date approaches, a press release is issued to announce the event and give relocation information on the company. The incubator hosts a reception that lasts approximately 60 to 90 minutes. Light refreshments are served.

Attendees include other incubator tenants, incubator board members, university personnel, and clients of the graduating tenant. The reception is an informal gathering at which the manager presents a plaque to the graduating tenant, who can make some parting remarks. Graduates also are given a marble desk replica of the plaque to take to their new location. The Wall of Fame is located at the front entrance so that people entering the building can see the names and types of graduating companies.

Tools

Some incubators have used various analytic tools or formal decision aids as they work with tenant companies to improve management functions. These tools might include software, checklists, or other comparable approaches.

The **GENESIS Technology Incubator** at the University of Arkansas-Fayetteville has developed a computer program to allow the staff to help tenant companies forecast the likelihood of bankruptcy. These calculations, known as the Z-score and the H-score, are business analysis tools taught in most academic business administration programs. This tool helps the GTI staff provide careful financial assistance and oversight to the tenant companies and permits reviews on a more frequent basis with less staff input. It permits tenant companies to get financial oversight and support at little or no additional cost, allowing them to concentrate on the substance of their new businesses.

The Z-score and H-score analyses have not been reduced to computer-generated algorithms because of their complexity and the variability of inputs. The GTI staff, working with graduate students who have expertise in computer and systems engineering, have developed a software package and practices for using the package. The software package requires some expertise to use, which the staff provides. The software is not prepared with user-friendly "front ends," which would allow individual company owners to use it. This requirement for interaction with GTI staff keeps tenant owners in closer contact. Incubator tenants have used the package on a continuing and recurring basis. Since its development, the package also has been part of the initial business planning for candidate companies.

Having the software available to the incubator management allows the coordinator of business services to stay in closer contact with business operations of tenant companies. It permits the coordinator of business services to extend the effectiveness of her work in support of companies by allowing more frequent and accurate analysis of company financial operations and progress. The tool also assists companies by providing continuing, frequent access to analysis of progress based on financial returns.

The **Center for Applied Technology** offers a business credit analysis service for its clients to help monitor business performance and the likelihood of success. The business credit analysis is performed by CAT staff free of charge, using a spreadsheet program and data provided by the companies. The companies' lease agreements require them to provide the information for analysis, which is generally conducted twice a year. Companies that entered the incubator prior to that requirement are not forced to undergo the business credit analysis but may take advantage of the service if they choose to do so. Business credit analyses are most useful to companies that have had at least two years of sales for comparison purposes. The analyses give the incubator manager a good idea of how the companies are doing, how they compare to similar businesses, and where they need help.

The tenant company provides a historical and projected balance sheet and a profit and loss statement. The figures are entered into a spreadsheet that generates ratio and financial performance information similar to a bank credit analysis. The analysis measures a company's liquidity, profitability, and management resources. The information is then compared to industry standards. Results are provided to the entrepreneurs for benchmarking purposes only. The incubator manager may discuss the report with the tenant. The analysis and discussion are confidential.

The incubator director and staff developed their business credit analysis skills from a course offered by the National Development Council for economic development finance professionals. This certification program is a four-week course that includes economic development finance, business credit analysis, real estate finance, and the art of deal structuring.

The Internet-based *Online Business Information Network (OBIN)* is a project supported within the Library of Congress by a generous gift from the Edward Lowe Foundation. The OBIN targets the needs of new businesses, small businesses, entrepreneurs, and the information providers and librarians who work with these groups. Several types of information are provided: basic technical information, provided mainly by the U.S. Small Business Administration; bibliographic information from the library and its partners, which directs users to a broad range of resources available in print and electronic formats; directories to volunteer and public agencies, such as SCORE chapters, Small Business Institutes, and federal offices for small and disadvantaged business utilization; basic regulatory and compliance programs and points of contact; and programmatic information on technical assistance and procurement that illustrate the range of services and opportunities available from the federal government to new and small businesses. Although much of this information is available from several sources such as Fedworld, OBIN provides pointers and programmatic information in a single place that can become a gateway to more specialized sources.

To access the database, users can telnet to marvel.loc.gov and log in as marvel, select research and reference on the first menu, and then select Online Business Information Network on the next menu.

Contact:
    Electronic Programs Office
    Business Research Center
    Library of Congress
    Washington, DC 20540-8005
    Tel (202) 707-5027

JIAN Software's *Employee Manual Maker* is a software package containing 110-plus policies and 30-plus benefits descriptions typed and formatted on diskette. The software includes sections on selecting qualified employees, an employment application form, sample interview questions, a new employee orientation guide, and a performance evaluation form. The user can either edit the text on hard-copy printouts or directly on a computer using existing word processing software. Also included are articles on wrongful termination, drug testing, harassment, family leave, and the Americans With Disabilities Act.

Contact:
    JIAN Tools For Sales, Inc.
    127 Second Street
    Los Altos, CA 94002
    Tel (415) 941-9191   Fax (415) 941-9272

Chapter 5

Business Planning

Transforming a technology into a successful business requires a detailed operational and financial plan. Many prospective business owners view the idea of a written business plan as "a lot of unnecessary paperwork." Nonetheless, the business planning process forces entrepreneurs to think critically about all aspects of the business including the organizational structure, funds required for start-up and expansion, possible sources of capital, market segment penetration, management team acquisition, sales, and the profit margin (Brett, Gibson, and Smilor, 1991). More importantly, the business plan (properly conceived and executed) can have direct implications for action. First, it is important to have a plan for internal use to guide the day-to-day decision-making process of the growing company. Second, a good business plan will convey a company's vision to outside sources of capital (see finance and capitalization). Moreover, no investor will seriously consider financing a business until the plan has been written and thoroughly reviewed.

At least two schools of thought surface when the business planning process is discussed in relation to incubators. One school believes that a detailed plan must be developed *prior to* admission or as part of the screening process. Further, it postulates that any tenant who has not developed a plan may not fully understand how to operate a business. Therefore, the principal (with limited assistance from incubator staff) must develop a plan to ensure a company's success.

An alternative approach says that the business plan is part of the learning process and can be completed *after* the company is admitted to the facility. The incubator instead emphasizes core technology, otherwise there can be no business. Often the "company" in a university setting may not have identified a business structure; therefore, a full-blown plan would be inappropriate. The stress placed on entrepreneurs to complete a plan sometimes stifles the creative process and may reduce the number of individuals seriously considering business formation. While both views have their supporters, neither approach removes the company from the business planning process. Each approach is open for future analysis and discussion.

Whatever approach is utilized, the business planning process involves more than just the development of a "master" document. Because tenants may not have assembled a true management team, staff can provide assistance with organizing technical reviews, evaluating competing technologies, identifying technical milestones, conducting cost analysis, evaluating financial alternatives, and organizing strategic marketing analysis and planning. Whether brokered or provided as a direct services, these tasks can prove crucial to business survival.

Technical reviews present an opportunity for the client company and a team of experts to analyze a technology's commercialization potential. This process can be used to avert anticipated problems by identifying any potentially fatal flaws in the company's technical or business plan. Some technical reviews may involve teams making a formal presentation to a team of experts about the company's technology, its product, and its markets. More importantly, a review can determine the technical knowledge of the entrepreneur as well as the viability of the product.

In a global economy, the window of opportunity through which any individual or corporation can capitalize on new technology is limited. "It is not just enough to build a better mousetrap; you have to build a better mousetrap company" (Abrams 1993). Therefore, it is always important to identify and evaluate competing technologies. In preparing a competitive analysis, one should focus on identifying the major competition, determining strategies for competing, defining the market niche and percentage, and discussing barriers to market entry.

Identifying technical milestones or markers is, in effect, benchmarking. Incubator staff and tenants discuss tasks and outline completion dates. Milestones should be realistic and attainable goals. The discussion should address strengths and weaknesses. It is always an excellent idea to "hope for the best and plan for the worst." Therefore, both parties should explore alternative solutions and their implications.

Strategic marketing and planning seems to be one of the most difficult tasks for entrepreneurs to complete successfully without assistance from incubator staff. It requires foresight and expertise, as well as knowledge of past industrial trends. In the next two sections, the reader will see the variety of business planning services and practices. In perhaps no other area of practice is the "model" of business development so influential. Depending on the incubator's perceived mission, and its view of its clientele and their needs, the services it provides may vary quite dramatically.

OVERVIEW OF PRACTICES AND SERVICES: BUSINESS PLANNING

We asked incubator managers to respond to a checklist of business planning services or practices provided to client companies. For each practice or service, managers were asked to indicate whether they provided the service or practice directly, brokered or referred the service or practice, did both, or did neither. The checklist had the effect of providing a scale of intensity for services and practices provided in the business planning area. Services have been arranged in order of occurrence. The summary results are presented in Table 5.1 (next page).

The most commonly provided or brokered services were evaluating financing alternatives and providing strategic marketing analysis and planning. The greater part of these services was provided directly by incubators. These two services may be viewed as fundamental to assisting start-up businesses.

The least frequently provided service was cost analysis of technologies. When provided, this service was usually brokered or referred. Many incubator managers believe that clients are better prepared to do cost analysis on their own, due to their knowledge of the technology.

We also made comparisons among different types of incubators. Incubators with close university

Table 5.1: Business Planning Practices (valid percent responses)

	no, rarely/never	yes, by referral	yes, directly	both
evaluate financing alternatives	7.3	21.8	52.7	18.2
analyze and plan marketing strategies	9.1	34.5	45.5	10.9
organize tech review of business plan	10.9	16.4	60.0	12.7
evaluate competing technologies	21.8	36.4	29.1	12.7
identify technical milestones	25.5	30.9	38.2	5.5
conduct cost analysis of technology	35.2	37.0	20.4	7.4

Table 5.2: Business Planning Practices by Incubator University Affiliation (valid percent responses)

	no, rarely/never		yes, by referral		yes, directly		both	
	university	non	university	non	university	non	university	non
evaluate financing alternatives	9.4	5.6	21.9	22.2	50.0	55.6	18.8	16.7
analyze and plan strategic marketing	12.5	5.6	34.4	33.3	43.8	50.0	9.4	11.1
organize tech review of business plan	15.6	5.6	18.8	11.1	59.4	66.7	6.3	16.7
evaluate competing technologies	28.1	5.6	28.1	55.6	28.1	27.8	15.6	11.1
identify technical milestones	31.3	11.1	34.4	27.8	28.1	55.6	6.3	5.6
conduct cost analysis of technology	38.7	27.8	38.7	38.9	19.4	16.7	3.2	16.7

relationships tended to be less likely to perform all of the practices in the business planning area than incubators not affiliated with universities, as shown in Table 5.2. An incubator was counted as providing a service if it answered that it provided the service directly, by referral, or both. There were no statistically significant relationships between university affiliation and any of the specific business planning practices, despite the overall trends just noted. It is unclear why university-affiliated facilities tended to be less involved in business planning. Perhaps they are dealing with a clientele that is much earlier in the development process and therefore more concerned with proving its technologies than with business planning in the usual sense of the term.

Comparing incubators in rural areas with those in urban areas, we found that rural incubators provide far fewer business planning services than do incubators in urban areas, as seen in Table 5.3 (next page). When examined for measures of association, we found a significant relationship between urban location and the practice of organizing technical reviews of business plans. Such a relationship

Table 5.3: Business Planning Practices by Incubator Location
(valid percent responses)

	no, rarely/never		yes, by referral		yes, directly		both	
	rural	urban	rural	urban	rural	urban	rural	urban
evaluate financing alternatives	21.4	2.4	14.3	24.4	57.1	51.2	7.1	22.0
analyze and plan strategic marketing	21.4	4.9	35.7	34.1	35.7	48.8	7.1	12.2
organize tech review of business plan	28.6	4.9	28.6	12.2	42.9	65.9	0.0	17.1
evaluate competing technologies	35.7	17.1	21.4	41.5	28.6	29.3	14.3	12.2
conduct cost analysis of technology	53.8	29.3	30.8	39.0	15.4	22.0	0.0	9.8
identify technical milestones	57.1	14.6	21.4	34.1	21.4	43.9	0.0	7.3

may exist because of the greater availability of outside technical expertise in urban areas. The practice of helping to identify technical milestones was also statistically significant, with urban incubators more likely to provide this type of assistance.

In the next section we will present the array of best practices that relate to business planning. As the data show, there is a heavy tilt toward using planning as a screening device and involving students.

BEST PRACTICES: BUSINESS PLANNING

Business planning implies both a product and a process. On the one hand, a tangible document called a business plan is usually produced and used as a reference and guide for the entrepreneur. Equally (or more) important is the *process* by which a plan is created. This involves gathering information, making comparisons, and drawing inferences, as well as changing, tuning, and improving the plan (as product). Most would argue that a business plan should be a dynamic product and that the process of planning should never end as long as the business is in operation.

Reflecting these observations, we have grouped best practices in business planning in the following categories: 1) selection and screening; 2) using students; 3) training; and 4) business planning tools.

Selection and Screening

Business planning services often are most intensive—albeit incomplete—when a company presents itself for admission to an incubator program. This is the opportunity for looking quickly and broadly at the business potential of the venture. The challenge is to make good choices (few false positives and/or false negatives) and to do it economically. Incubators need entrance review methods to judge the viability of a technology and the capabilities of the entrepreneur to start a business. Several programs adopt explicit or implicit decision models. These face-to-face interactions result in the development of a contract or set of expectations with the client company.

The **Advanced Technology Development Center (ATDC)** has developed a relatively quick process to review applications to the incubator, which they call "*mini-due diligence.*" A first cut eliminates those applicants whose technologies will demand huge investments and a long development cycle. A second "Kentucky windage" assessment will eliminate those companies and technologies that have limited commercialization potential (limited markets in size and/or margins). The balance of applicants undergo the mini-due diligence, which takes about a month. Applicants submit a draft business plan. Staff evaluate several areas: technical risk in developing the technology; business risk, particularly "sustainable competitive advantage"; intellectual property strategy; and distribution channel assessment. If admitted, the tenant is given a letter describing expectations or milestones in each of these areas. Companies are admitted on either "developing company" or "full company" status. The latter will have most of the ingredients of a developed technology, a management team, and capitalization. The former will lack one or more of these elements.

The **Austin Technology Incubator's** selection and screening process is quite exhaustive but is designed to ensure the quality of new tenant companies. ATI's success rate for companies that have come through the incubator and are still in business stands at more than 90 percent—an outstanding achievement in light of the national average for entrepreneurial success. The selection process is rigorous and requires a good deal of effort on the part of the companies' management and ATI's staff.

The principle criteria used in selecting companies for admission into the incubator are few, yet stringent. The product or service should be based on new technologies or technologically innovative concepts. Product-based companies should seek to develop a proprietary position; with service-based companies, ATI looks for market barriers to entry. The company should endeavor to create jobs that contribute to Austin's economic development. The product or service should respond to market needs and have market growth potential. The company should able to graduate from the incubator in two or three years and continue growing. The company should have a detailed, written business plan that includes market analysis, financial projections, funding requirements, management background, and related information. The entrepreneur should demonstrate team-building potential. The CEO should be willing to accept guidance and share management responsibility with others to build a strong management team for the success of the business. With these criteria in mind the incubator staff can begin the selection process.

The first step on the path to admission is first contact with an ATI staff member. This usually takes the form of an inquiring phone call fielded by an MBA student intern. ATI receives from 10 to 40 calls per day. The intern tries to obtain as much information about the prospective company as he or she can, and if it is determined that there is a possible "fit," the intern requests a brief one-to-two page product summary. This summary is a general description of the company and its main product and contains no proprietary information. This description serves as the supporting document to the initial "first contact" conversation.

Once this survey is received and reviewed by ATI's staff, an initial meeting is scheduled between incubator management and the entrepreneurs. The purposes of this meeting are to better understand the foundations for the company, assess the managerial and entrepreneurial capabilities of the principles, describe the incubator in greater detail, and decide whether or not to ask for a fully written business plan. Basically, ATI attempts to spot any glaring weaknesses in the business idea.

The submission and review of the business plan are the next steps toward admission. The business plan serves as the formal application to the incubator and should meet the criteria mentioned above. ATI uses a standardized "Business Evaluation Form" for its review process, which consists of both internal and external reviews. The internal review gives the incubator interns and staff the opportunity for an in-depth examination of the company. The internal review consists of evaluation by engineering and MBA student interns and the director. This review also serves as an initial critique, and the entrepreneurs may be asked to rework or add some sections to the plan before continued processing. The business plan is then submitted for external review. These external reviews provide candid, unbiased opinions from individuals familiar with the technology, the market, and the end use of the company's product. A minimum of three external reviews are required.

Once all reviews have been completed and all evaluation forms are in, a final decision for admission is made and presented to the ATI advisory board. Results from all reviews (both internal and external) are summarized and a final meeting is held with the entrepreneurs. At this meeting any questions that arose from the reviews are posed, and the company presents proof that it has the ability to sustain itself financially for the first three to six months. More specific requirements are then discussed, such as space, and other logistics. A recommendation for acceptance of the company into the incubator is submitted, with supporting materials, to the board of directors for formal approval.

It should be noted that ATI has been very selective because of the voluminous amount of inquiries and plans received by companies seeking admission. This is primarily attributable to the marketing efforts of ATI's staff, in particular the director, and the excellent reputation ATI enjoys in the community.

The **Iowa State Innovation Center** has a somewhat similar approach, albeit a different set of metaphors. It likens its process to a *medical model*, which begins with an intake interview to gather basic entering "symptoms" and then proceeds through a series of interactions that result in a "diagnosis." The diagnosis identifies key points of the business that need to be treated and "prescribes" actions to be taken by the client and incubation management. At some point the "patient" is released and moves into larger facilities in the community, which may involve "aftercare" on the part of the incubator. This conceptual model also drives specific actions and practices. For example, because the incubator works in partnership with the SBDC in the research park, the SBDC functions as the family physician or case manager, routing both internal and external (consultants) specialists to the client. It also provides a running case history for the client and quarterly progress reports. At the onset of the client relationship, the diagnosis and set of expectations are communicated to the client.

The **Metropolitan Center for High Technology** in Detroit has developed what it describes as an interaction agreement that results from their initial discussions with the prospective tenant company. This involves face-to-face meetings with the entrepreneur, during which the developmental *needs* of the company are articulated, which in turn establishes a set of behavioral *expectations* for the first six months or so of residency in the incubator. These expectations apply to the incubator management as well as the entrepreneur and are written down in the form of a memorandum for both sides. The agreements are specific and identify timelines and deliverables. For example, the agreement might specify five or six goals for the company, but it will also specify the role that MCHT will play, working with the entrepreneur, to accomplish those goals. One of the goals might be to "find a corporate partner to commercialize XXX product." The roles MCHT might play include working with the entrepreneur to assemble a marketing package on the product and the company, and identifying likely prospects and initiating contact. The interaction agreement operates, in effect, as a contract between the incubator and the entrepreneur. If either side reneges on the understandings, they are likely to part company.

The **Technology Innovation Center** requests a fairly simple statement of business/investment opportunity from a candidate company. Often the "company" in the university setting will not yet be incorporated and will not yet need a full-blown business plan. The opportunity statement is typically a three-to-five page document without a lot of "spreadsheet gymnastics." This is only a precursor to a formal plan but serves as a basis for discussion with the incubator and/or with potential regional investors. Candidate entrepreneurs follow an outline in the creation of the opportunity statement, which is then passed on to a review panel, consisting of incubator staff, faculty, potential investors, or others selected on an *ad hoc* basis. The statement should answer three questions: 1) Is the product/service technically feasible? 2) Is the product/service commercially viable? and 3) Can the people involved pull it off?

Incutech Brunswick Inc. requires a business plan from firms entering the incubator but prefers that the plan be written in the entrepreneur's own words rather than in a "canned," fill-in-the-blanks format.

This encourages the client to truly understand what the business plan is about and have owner-ship of it. If an entrepreneur has no idea how to format a business plan, the manager will sometimes provide a brief outline with section headings. This is usually not necessary, as most entrepreneurs have some business acumen. The entrepreneur's own business plan, even with mistakes, is a useful diagnostic tool to see if the idea is viable and the entrepreneur has the capabilities to pull it off. The initial plan goes to the incubator manager, who screens it and helps rework it structurally if necessary, before it is forwarded to a screening committee. The screening committee set up by Incutech's board of directors then reviews an applicant's business plan, to decide whether to allow the company to enter the incubator.

The **Montgomery County Technology Enterprise Center (MCTEC)** uses 12 criteria to evaluate an applicant's business plan and decide if the incubator is a good match for that company's needs. All applicants to MCTEC are required to submit an MCTEC application and completed business plan. Using these documents, the incubator manager evaluates the potential tenant by asking the following 12 questions: 1) Is the business one that is targeted for the incubator? 2) Will the business fill an identified gap and an identified market need in the economy? 3) Is the product/service innovative and technology-based? 4) Is the business in need of the incubator environment? 5) Will the tenant fit in well with other tenants and serve as a contributor? 6) Does the owner have the requisite entrepreneurial skills to run a business? 7) Could the business benefit from specific management services the facility can offer? 8) Does the applicant have a business plan, and is it well thought out and researched? 9) Has the owner participated in previous business programs to learn the basic business skills and talents needed to run the business successfully? 10) Is the owner willing to trade a portion of equity for the services the company will receive while in the incubator? 11) Does the business compete with other firms in the local community or complement market gaps? and 12) Does the business show evidence of a reasonable expectation to be able to pay the first six months' rent?

If the MCTEC manager makes a preliminary determination that the potential tenant meets the entrance criteria, the incubator advisory board then completes a technical review of the business plan and conducts a personal interview for final admission approval.

The **Technology Advancement Program (TAP)** at the University of Maryland, College Park, has an application form followed by a three-step review process for entrepreneurs interested in entering the incubator. Applicants undergo an informal review with the TAP director, meet with a panel of technical reviewers, and then go before a business review panel prior to admission.

The first step of the process is the submission of a one-page application form. This application asks for brief descriptions of the nature of the business, the background of principal officers, the status of the business, current sales revenue, date the business was established, number of employees, type of financing obtained, facility and space requirements, and status of the business plan. TAP also looks for companies that conduct, or plan to conduct, a significant portion of their business in-state.

Once the written application in received, a meeting is scheduled with the TAP director and at least one person from the university's Engineering Research Center who is knowledgeable about the technology involved in the business. This meeting is informal but is oriented toward ensuring that the company is compatible with the university's policies, gauging the commitment and technical ability of the principals, and determining the potential market for the product. If the director determines the company suitable, he works with the company to prepare for the two formal stages of the application process, the technical review and the business review.

Both reviews are conducted as seminars in which the applicant makes a formal presentation to a panel of experts who serve as unpaid consultants to the company. The review process is intended to identify any potential fatal flaws in the company's technical or business plan, in order to avert problems ahead. Before each review, panelists are given the company's plan (technical or business), and the company is informed of the names and affiliations of the panelists.

The technical review involves the company making a formal presentation to a panel about the technology, the product, and its market. Panelists are experts in the technical field from academia or government laboratories, not competing businesses. They are usually drawn from the Engineering Research Center, although representatives of the University College of Business and Management may also be involved; the TAP director and staff are also panelists. The session addresses the product strategy, planning, scheduling, performance specifications, and most importantly, the potential customer. The focus is to determine the technical feasibility of the product by ascertaining if it can be developed to a commercial state within three years with resources that can be reasonably obtained by the company. Also examined are the technical risk of the product and its technical innovative edge over current or potential competition. The session determines the technical knowledge of the entrepreneurs as much as it does the viability of the product. Proprietary and confidential information need not be revealed, and panelists agree to honor all nondisclosure provisions. The topics covered in the session generally follow the sequence of the submitted technical plan.

The entrepreneur makes a brief presentation to the panel and answers panelists' questions in a session lasting a total of about one-and-one-half hours. Following this, the company personnel leave and the panelists make any further comments to the incubator management. After the session, a report is circulated to panelists for accuracy and then given to the entrepreneur. Normally, the entrepreneur is notified of the panel's opinion within 48 hours. If the review is unfavorable, another technical review can be scheduled when recommended changes are made.

If a company passes the technical review stage, it proceeds to a formal business review, which takes the same format as the technical review, but functions as a mini-due diligence. Business review panelists include faculty from the College of Business and Management, members of the Dingman Center for Entrepreneurship, venture capitalists, and professional service providers, such as accountants, attorneys, and bankers. This panel of 12 provides valuable advice to the entrepreneurs about the market of interest, based on the experience of the panelists. The panel, acting as *de facto* consultants to the company, attempts to identify any serious flaws in the business plan. This review session generally lasts between one-and-one-half and two-and-one-half hours. Companies are advised to use visual aids in their presentations.

The panel advises TAP management immediately following the review of the suitability of the company. A final decision to admit the company to the incubator is made within a few days, incorporating the decisions of the two panels and other factors.

If a company has passed the technical review but is not ready for the business review, it may be granted provisional participation program status for 90 days, with another 90-day extension possible. This program allows a company residence in the incubator in order to further develop the business plan and prepare for the business review. During this time the company is encouraged to use the business support services available in the incubator and is required to prepare for the business review.

The process may take a company between two and four months to complete, depending on the readiness of the company. It may also take time to schedule appropriate panelists.

This process gives applicant companies valuable insights into the prospects of success and identifies flaws the companies must address, based on the combined broad-ranging expertise of the panelists. The process also allows TAP to accept into the incubator only companies likely to be successful. Additionally, once a company has succeeded in this process, it has attained credibility in the local venture capital community.

No idea is too big or too small to discuss with the incubator manager at the **Carleton Technology Innovation Center (CTIC)**. He has established an unwritten "one-hour rule" which gives anyone in the region an opportunity to talk with him. This includes individuals who have a new technology or venture idea and are looking for ways to develop it. Working with potential tenants and tenants is seen as a "case-driven" activity. Anyone in the Ottawa-Carleton area can contact CTIC and arrange to sit down and talk with the incubator manager. This open-door policy enables CTIC to assess the entrepreneur and his or her technology, identify resources, and select the proper business planning tool for the entrepreneur. Where a liaison makes sense, the two parties work to form the relationship.

Use of Students

Start-up technology companies lack the personnel and expertise to perform all the market research and business planning needed to launch a successful business, and they cannot afford to contract for these services at market prices. In addition, graduates and undergraduates need "real world" experiences to test theories they have learned in the classroom. As a result, incubators linked to or located near universities often develop programs for student teams to assist incubator companies. Programs take on many forms. Some universities give course credit to the students in return for their work with start-up businesses, while others work out a fee arrangement to compensate for assistance. In addition, both undergraduate and graduate students are utilized.

The **Evanston Small Business Incubator** is located in a research park that is a joint venture of the city of Evanston and Northwestern University. Because of its location, the incubator has made connections between businesses in the incubator and students at the Kellogg School of Management at Northwestern. Students may work with incubator companies to undertake projects as part of classes in marketing, business planning, or entrepreneurship. Although the incubator is a nonprofit organization separate from the university, two of its board members are vice presidents of the university.

The "Entrepreneurship Laboratory" is a course offered by the J.L. Kellogg Graduate School of Management at Northwestern University. The course is designed to bring "real life" into the classroom by involving students in a consulting exercise. Student teams undertake consulting assignments with start-up companies, many from the Small Business Incubator. The incubator is one of two organizations from which companies are solicited as "clients."

Companies are solicited twice a year for participation in the program. A professor provides a short description of the course to the companies in the incubator, and the incubator manager helps recruit businesses to participate. The companies develop a five-to-ten minute presentation of what they are about, along with a page of descriptive material. The first two weeks of the class are devoted to company presentations. The students then form into teams and select whom they want to work with, based on their own interests and how they match up against particular companies.

The student exercise is based on an evaluation of the business in its current stage and what is most pressing or necessary for business success. In effect, these are highly focused case studies. The course emphasizes the need to understand a situation, create an integrated cross-functional strategy, and implement for results. The teams hold client meetings with the companies and present progress reports to the class.

Northwestern's business school is a useful resource for the incubator companies. Because students are limited in their time commitment, however, the kind of structured project offered by the Entrepreneurship Laboratory provides an effective way to use that resource. Both the students and the businesses know up front what time commitments are needed to attain the projected outcome, yet the project itself is flexible enough to respond to the particular needs of an incubator company.

The **Business Technology Incubator** at Bradley University and the **Akron Industrial Incubator** utilize students affiliated with the Small Business Institute (SBI) program. This federally funded program uses college of business senior-level students and faculty to assist small businesses. Access to the Bradley College of Engineering and Technology is also accomplished through the Technology Center, which was a state-funded program until 1991 and is now a privately funded program located in the incubator. All graduating seniors in engineering and business at Bradley are required to work with a real business, so every firm in the incubator has access to these student project programs through the Small Business Institute or Technology Center.

The student project programs utilize up to 500 students and five to 10 faculty per year to work directly with clients. Bradley's Small Business Development Center, which is colocated with the incubator, selects firms based on need, and the coordination of students is done through business and engineering professors. The professors put together the teams based on the background of the students. A SBI team may include senior-level students in marketing, finance management, economics, or international business. The university provides two graduate students who coordinate student work on projects and determine scope, objectives and method.

Both undergraduate and graduate students work with tenant firms. The SBI undergraduate projects, typically marketing studies, are free to the client. The projects take from 200 to 600 hours during a semester, and students track their work by completing a time and effort sheet. For studies involving exporting or international business relationships, the client pays for out-of-pocket costs such as international phone calls. The federal government reimburses the institutions for several cases each year through the SBI Program. To date, more than 3,000 student projects have been completed at Bradley since 1972.

The **Austin Technology Incubator** (ATI), through its close association with the University of Texas, utilizes a wide variety of student interns. Interns have been hired from the Schools of Business,

Engineering, Communication, and Liberal Arts. Most interns fall within three areas: volunteers, independent studies with course credit, and paid interns. ATI provides "experiential learning" in a high-tech, entrepreneurial setting for the interns while fulfilling its staffing needs and aiding its tenant companies. Most interns work on live case study projects for tenant companies, as well as provide administrative support for the incubator. ATI's tenant companies actively seek the involvement of students to assist them with current, critical-stage issues. Students have provided valuable support through research and recommendations on such issues as price, distribution channels, competitive analysis, and promotional literature. The benefits of the intern program for both ATI's tenant companies and interns have been substantial, as evidenced by the recent hiring of a number of graduate MBAs by in-house companies.

The **Business Technology Center** of Columbus, Ohio, uses MBA students to assist tenant and non-tenant companies in preparing and improving business plans. Students participating in these activities receive course credit in the Franklin University MBA program.

Students working in four and five-member teams assist tenant companies in improving their business plans and help non-tenant companies, identified by the incubator as potential tenants, in developing or improving business plans.

The **Enterprise Development Center** at New Jersey Institute of Technology (NJIT) uses volunteer MBA students to assist its tenant companies in marketing and other business development needs. In addition, upper-level undergraduate students in a new program at the School of Technology Management have volunteered to assist incubator companies with such activities as market research. The students provide these services on an unpaid basis in return for class credit. While the technology management program is a good fit with the incubator, the shortcoming of this arrangement is the limited amount of time students spend on the project.

The Enterprise Development Center also uses work-study students to assist its tenant companies and the incubator management. It arranges for about 15 students to work at the incubator each semester. These students receive "work-study" financial assistance, earning between $6 and $9 per hour, a large portion of which (currently about 75 percent) is subsidized by the federal government. Thus, the incubator or the tenant company employing the student pays a very low rate for the student labor. Students are usually used to perform general office work but some more technical work is performed by mechanical and electrical engineering students.

While the low cost of this labor makes the use of students worthwhile, the limit on the number of hours each can work weekly (20) and the unavailability of students during vacations and exam periods, causes some frustrations. On the other hand, some companies have found the students to be so helpful that they have taken on the full wage for student employees when federal funds have run out at the end of the fiscal year.

As a facility based at a technologically oriented university, the **Rensselaer Polytechnic Institute (RPI) Incubator Center** makes heavy use of students from academic programs. RPI's MBA program is focused on management and technology, and as part of coursework, students are required to participate in the Practicum Program. They also bring to this experience extensive coursework in areas of relevance to a technology-based new enterprise: information systems, manufacturing, management science, and so on.

Students are expected to invest approximately 150 hours over the course of the semester in

Practicum experience. In some courses, the majority of time is spent on a field project; in others, the project is only part of their course responsibilities. The quantity and type of work varies depending on the capabilities of the student, the nature of the project, the cooperation of the company, and a host of other factors.

Students are expected to work with their client company and their professor to define the project and complete the work. The Rensselaer professor provides oversight and guidance but does not do the work for the students. The professor generally will facilitate communication with the company, especially at the beginning when project definition is so important, as well as at the end when companies receive the results.

The responsibilities of companies vary from course to course but most often include some or all of the following: 1) The company assigns a liaison to work directly with the student (ideally a manager in a position of responsibility); 2) Companies agree to absorb out-of-pocket expenses, not to exceed an amount agreed upon in advance; 3) Companies send a representative to the oral presentation at the end of the report; 4) Companies do not send proprietary or confidential information to the program or a student without the express consent of the professor in charge of the program; and 5) The companies understand that the students may need to publish all or part of their experience in the program, including the project requested by any company. The program is open to external affiliates and regional companies, but incubator firms usually receive preference. Also, students are surveyed. They are asked to rate the professor and the educational experience. Not every project submitted for consideration will be selected. In addition, companies may have to wait a semester before the right course or team of students is available. However, the program tries to ensure that companies and student teams are the "right fit."

A typical project goes through the following stages: An initial meeting is held between the student(s) and the "client" company to define needs and to scope out the potential project. The professor usually reviews the approach to be taken (e.g., survey case study) and the methods to be used. Over the course of the semester, various oversight meetings are held with the corporate liaison and/or the professor. At the close of the project, an oral presentation is made before the class, the company representative, the professor, and an independent panel of judges that has been invited to review the quality of the presentation. This oral presentation lasts approximately 15 minutes and consists of a project overview and recommendations. A written report is given to both the professor and the company.

The outcomes depend on the relationships between students and companies and the quality of the student teams. The most successful projects are those in which the company clearly defines the projects and keeps the students on track—in effect, functions as a good client. RPI surveys tenant companies after each project has been completed.

Since its inception, the Practicum Program at Rensselaer's School of Management has provided 50 incubator clients with useful products and recommendations. When companies are surveyed, they typically say, "The student project would be worth several thousand dollars if it were performed by a paid consultant." Typically, students rate the Practicum-based course as among the best in their educational experience at the university. These responses strongly suggest that the Practicum Program works.

Tenants of the **Rutgers/CARR Business Innovation Center** have access to teams of MBA candidates to assist in business planning. The MBA curriculum is especially strong in quantitative analysis. Student consulting teams provide assistance to incubator companies for an entrepreneurship course run through the SBDC at Rutgers. Usually the students focus on updating the business plan, but more specialized services may be provided, such as market research, setting up charts of accounts, and developing loan packages. Teams of students may range from one to four individuals. Generally, two companies are assisted per semester.

In the two years that the program has operated, student consulting teams have assisted about seven companies. Due to the strength of the MBA program and its quantitative focus, companies report positive results when they use student consultant teams.

The **St. Louis Technology Center** uses a 12-person business development planning staff, including five retired executives with industry backgrounds and experience in commercializing technology, five MBA or technology management/marketing graduate students, one full-time strategic planner who is also the director of commercial development, and a full-time financial analyst. The director of commercial development does the first screening of companies, tracks clients, and coordinates the team for each company, including the graduate students. The retired executives work without compensation.

The incubator director sets the legal, reputational parameters, but the team is basically self-directing. Tasks include focus groups, phone surveys, and literature searches. To look for a match, the team compares market requirements with the characteristics of the technology.

The planning process lasts from six months to one year. Generally, a client is in the incubator an average of two years. A scope-of-work document is adopted with each company after two or three months, so that all sides know the expectations.

Companies pay a $5,000 fee for the planning process, although it costs the incubator about $10,000 to provide the service. This payment may be deferred until the company can afford to pay. Nonetheless, a nominal fee is charged so that the company takes the service seriously. Cost is based on the number of hours dedicated to the planning process.

Graduate students are from the four local universities, and all are in the top 10 percent of their class. They typically have at least two years of industry experience before returning to graduate school. Resumés are solicited though university contacts, such as assistant deans. The incubator tries to rotate among universities to fill graduate student positions, with the minimum commitment from graduate students being one year.

This team approach is an intensive process that leads to a well-developed business plan. This process can be done at any stage of the company's development. The incubator does not require a business plan for entry, so the process may be completed before or after the company enters the incubator. A concept may be researched before a prototype is developed, and the user characteristics may help determine what the prototype will look like. One program objective is for clients to understand the research process so they can replicate it on their own after they leave the program.

Training, Workshops and Seminars

For a variety of reasons, incubators may emphasize a **training** approach to the business planning process. That is, rather than providing direct or brokered assistance, the intent is to encourage incubator tenants to acquire planning skills and perspectives. Training also may be combined with various types of direct assistance. Some training programs may emphasize only one important component of the business planning process (e.g., technology commercialization), while others will be more inclusive. Although tenants of technology incubators may be experts in their fields, few possess all of the skills necessary to run the business. Entrepreneurs obtain skills through training, workshops, and seminars. Many incubator managers focus on business planning workshops, but other types are also provided. The incubator manager must balance the number and variety of workshops offered with the needs of tenants. The major challenge is to provide training that not only teaches new skills but motivates future attendance.

The **Idaho Innovation Center** has developed a commercialization plan workshop to help its entrepreneurs. Commercialization plans examine potential ways in which a technology can be commercialized and serve as a precursor to a business plan, especially for entrepreneurs coming out of a research setting.

The Innovation Center's workshop is based on the NIST Energy Related Inventions Program (ERIP) Business Development Orientation. The goal of the workshop is for each participant to develop a business or commercialization plan by the end of the session. For many start-up entrepreneurs, the focus is on developing a commercialization plan that determines the options for bringing the product to market, such as licensing, joint venturing, and selling the technology directly. The next step is to select the best option to try, with the assumption that the strategy is not yet developed at this stage in the process. Thus, the commercialization plan workshop serves to make the transition from invention to business—a transition that should be made as quickly as possible. The commercialization plan also examines the costs, staffing, and time involved in developing, marketing, and selling the technology. These costs are projected for each of the first five years. The final commercialization plan is a document useful to the entrepreneur when dealing with venture investors and prospective licensees.

The workshop is concerned with the business aspects of the product. In the words of the program director, "We don't want to hear a damned thing about your technology." Rather, the workshops seek to ensure that the entrepreneur is prepared to handle the business end of the company and that a real market for the technology exists. Since the concern is whether the entrepreneur is ready, the technology may be at any stage in its development when the entrepreneur goes through the workshop. The workshop conveys to entrepreneurs that technology development should take only a fraction of their time, and that they also need to address marketing and business issues and identify problems ahead of time. To further hone the business skills of the entrepreneurs, the last part of the workshop is a presentation by each entrepreneur, which is videotaped and critiqued by the whole group.

The Innovation Center workshop allows for no more than five entrepreneurs at a time so it can be individualized. Such a group will usually be advised by faculty from the local technical college and from Idaho State University, as well as the Innovation Center director. Videotapes of the NIST Business Development Orientation also will be used.

The Innovation Center requires all tenants to have either a commercialization plan or a business plan; thus, most of their tenants go through the workshop at some point. Generally, the workshops have been held every two months.

A Small Business Development Center (SBDC) is housed in the **Business Technology Incubator** facility. The incubator hosts semimonthly workshops for entrepreneurs who have contacted the incubator or SBDC. The workshops, which cover basic business planning, typically attract from five to 15 participants and last two to three hours. The SBDC program manager conducts the workshops, introducing the participants to the business planning process as well as to the incubator's role in business development. Outside entities such as loan program advisors sit in on some of the meetings, although the workshop organizers do not make access to loan funds a big issue up front in order to prevent attracting businesses that are merely interested in capital access.

Notices of workshops are sent to people who have contacted the SBDC or the incubator. After a client completes the workshop, he or she may or may not pursue further assistance. In effect, the workshop serves as a soft screening device for admission. If participants are serious about starting a business, most will make a follow-up appointment at the end of the workshop. The SBDC follows-up any workshop participant who has not made contact within 30 days.

Most incubator facilities require potential tenants to submit a business plan. The real issues become how to evaluate the plan, and work with individuals to improve it over time. The **NET Ben Franklin Technology Center** uses a business planning workshop to address these concerns. By the end of the session, companies will have identified strengths, weaknesses, opportunities, and threats (SWOT).

Three to four incubator companies are selected to participate in a two-day business planning session. Sessions are held two to three times a year. The SWOT analysis is free, although not every tenant company will participate in the process. The incubator manager is responsible for selecting the companies, with an emphasis on choosing those that are at a crossroads with regard to their operation. For example, will the company need additional funding or employees? Is there a window of opportunity for new technology? Is the company likely to listen to the advice of or need specialized assistance from the SWOT team?

The sessions are handled by the SWOT team, composed of a venture consultant, an accountant, a corporate attorney, and an intellectual property attorney. Business plans are given to the team prior to the sessions for review.

Day one is conducted by the venture consultant. Tenants receive a four-page handout that outlines the agenda and activities for the session. In order to foster intercompany perspectives, all of the companies work together in one room. The incubator manager remains out of the process to serve as a friendly facilitator. The session starts with a 30-minute icebreaker with coffee and donuts. Each company is given 10 minutes to talk about its business or plans for the company's future. Next, an overview of the day's activities is discussed. The manager introduces each company. Step One in the workshop process requires that each company develop a clear, concise description of itself. Examples are provided in handouts, and participants are given an opportunity to develop their own descriptions. This process lasts for approximately two hours.

In Step Two, workshop participants are asked to perform a SWOT self-analysis. That is, for each factor (strengths, weaknesses, opportunities, and threats), workshop participants are asked to list specific examples in their company. Strengths and weaknesses are considered internal factors, while opportunities and threats are considered external (to the company) factors.

On day two, companies meet individually with the SWOT team. Each company is given two hours in which to review the SWOT profile with the team and to determine specific follow-up action items. Companies do develop a "to do" list of the action items. If a more complex analysis is required from the SWOT team, that task will be arranged at this time—including partial compensation.

Follow-up is conducted within four to six weeks during "one-on-one" meetings with the incubator manager to ensure that companies have begun to implement recommended actions. Additional follow-up is done on a case-by-case basis.

The Akron Industrial Incubator in conjunction with the University of Akron has developed advanced business planning seminars for both tenants and non-tenants. Although the normal business planning process results in an eight-to-ten page operating plan, a more detailed and thought-intensive process is needed to develop a successful business plan. That observation has led this program to develop a much more extensive training experience.

Two 10-week business planning seminars are conducted. Each session lasts for approximately four hours per week. This first seminar focuses on wholesale, manufacturing, and research and development businesses. The second seminar focuses on the retail industry. All sessions are open to incubator tenants, potential tenants, and local business owners.

The **Austin Technology Incubator (ATI)** provides its tenant companies with a number of venues for educational training, networking, and promotional exposure. As part of the IC^2 Institute, ATI is able to offer its tenant companies access to a number of Institute-run programs. The Austin Software Council (ASC)—an academic, business and government coalition dedicated to creating and building a world-class software engineering center in Austin—is one such entity. This relationship affords ATI's tenant companies the full benefits associated with ASC membership at no charge. Affiliation with the ASC provides benefits to tenant companies through monthly dinner presentations, mentor programs for start-up software firms, major conferences, and workshops on such business innovations as cutting edge technology and market trends. All of these events furnish beneficial networking opportunities for ATI's member companies, as the ASC has among its membership Austin's premier business professionals.

The Capital Network (TCN) is another IC^2 Institute program in which ATI's tenants enjoy benefits. The Capital Network is an innovative, proven program designed to introduce investors to entrepreneurs based on their mutual business interests. Benefits to ATI's tenant companies include free membership and admittance to TCN's venture-related seminars. TCN has made many lucrative introductions for ATI client companies and has assisted entrepreneurial ventures in raising more than $20 million.

ATI also provides its tenants with in-house programs structured around their needs. Each month the Austin Technology Incubator invites one of its tenant companies to showcase itself in a planned, publicized forum at its Tenant Round Table. Typically, company CEOs prepare and deliver a 30-minute presentation about their companies and its products. The presentations are well attended by other tenant companies' officers, interested business professionals, and the press. This showcase provides a forum for ATI's CEOs to get to know one another and cooperatively exploit synergies.

Another monthly event on ATI's calendar is the CEO Luncheon. Each month ATI provides lunch and a guest speaker for tenant companies' CEOs. Ideas for speakers and topics are drawn from the companies and deal with critical issues and problems typically faced by entrepreneurs. Like the Tenant Round Table, ATI hopes to foster a community spirit among its CEOs by pointing out mutual problems and shared experiences. ATI hopes that companies will work together for reciprocal benefit.

Business Planning Tools

The market is full of books, publications, checklists, software, and other decision tools to assist individuals with the development of business plans and commercialization of technology. However, several incubator managers have uncovered tools that aid in the development of technology companies. Some of these have been developed by incubator programs themselves. Others have been recommended as having particular value in the context of the incubation process. In general, tools of this sort have the advantage of saving staff time, often being self-executing. However, no tool is as valuable as a one-on-one with a creative expert, and there can be a one-size-fits-all limitation of tools as well. Nonetheless, they are useful adjuncts to incubator services.

The **Center for Innovation and Business Development** (CIBD) at the University of North Dakota developed a checklist for evaluating new ideas and ventures. The checklist provides entrepreneurs with a quick method to quickly assess a new product or venture against key factors for success. The 25-page document sets out criteria for evaluating the venture. Four primary areas are assessed: a comparison with competing technologies, market opportunity, economic feasibility, and management factors. There is a checklist of 42 specific criteria and a method of deriving a score in each of the four areas.

The checklist came out of a three-year demonstration project for the Northwest Area Foundation on starting manufacturing companies in rural areas. About 40 start-up companies were studied to determine key factors for success. Out of that study came a methodology to evaluate the technology or product, the market, and the economic and management factors.

The checklist is applicable for most new ventures and products, but not all. It can be used for services. Specialized industry or product knowledge may be required for proper evaluation and assessment. The checklist is designed to be thorough and requires critical thinking skills for realistic self-assessment, but it is also user-friendly. The company needs to have an idea of how its product idea compares with similar products and technologies, who its customers might be, and who its competition is.

The CIBD goes through the evaluation tool with clients in a two to three-hour session, and then there are one or two follow-up sessions in which the company may bring back more information. The evaluation serves as a screening tool for the center. The reviewer gives an evaluation of the strengths, weaknesses, threats, and opportunities, as well as recommendations for further development.

This tool is very helpful because it is a quick and dirty evaluation that can be done in a few hours with a client. Both the company and the center find out what factors need to be addressed and if there are fatal flaws that will keep this from being a successful company. It is most useful when staff assist the firm members to dig a little bit, face the facts of the marketplace, and acknowledge what they don't know.

The **Idaho Innovation Center** program uses the *Commercialization Planning Workshop Workbook* by Marcia L. Rorke and Harold C. Livesay, 1984, (Mohawk Research Corp., 915 Willowleaf Way, Rockville, MD 20854). The workbook contains the following sections: overview of the commercialization process, writing your commercialization plan, engineering and prototype development, market analysis, licensing, sources of capital, planning to license or venture, and an appendix presenting supporting materials about the innovation process. The appendix contains a table that breaks down the innovation process into three stages: the innovation stage from concept to prototype, the entrepreneurial stage from prototype to production, and the managerial stage from production to major market penetration. The steps for each of these stages include parallel technical, market, and business steps, along with skills required and people involved for each step.

The **Madison Gas and Electric (MGE) Innovation Center** provides early-stage tenants with a business plan outline to use as a tool in preparing a plan for potential investors. The MGE Innovation Center is managed by Venture Investors of Wisconsin (VIW), a venture capital fund that provides business services as part of managing the incubator facility. The business plan outline addresses background information about the company and its employees as well as information about the industry, financial projections, markets, and future capitalization. The outline is not a "fill-in-the-blanks" tool. Rather, it is intended as a stimulus for further research by the entrepreneur. It identifies issues, asks questions, and so on.

The Business Plan: A State-of-the-Art Guide is published nationally and available through the **Center for Innovation and Business Development (CIBD)** at the University of North Dakota. The publication was written by a business consultant who is an alumnus of CIBD and edited by the CIBD director. The Center provides business and technical support services each year to hundreds of individuals and businesses who have product ideas.

The step-by-step workbook, published in 1989, is specifically targeted for manufacturing companies and entrepreneurs with a new product or new technology. It is designed not only to assist in obtaining financial support from investors and bankers but also to help set up the management team, establish strategic goals, and avoid mistakes.

Each chapter outlines how to research, analyze, write, and implement the important elements of a business plan. The guide is written in modular format, in which each module represents a section of a good business plan. Sections include: the executive summary, technology analysis, market analysis, management and ownership, milestones, schedules and strategic planning, and financial data and projections. Modules are designed to stand alone or can be viewed as a series of mini-lessons that can be attacked one at a time. Each module is an exercise that will result in a section of the business plan. The guide tells the entrepreneur what to do but not how to do it. For each section, it details the suggested length, the objective, a series of questions that must be answered, a suggested sequence of presentation, subheadings to include, and common mistakes to avoid.

CIBD also sells software on business planning to accompany the guide. The customized workbook and software is used with the client's own word-processing program. The software and workbook combination is $79 plus $3 shipping. A video on "The Business Plan" is also available, which includes presentations by the author on each module in the workbook. The video is available for $125 plus shipping.

The guide is the most valuable tool used by CIBD in working with people whose businesses are at different stages of development. It is most useful when someone goes through the process with the entrepreneur. The guide has given the Center a great deal of national exposure and been extremely successful with clients. CIBD has sold approximately 43,000 copies since 1989 at a cost of $30 plus shipping. The center receives royalties from the publisher.

The **Center for Applied Technology** sometimes refers its clients to *Business Planning for Scientists and Engineers*, prepared for the U.S. Department of Energy by Dawnbreaker, May 1991. The book is intended for use by individuals and firms having received Phase II SBIR (Small Business Innovation Research) funding.

The Department of Energy found that there was a need for commercialization and business planning assistance, among companies that had received SBIR awards from the federal government. The authors of the book recognized that individuals and small companies often need a business plan when they have the fewest resources to develop one. It also recognizes that many scientists and engineers find that something written in their language is more helpful than the standard business planning references. This is especially true if the researcher does not realize he or she needs assistance.

Business Planning for Scientists and Engineers is designed for companies that are developing a product or technology but do not have a business plan. It either provides the information that entrepreneurs need to write a business plan or tells them where they can access the information. It is a combination textbook/workbook that focuses on the how-to's of business planning: finding information, researching market potential, developing the plan, and, finally, selling the plan to investors. The approach is to start with the entrepreneur's initial assumptions about the technology or product and, through a gradual process of adding more facts, to move "from conjecture to certitude."

The book provides entrepreneurs with benchmarks to follow as they go through the business planning process. Additionally, it is organized into three simple sections. The first gives introductory information on the commercialization process and potential funding sources and outlines a business plan. It also discusses finding the commercialization team, licensing, and joint ventures.

The second section focuses on the business planning process and includes information on planning tasks, how to schedule your time, and data-gathering resources. In the chapter, "Benchmarking Your Starting Point," the book provides a roadmap to project planning to increase the likelihood that the entrepreneur will make it successfully through the process and emerge with a completed business plan.

Section three is a workbook. There are more than 40 questionnaires, checklists, and worksheets for the entrepreneurs to complete. These include an assessment of the technology and its applications, possible users and competitors, and market size and growth. There are also questions about the company's vision and organizational structure, as well as timelines and financial requirements. A chapter on strategy development takes the company through the process of putting together the business plan, including market strategies, R&D strategy, manufacturing strategy, and the human resource plan. There is also a chapter on how to use and distribute the plan. An appendix lists venture capital firms that provide seed money.

CAT has two copies of this book available to lend to tenant companies. A limited number of copies are available for SBIR companies from the Department of Energy SBIR Program. The book is also available in microfilm in the Government Documents section of some libraries.

The incubator management lets the companies do the work themselves; this way, they are more likely to learn how to do the business plan. The book has proven to be a good resource for CAT for that reason. The tenants like it because it makes sense and makes the business plan process more logical.

The **Carleton Technology Innovation Center (CTIC)** uses the book *University Spin-off Companies: Economic Development, Faculty Entrepreneurs, and Technology Transfer* as a tool for potential tenants. The book was edited by Alistair Brett, David V. Gibson, and Raymond W. Smilor (Rowman and Littlefield, 1990).

In this volume, 14 contributors provide an overview of the opportunities in and barriers to creating spin-off ventures and discuss relevant university case studies. Individuals contributing to the book believe more emphasis should be placed on spin-offs, which would allow the nation's universities to play a role in increasing industrial competitiveness, creating wealth, providing greater return on the investment in higher education, and enhancing their traditional role. This 300-page book is organized into four distinct parts: the university and economic development, university faculty as entrepreneurs, technology transfer—issues and initiatives, and turning university research into business opportunities. Appendices for the book discuss obtaining venture capital, understanding the legal framework for spin-off companies, and dealing with unrelated business income taxes. The book provides excellent articles on the characteristics of spin-off companies, which enable companies to compare themselves to others in related fields.

CTIC also uses the book *Making Technology Happen* as a business planning tool for potential tenants. This book is subtitled *A Handbook for Entrepreneurs, Investors, Scientists, Economic Development Officers, Public Servants. Tools and Techniques for Finding It, Exploiting It, Managing It.* It is produced by Doyletech Corporation, Kanata, Ontario. This slim, 130-page volume is very hands-on in its approach. Organized into seven chapters, from "taking the first step" through organizational and personnel issues (plus appendices), it takes the would-be entrepreneur through many of the steps involved in entrepreneurship.

Another book used and recommended by Carleton is *From Technical Professional to Entrepreneur* (Wiley-Interscience, 1991). This, too, is treatment-oriented toward the research scientist or engineer who is confronted with the possibility of launching one's own company.

Tools

Outline for a Business Plan is available free-of-charge from Ernst & Young's National Entrepreneurial Service. It is a quick and simple reference for writing a business plan, which, along with more hands-on assistance, may be used to help entrepreneurs determine the feasibility of financing a new company, anticipate the questions that potential investors may ask, and develop a more detailed operating plan. The 16-page guide instructs the user on how to create a business plan outline with the following steps: executive summary, market analysis, company description, marketing and sales activities, products and services, operations, management and ownership, funds required and their uses, financial data, and appendices or exhibits.

Contact:
Ernst & Young LLP
National Entrepreneurial Services
2001 Ross Avenue, Suite 2800
Dallas, TX 75201
Tel (214) 979-1700   Fax (214) 979-2333

Bizplan Builder is a strategic business and marketing plan software package that works with a user's existing word-processing and spreadsheet software. The package contains a 90-plus page business plan template with much of the text already written, including headlines, written paragraphs, tables and lists. The user fills in and edits the existing business plan. The software prompts the user and makes suggestions on content. Formulas are predefined in the spreadsheet portions. The template includes sections on management, product/service description, market analysis, marketing strategy, manufacturing, and financial projections. An indexed reference guide and sample completed plan are also provided.

Contact:
JIAN Tools For Sales, Inc.
127 Second Street
Los Altos, CA 94002
Tel (415) 941-9191   Fax (415) 941-9272

Growth Company Starter Kit, published by Coopers and Lybrand (1992) is designed to help founders and managers of growth companies launch their businesses. The kit's purpose is to provide the entrepreneur with easy, comprehensive checklists needed to develop a strategy for the future success of a company. The user works through the checklists, which cover topics such as market research, financing, insurance, and personnel. The manual then provides a roadmap for writing a business plan, also in checklist form, including do's and don'ts. The appendices contain information on information/support sources such as trade and industry associations, SBA programs and contact numbers, model financial statements, and instructions on tax filing requirements. The cost is $8 for NBIA members and $10 for nonmembers.

Contact:
    NBIA Publications
    20 East Circle Drive, Suite 190
    Athens, OH 45701
    Tel (614) 593-4331   Fax (614) 593-1996

Start-Up: An Entrepreneur's Guide to Launching and Managing a New Business (1994) focuses on entrepreneurship and the problems commonly associated with starting and maintaining new businesses. Targeted to those individuals who are actually considering starting businesses, *Start-Up* spans over 50 chapters addressing such issues as developing business plans, dealing with venture investors, accountants, bankers, and lawyers, and marketing, obtaining loans, and seeking government assistance. The book explores such areas as what makes an entrepreneur, succeeding as a woman business owner, decision-making, and goal setting. The author, Bill Stolze, is a Sloan fellow at the Graduate School of Management at MIT, the founder of several successful businesses, an investor and director of numerous start-up companies, and the founder of the Rochester Venture Capital Group. Stolze teaches new venture management and entrepreneurship at the University of Rochester and the Rochester Institute of Technology. Several contributing authors contributed to the latest addition, including a chapter on "25 Entrepreneurial Death Traps" written by Frederick J. Best, CEO of the General Partners of NEPA Venture Funds. The book's cover price is $16.95.

Contact:
    Career Press
    180 Fifth Avenue P.O. Box 34
    Hawthorne, NJ 07507
    Tel (800) CAREER-1 or (201) 427-0229 (outside U.S.)
    Fax (201) 427-2037

CHAPTER 6

LEGAL/
REGULATORY

New entrepreneurs become involved in launching a company for a variety of reasons and motivations. One set of motivations involves attaining the freedom to set the course of their own destiny. Then they are forced to encounter lawyers.

Entrepreneurs and new enterprises need legal help for a variety of reasons, and those reasons expand when the core of their business involves new technology. In this area, they need help in establishing and maintaining intellectual property protection through copyrights, patents, trade secrets, trademarks, and combinations thereof. Despite the cost and hassle, entrepreneurs are advised not to be their own attorneys when dealing with the U.S. Patent and Trademark Office.

Technology-based ventures, particularly in certain technical areas and industries, also bump up against various federal and state regulations and standards. Sometimes these issues relate to research currently underway within the company that may involve hazardous materials or the use of human subjects. Downstream in the development process there may be legal issues related to product certification.

Finally, very few new companies—given their typical level of capitalization—can afford the usual hourly rate of first-rate legal assistance. Not surprisingly, one of the major preoccupations of incubator managers is to broker or arrange subsidized or free legal services, at least early in the history of the company.

OVERVIEW OF PRACTICES AND SERVICES: LEGAL/REGULATORY

We asked incubator managers to respond to a checklist of likely legal services and practices provided to client companies. For each practice or service, managers were asked to indicate whether they provided the service or practice directly, brokered or referred the service or practice, did both, or did neither. The checklist had the effect of providing a scale of intensity for services and practices provided in the legal area. The summary results are presented in Table 6.1 (next page).

Table 6.1: Legal/Regulatory Practices (valid percent responses)

	no, rarely/never	yes, by referral	yes, directly	both
assist in enterprise incorporation	7.5	67.9	20.8	3.8
develop/facilitate license agreements	7.5	49.1	32.1	11.3
facilitate intellectual property protection	9.4	54.7	24.5	11.3
facilitate nondisclosure procedures	15.1	34.0	35.8	15.1
assist with government procurement issues	21.2	53.8	17.3	7.7
develop financial prospectuses or offerings	28.8	57.7	11.5	1.9
review U.S. and international patents	32.1	50.9	13.2	3.8
arrange for contract services	32.7	44.2	17.3	5.8

The most common practices are assisting in enterprise incorporation and developing and facilitating license agreements—services that are essential to the development of a technology business. Both of these services, as is the case with all of the practices in this area, are more frequently referred than provided directly by the incubators.

The least frequently provided services include developing financial prospectuses and offerings, reviewing patents, and arranging for contract services. These services are generally not in the scope of incubator direct support functions.

In comparing university-affiliated incubators with incubators not closely linked to universities, we found a statistically significant relationship in only one practice, that of assisting in enterprise incorporation. Frequencies of service provision by incubator university affiliation are found in Table 6.2.

Table 6.2: Legal/Regulatory Practices by Incubator University Affiliation (valid percent responses)

	no, rarely/never		yes, by referral		yes, directly		both	
	university	non	university	non	university	non	university	non
assist in enterprise incorporation	6.5	11.8	80.6	47.1	12.9	29.4	0.0	11.8
develop/facilitate license agreements	6.5	11.8	48.4	47.1	35.5	23.5	9.7	17.6
facilitate intellectual property protection	9.7	11.8	51.6	52.9	32.3	11.8	6.5	23.5
facilitate nondisclosure procedures	19.4	11.8	29.0	47.1	38.7	29.4	12.9	11.8
assist with government procurement issues	23.3	17.6	56.7	58.8	20.0	5.9	0.0	17.6
develop financial prospectus or offering	23.3	29.4	66.7	52.9	6.7	17.6	3.3	0.0
review U.S. and international patents	29.0	29.4	51.6	58.8	16.1	5.9	3.2	5.9
arrange for contract services	40.0	23.5	46.7	52.9	10.0	17.6	3.3	5.9

Analysis was also performed on the relationship between legal practices provided by incubators and incubator location. There was a significant relationship between the practice of organizing and facilitating intellectual property protection and location in an urban area. In addition, there was a highly significant relationship between the practice of developing financial prospectuses and offerings and location in an urban area. Both of these practices were most commonly referred to outside providers, rather than provided in-house by the incubator, and the availability of such outside providers appears to be more common in urban than in rural areas. Frequencies of practices provided by incubator location are found in Table 6.3, below.

Table 6.3: Legal/Regulatory Practices by Incubator Location (valid percent responses)

	no, rarely/never		yes, by referral		yes, directly		both	
	rural	urban	rural	urban	rural	urban	rural	urban
assist in enterprise incorporation 7.7		7.5	84.6	62.5	7.7	25.0	0.0	5.0
develop/facilitate license agreements 15.4		5.0	46.2	50.0	38.5	30.0	0.0	15.0
facilitate intellectual property protection . . . 23.1		5.0	38.5	60.0	38.5	20.0	0.0	15.0
facilitate nondisclosure procedures. 30.8		10.0	38.5	32.5	30.8	37.5	0.0	20.0
assist with government procurement issues. . 23.1		20.5	38.5	59.0	38.5	10.3	0.0	10.3
arrange for contract services. 46.2		28.2	38.5	46.2	15.4	17.9	0.0	7.7
review U.S. and international patents 53.8		25.0	30.8	57.5	7.7	15.0	7.7	2.5
develop financial prospectus or offering. . . . 69.2		15.4	30.8	66.7	0.0	15.4	0.0	2.6

BEST PRACTICES: LEGAL/REGULATORY

Based on the interviews with incubator managers, we have grouped the best practices in this area into three broad categories: free or reduced cost legal services; intellectual property; and regulatory compliance. The last two categories are particularly relevant to new companies with a technology focus.

Free or Reduced-Cost Legal Services

Quality legal services are important to new and developing companies but are often prohibitively expensive if no special fee arrangements are available. Several incubators have been able to work with the legal community to match emerging companies to attorneys who specialize in areas important to those companies. These attorneys are also willing to provide legal advice free or at a reduced rate, usually in hopes of securing a long-term client. The various attorney-matching programs allow start-ups to get answers to legal questions they may not pursue if a fee is involved, and they help firms establish relationships with area law firms.

The Calgary, Alberta **Technology Enterprise Centre** assists its client companies in obtaining access to legal advice through its Shingle Out Program. This program arranges for local attorneys to provide *pro bono* assistance to incubator companies during a day on-site.

During the "Shingle Out Session," an attorney from a local firm comes to the incubator for a day, usually once or twice per year. Each company is entitled to sign up for a half-hour of free legal advice from the attorney. Time is restricted so that all incubator companies have access to this service. The Technology Enterprise Centre has found that its companies are most comfortable with lawyers from small firms. Bringing a local attorney to the incubator provides companies with useful information without their having to spend money and allows the attorney to develop business among growing companies. Because the time is limited, the session is most useful to gain brief factual information and/or to obtain an estimate of how much it would cost to retain a lawyer to perform a particular service.

CYBER Center (York, Pennsylvania) tenants can take advantage of free legal advice provided by members of the York County Bar Association. Six to 12 attorneys operate a local telephone bank to provide legal advice. The number of attorneys who work during the free day is limited by the number of telephones lines available. Free days usually take place on Saturday mornings from 8:30 a.m. to 12 noon, perhaps once or twice a month. Attorneys usually spend as much time as necessary with a caller to answer his or her legal questions. Calls are taken on a "first come, first served" basis.

The York Bar Association initiated this service for anyone within the community, not just incubator tenants. The impetus for the program (and similar ones across the country) is the opportunity for state bar associations to identify new service areas for consumers. While the service was not initiated by CYBER Center, the bar association does make sure the incubator is aware of scheduled free days. Since there is no cost, tenants may be willing to get answers to questions that they would not necessarily pursue otherwise. Ultimately, most tenants prefer to use the attorney whom they consulted early in their life cycle such as during incorporation.

The **Chicago Technology Park** offers a free, on-site, weekly legal clinic in which tenants can get answers to quick legal questions without having to make an appointment or to be charged for the consultation. A law firm in the area conducts the clinic in the incubator facility, focusing primarily on corporate law. The program is open to tenant companies in the incubator, as well as university faculty members who are interested.

The **Arizona Technology Incubator** (**ATI**) has a raft of attorneys that will work 12 hours per year free for ATI companies. ATI also has an arrangement with one firm that offers a $2,000 "clean up your legal status and board of directors advising" deal; the firm will attend all board of directors' meetings, advise companies on how to keep minutes and deal with particularly sensitive issues, and so forth.

Tenants of the University of Maryland College Park **Technology Advancement Program**, the **Technology Enterprise Center** at University of Maryland Baltimore County, the **BayView Alpha Center** of Johns Hopkins University, and the **Technology Development Center** of Baltimore incubators have access to the Law and Entrepreneurship Program of the University of Maryland School of Law. This program uses second- and third-year law students, under guidance of corporate law firms, to provide low-cost legal assistance to small companies.

Two or three area law firms that specialize in representing start-up businesses, especially in technology fields, serve as supervisors for selected student interns, the **Law and Entrepreneurship Fellows.** Student participants, usually five to six during a given semester, are also supervised by school of law faculty and are prepared by coursework relevant to business law and issues of relevance to entrepreneurs. The fellows provide assistance on specific legal problems, e.g. they might perform audits, develop contracts, draw up licensing agreements, and perform legal research—all under the supervision of the corporate law firm. Companies usually receive a specified number of free hours and are then charged only a reduced rate (usually a 10 to 20 percent discount) for the oversight provided by the firm. They are not charged for the hours of work of the student fellow. If there is no student who meets a specific need of a company, the law firm will charge a reduced rate, on a sliding scale, for a specific service. Fees may be deferred until a company has obtained sufficient financing. Access to the program is facilitated by the incubator manager. At the outset of the relationship, all parties discuss and clarify expectations. The program, started in 1990, was initially funded by a private foundation, the Maryland Office of Technology Development, and the University of Maryland School of Law.

This program serves the legal needs of incubator companies at a much lower than normal expense and builds relationships between start-up businesses and area law firms. The program also benefits the students—who gain valuable experience and course credit—and the law firms—who gain exposure to potential paying clients, as well as to potential employees.

The **GENESIS Technology Incubator** at the University of Arkansas-Fayetteville helps clients navigate through the legal community by maintaining a list of attorneys who have had experience with prior tenants or who have expressed interest in working with new and developing companies. These attorneys have agreed to work with tenant companies at discounted rates in return for having information on their services and capabilities maintained by the incubator. The database is maintained in paper form, not electronic, and also contains information from tenant companies that have worked with various attorneys listed in the database. In effect, the database is a consumers' directory that enables users to choose attorneys on the basis of cost, specialization, and quality of services.

Intellectual Property

Intellectual property is a key legal issue for technology-oriented companies. Often the key to business success is the ability of a company to protect legally its core technology. Every incubator brokers or facilitates access to legal assistance in this area; however, some incubators spend extraordinary effort helping entrepreneurs to understand, plan, and "position" the intellectual property embedded in their product or process. Most notable is the approach taken by the **Advanced Technology Development Center (ATDC)** at the Georgia Institute of Technology. Entrepreneurs often overestimate the uniqueness and relative advantage of their core product or process technologies, and academics may be ignorant of the patent literature. They need to make the effort to analyze how their technology compares to other competing technologies that may already be patented or otherwise protected.

ATDC uses a one-on-one mentoring approach on intellectual property issues. Incubator staff give the entrepreneurs guidance on how to conduct a patent search, how to use regional Patent Office collections, and how to use various tools (databases, CD-ROMs). However, the staff feels that it is very important that the entrepreneur *do the actual work* in a process of self-discovery. For example, the entrepreneur is encouraged to develop a pictorial "patent map" that depicts the company's technology in relationship to that of potential or actual competitors. This will illuminate the "patent minefield" that is out there, as well as the distinctiveness of their product or patent.

Entrepreneurs will presumably come out of this exercise with a better understanding of what additional protection (e.g., patents) they will need to pursue. Another outcome may be a decision to forego further development of their technology (and company). A third outcome might be an awareness of needed additional R&D to strengthen their competitive advantage.

The commercialization of technology through start-ups increasingly involves information resources that are not resident in the organization managing the process. These may include specialized databases, niche expertise, and the like. The **Ohio University Innovation Center**, working through its colocated university Technology Transfer Office, has developed a *virtual licensing office (VLO)* that is available through the Internet. It is a compilation of services available through the World Wide Web and includes the following: patent resources, which identify public and private databases or services (e.g., CNIDR U. S. Patent Database on AIDS-related patents); industry and economic resources, which identify public (and free) databases (STAT-USA) and private databases (e.g., DIALOG) on industries, companies, and economic trends; and technology transfer resources which identify databases, home pages, and news groups, all dealing with technology transfer as either a practitioner, source of technology, or source of information. The links are updated and new ones will be added as VLO expands. The Virtual Licensing Office can be accessed on the World Wide Web at URL http://ra.cs.ohiou.edu/gopher/nonacademic/tto/vlohome.html.

Regulatory Compliance

Along with cash flow, marketing, and everything else involved in running a business, start-up technology companies are responsible for regulatory compliance and safety issues. Incubators help tenant firms with these important regulatory issues in various ways, including assistance in federal/state compliance and hazardous waste disposal. This assistance is often important in technology-based incubators because of the increasing number of biotech firms and the use of development or production processes that are subject to regulatory review.

Companies must be aware of health and safety laws and regulations and be able to meet stringent guidelines relating to materials handling, disposal, and manufacturing practices. Federal, state, and local regulations can be obstacles to start-up companies operating laboratories. The entrepreneur needs to comply with them all. Radiation licenses and disposal of radioactive materials are significant issues, especially for biotech companies using isotopes. New firms need to know what regulations apply to them and what permits are required. Gathering all this information can be an overwhelming task for a small company and may be an important part of start-up assistance.

The **Colorado Bio/Medical Venture Center** (CBVC) is involved heavily in FDA and environmental compliance issues for its client companies and has even created a user's guide, *How to Permit a Biotech R&D Facility in Colorado,* for their use. The user's guide includes information on air regulations, water regulations, radiation regulations, community right-to-know laws, Occupational Safety and Health Administration (OSHA) hazard communications, waste management regulations, blood-borne pathogens, and animal welfare. Each section includes a page summarizing regulations and possible applications to biomed companies. The guide covers issues such as what to do with hazardous material, spills, blood-borne pathogens, nuclear or radioactive waste, air emissions, and water emissions, and covers other OSHA considerations. The guide also includes copies of the relevant regulations.

In assembling the guide, CBVC went through all of the appropriate federal and state regulations, guidelines, and application materials. In addition to assembling all of that information, summarizing it, and providing excerpts of safety manuals, the center also tried to provide a brief analysis on how the regulations apply to young companies.

The guide is available only to CBVC client companies. While not comprehensive, it serves as a starting point for the companies to develop their own operational procedures.

In addition to the user's guide, CBVC also provides hands-on assistance in the area of regulation. Using their Bio/Medical Friends Group, a network of industry professionals, CBVC can help tenants to obtain licenses and to access appropriate disposal sites. CBVC will call the state regulator for client companies to help get the correct information. CBVC has safety committee meetings on a regular basis to verify the progress of companies. Formal training is provided through the Colorado Safety Association, as well as books and videos.

The **Massachusetts Biotechnology Research Institute (MBRI) Innovation Center** takes on all liability for regulatory compliance by tenants and holds most necessary permits for laboratory activities. Licenses held include a Nuclear Regulatory Commission (NRC) Broad Scope license, which fulfills the need for NRC licenses that can take more than five months to obtain. Holding these "long-lead" permits saves companies time and allows them to focus on research and development, rather than on regulatory issues. Permits not held by the Innovation Center are those that can be obtained by companies within a two-week period. Thus, companies may be able to begin their lab work in four to six weeks under this arrangement.

In order to support this arrangement, the Innovation Center staff includes a radiation safety officer (RSO) to ensure that NRC license compliance is followed. The NRC Broad Scope license allows the RSO to determine who is qualified to work with radioactive materials and the quantity and type of isotopes. Thus, the license does not need to be updated and authorized by the NRC before a new start-up can access radioactive materials. Additionally, the RSO develops safety procedures, training, and waste requirements for the Innovation Center as guided by the NRC.

The Innovation Center also has on staff an occupational health and safety manager who assists start-ups with necessary policy manuals, employee training, safety procedures, waste requirements, and other procedures required by OSHA, EPA, DOT, and DEP regulations. Formats for policy manuals, including general precautions and chemical hygiene plans required of tenants to remain in compliance, are available on disk at the Innovation Center.

By absorbing all liability for regulatory compliance for tenant companies and providing supervision on regulatory issues, the MBRI Innovation Center saves tenant companies the time and hassle of obtaining their own laboratory permits. This practice allows entrepreneurs to "get into the lab" in a relatively short amount of time.

Tenants of the **Rensselaer Polytechnic Institute (RPI) Incubator Center** consult with the university Office of Risk Management and Loss Prevention concerning regulatory issues. The Office of Risk Management and Loss Prevention deals mainly with the university itself to ensure that it complies with regulatory requirements. Because the incubator is owned by the university, however, those same requirements apply to the incubator facilities. As an extension of its role, the office has been helping tenants deal with regulatory issues. In some situations, the office will require action by the incubator companies.

At an early stage of development, access to disposal services for toxic and hazardous materials at a reasonable price can be important to a company. As an operating department of the University of

Arkansas, the **GENESIS Technology Incubator (GTI)**, located in the university's Engineering Research Center, has access to the university's hazardous waste disposal service. At nominal cost, the university environmental health and safety office will provide for the receipt, handling, and disposal of toxic and hazardous waste in accordance with state and federal environmental protection regulations.

The costs of this office are generally charged back to organizations on the basis of the materials they require. The ongoing costs of this service are part of the university's indirect cost pool. Since the GENESIS Technology Incubator is considered an activity of the University, its environmental health and safety service serves the incubator and its tenants. The service is billed by the university to the incubator on an interdepartmental transaction basis. The incubator management then bills back to tenants as part of its service menu, for the specific services provided to each tenant. As a way of providing background, incubator management has also prepared a guide for the handling and disposal of toxic and hazardous wastes in collaboration with the environmental health and safety service.

In addition, research undertaken by tenant companies of the GENESIS Technology Incubator often requires either approval of research involving human subjects by an institutional review board or of research involving animals by an institutional animal care and use committee. Other research or laboratory activities often require licensure under prescribed good laboratory practices (GLP) rules and regulations. GLP certification is required by the federal Food and Drug Administration and by the U.S. Environmental Protection Agency. The GTI provides tenant companies access to institutional committees and review boards to obtain proper clearances for research projects, and also provides access to expert university assistance in complying with GLP licensure standards.

The University of Arkansas research services offices provide the same support to GTI tenant organizations that are provided to regular university research laboratories, departments, and centers. These services are provided at no cost as long as staff and facilities are available. As noted, out-of-pocket expenses related specifically to the needs of a tenant company are charged back to the company through the incubator.

Laboratory Associated Businesses, Ltd. of Madison, Wisconsin is a for-profit corporation that provides laboratory space to emerging biotechnology and medical testing companies. The corporation has a license for radioactive material disposal that the tenants can use. The laboratory is responsible for maintaining it and monitoring its use. The tenant companies pay for the control swatching. This is a great benefit to the companies because, on their own, it can take them years to obtain a permit. Many of the tenant companies are involved in gene therapy, bacteriology, organic chemistry, testing metabolites, etc. Laboratory Associated Businesses also has an incinerator that handles disposal of animals and other hazardous waste.

A representative from each client company in the **Chicago Technology Park** serves on a park-wide Health and Safety Committee that addresses any health and safety issues within the park and makes recommendations to management of the facility. If there is any indication that a company is utilizing unsafe practices, a committee member is delegated to audit that company and recommend changes. If the company does not make the recommended changes within a specified period, it must leave the facility.

CHAPTER 7

PHYSICAL INFRASTRUCTURE

It is impossible, almost by definition, to incubate technology-based technologies without access to technology. In an earlier chapter we described the "soft" side of technology access—people and organizational relations. In this chapter we will address the hardware and software of technology business incubation.

Depending on the product and process technologies of a start-up company, the entrepreneur may need access to significant laboratory or equipment assets. Only a few incubators (mostly with a single technology focus) have such assets on-site. Nonetheless, many incubators have internal facilities or equipment that support general business development. These may include libraries of software, a small suite of machine shop tools, telecommunications services, and the like.

This does not solve the problem of access to major facilities. As a result, a major theme of practices and services lies in the brokering or facilitating of external access. Usually colocation helps in this process; as will be seen in the descriptive statistics in the next section, urban incubators have a clear advantage.

Finally, there is often a need for small, bench-level types of equipment. Often these have fairly specific applications, which may be idiosyncratic to a single tenant company but may also involve continuous or frequent use. Thus, a third major category of best practices is related to various deals and arrangements involving equipment.

What is not clear from either the quantitative or qualitative practice descriptions is the best "mix" of physical infrastructural arrangements. This has implications for public policy and program investments. For example, is it better to broker or facilitate access to labs that can be supported from other pools of money, or is it better to launch specially focused and dedicated laboratory space? More discussion is needed on these and related issues.

OVERVIEW OF BEST PRACTICES AND SERVICES: PHYSICAL INFRASTRUCTURE

We asked incubator managers to respond to a checklist of likely infrastructure arrangements available to client companies. For each arrangement, managers were asked to indicate whether they provided it directly, brokered or referred access to it, did both, or did neither. The checklist had the effect of providing a scale of intensity for infrastructure services. The summary results are presented in Table 7.1.

Table 7.1: Physical Infrastructure Practices (valid percent responses)

	no, rarely/never	yes, by referral	yes, directly	both
Internet/network/telecom services	5.7	15.1	77.4	1.9
special technical facilities	7.7	23.1	59.6	9.6
software libraries/directories	20.4	14.8	53.7	11.1
computer technical support	25.9	33.3	35.2	5.6
machine shop facilities	29.6	46.3	22.2	1.9
specialized equipment leasing/purchasing	32.1	39.6	24.5	3.8
computer equipment leasing	32.7	38.5	28.8	0.0
production processes/systems development	39.6	45.8	12.5	2.1

The most frequently provided service is access to Internet, network, and telecommunication services. Access to special technical facilities such as wet labs and clean rooms is also provided by a majority of incubators. These services are generally provided in-house by the incubators. Such facilities are often the drawing card that brings start-up businesses into incubators.

Few incubators develop or adapt production processes and manufacturing systems for their clients. Although these are the least common practices in this area, they are not infrequently referred to other providers. Since most technology incubators do not get involved in manufacturing, it is not surprising that incubators rarely provide this service directly.

We found no statistically significant relationships between infrastructure practices and university affiliation of the incubator. Table 7.2 (next page) shows the frequency of infrastructure practices provided by university and non-university incubators.

We also compared infrastructure services provided by rural incubators and those provided by urban incubators. Inspection of Table 7.3 (next page) indicates that urban incubators were more likely to provide virtually all infrastructure services. Statistically significant relationships were found in two of the categories. Urban incubators were more likely to have available software libraries and/or directories. They were also more likely to provide for the lease/purchase of specialized equipment.

Table 7.2: Physical Infrastructure Practices by Incubator University Affiliation (valid percent responses)

	no, rarely/never		yes, by referral		yes, directly		both	
	university	non	university	non	university	non	university	non
Internet/ network/telecom services	3.1	11.8	15.6	11.8	78.1	76.5	3.1	0.0
special technical facilities	3.2	12.5	22.6	25.0	61.3	56.3	12.9	6.3
software libraries/directories	25.0	17.6	9.4	17.6	59.4	47.1	6.3	17.6
computer technical support	28.1	23.5	31.3	41.2	34.4	29.4	6.3	5.9
machine shop facilities	31.3	23.5	40.6	58.8	25.0	17.6	3.1	0.0
computer equipment leasing	33.3	35.3	30.0	52.9	36.7	11.8	0.0	0.0
specialized equipment leasing/purchasing	38.7	23.5	25.8	58.8	32.3	11.8	3.2	5.9
production processes/systems development	40.7	37.5	40.7	50.0	14.8	12.5	3.7	0.0

Table 7.3: Physical Infrastructure Practices by Incubator Location (valid percent responses)

	no, rarely/never		yes, by referral		yes, directly		both	
	rural	urban	rural	urban	rural	urban	rural	urban
Internet/ network/telecom services	7.7	5.0	23.1	12.5	69.2	80.0	0.0	2.5
special technical facilities	23.1	2.6	30.8	20.5	38.5	66.7	7.7	10.3
computer equipment leasing	33.3	32.5	33.3	40.0	33.3	27.5	0.0	0.0
computer technical support	38.5	22.0	30.8	34.1	30.8	36.6	0.0	7.3
machine shop facilities	38.5	26.8	38.5	48.8	23.1	22.0	0.0	2.4
production processes/systems development	41.7	38.9	41.7	47.2	16.7	11.1	0.0	2.8
software libraries/directories	46.2	12.2	7.7	17.1	46.2	56.1	0.0	14.6
specialized equipment leasing/purchasing	61.5	22.5	15.4	47.5	23.1	25.0	0.0	5.0

BEST PRACTICES: PHYSICAL INFRASTRUCTURE

For the purposes of this project we have defined infrastructure in terms of capital facilities, laboratory access, and specialized equipment necessary to conduct research and development. In a few cases, the practices described here may pertain more to equipment or facilities more germane to other aspects of business development (e.g., marketing). We have categorized the practices into three areas: 1) on-site labs and facilities; 2) access to external labs and facilities; and 3) equipment deals.

On-Site Labs and Facilities

Almost by definition, technology-based companies need access to specialized equipment, laboratory space, and other facilities. Some of this is available on-site in the incubator's building. In many cases, these reflect the particular technical focus of the program and the tenant companies. In other cases, the facilities will be oriented toward general business needs.

The **Office for the Advancement of Developing Industries (OADI)** incubator at Birmingham, Alabama provides a safe and secure repository for electronic records for its tenants and associates. This repository is known as a data safe and provides an on-site location to store safely irreplaceable electronic media.

Companies involved in the development of customized software store their work products magnetically either on disks or tape. These records usually back up a day's worth of work on program code for software development companies. Other companies might have key financial or other business transactions stored on disk or tape. In the event of equipment failure, or any other event (fire, flood) that might damage or destroy computers or materials stored in an office, the loss of the work product could be a serious setback for a new software development company. In order to meet this need for a secure, disaster-proof storage site for such electronic records, companies are often forced to use safe deposit boxes in banks or similar storage sites, which can be an inconvenience.

The OADI incubator has a fire-resistant, explosion-proof, waterproof storage cabinet with 20 separate lockable compartments. Tenant companies have access to the data safe during normal business hours and can secure their own separate data in a locked area. The data safe is available at no additional cost.

The **Chicago Technology Park** has a media production lab that client firms can use free of charge to develop presentations to financiers, patent officers, and other business contacts. The lab includes two "video toasters" for animation, 3-D modeling, photo digitizing, and video looping. Outside groups donated the equipment, with the understanding that the incubator would reciprocate with some media services.

To staff the facility, the incubator uses students from the computer science and computer graphics departments of the university for production work and to train clients on the equipment. Students typically work in exchange for the use of the equipment for their own projects. Volunteer consultants for the incubator can also use the equipment. A common use of the facility by tenant firms is to create high-tech presentations for patent officials. In addition, those companies seeking capitalization can also create presentations of their business plans.

The Chicago Technology Park also has an extensive on-site software library that tenant firms can use as part of their membership in the technology park. This includes $500,000 worth of software in the areas of business development, personnel management, spreadsheet, word processing, molecular modeling, macromedia, and database software packages. A tenant committee is used to decide on the acquisition of even more highly specialized software, which is purchased jointly by client firms and the incubator. Companies affiliated with the park can use this software at no charge.

Incubators are noted for their ability to provide shared services. **CYBER Center** has expanded the traditional services to include a forklift, and tenants routinely use the forklift for loading and unloading of equipment and supplies. When CYBER Center was built, a local company donated the machine. Tenants use it on a first-come, first-served basis and are not required to pay a monthly fee for use. However, companies that do use the forklift are asked to contribute to maintenance and repair costs. Quarterly preventative maintenance is scheduled; otherwise, it is conducted when necessary. If the forklift maintenance is more than one or two hours, tenants are notified. No arrangements for replacement forklifts are made. Since the forklift is community property, no single tenant has to purchase or assume the liability and maintenance for the machinery, which depreciates quickly.

In May of 1995, the **Austin Technology Incubator (ATI)** moved its operations to the Microelectronics and Computer Technology (MCC) building on the University of Texas' J.J. Pickle Research Campus in northwest Austin. The move was extremely beneficial for ATI. First, the building was designed specifically for technological development and, as such, is an excellent environment for the emerging technology companies ATI nurtures. Furthermore, the new facility has sufficient space to allow the incubator to expand its operations. In addition to providing space for expansion, the new facility provides tenants with such benefits as a full service cafeteria, auditorium, 24-hour security, strategy center, Internet connections, and many conference and break rooms.

The Austin Technology Incubator also maintains a wet lab/manufacturing facility off-site. This facility contains two lab areas, one mixed office and lab, and one manufacturing and office area. The labs are equipped with fume hoods, eye washes, emergency showers, high voltage electricity, and some instrumentation such as a wave analyzer and centrifuge.

ATI also has an electronic meeting room, known as the "Strategy Center." The Center contains 13 networked computers with color monitors, loaded with a variety of software packages including Microsoft's Office and VisionQuest, an interactive groupware developed by Collaborative Technologies, Inc., an ATI graduate company. The facility also contains a laser printer, a large screen computer/video projector, an overhead projector, a VCR, modem hook-ups, and whiteboards, all for meeting facilitation.

Tenant firms or outside groups can use this facility for software demonstrations, training sessions, presentations, and interactive meetings. For software companies, including ATI tenant firms, the Strategy Center provides the ideal vehicle to showcase their products to potential clients and to train customers. ATI's companies can also use this space for electronic conferencing and strategic planning. Incubator tenants can use the facility at no charge. ATI rents the space to outside groups as well.

The **GENESIS Technology Incubator (GTI)** at the University of Arkansas-Fayetteville provides its tenants with a resource room at the incubator facility, which in effect is a business-oriented reference library. The resource room includes materials on financing sources, a compilation of supporting sources at the University of Arkansas and how to access them, and general reference materials of common interest to tenant companies.

GTI staff continually seek to acquire materials that they believe will be helpful to tenant companies and try to fill specific requests made by tenant companies for needed reference materials. Materials are usually available for use at the reference room but in specific circumstances may be checked out to individual users. Recently GTI also has begun acquiring computer software that can be licensed for multiple use in each of the tenant companies' spaces or used on the resource room's computer.

Incutech Brunswick Inc. owns a trade show booth that clients can rent for trade fairs at a rate of $10 per day. The rental fee helps recover the cost and maintenance of the booth. The booth itself is adaptable, so that it can effectively display the logos and marketing materials of any tenant firm. It enables companies to have a professional-looking presence at important marketing events without the significant up-front costs of acquiring their own booth.

The **North Central Idaho Business Technology Incubator** worked with a tenant company to facilitate the company's ability to provide commercial Internet services to other tenants. The incubator paid half the cost of the hub. The only Internet access previously available was for educational use through the University of Idaho and was not appropriate for tenant companies needing commercial services.

A tenant company, First Step Research (which specializes in computer networks), was willing to provide the commercial Internet hook-up, and the incubator agreed to contribute half the funding for installation. Other incubator companies knowledgeable about computer networks purchased cabling and related materials, and over one weekend, tenant companies "wired themselves up." The incubator's contribution to the cost of the hub was about $500, and each company pays its own access fee. The Economic Development Council, which manages the incubator, receives free access and a home page, while the incubator itself pays the standard business fee for access and a home page presence.

As a byproduct of common Internet access, which includes two-thirds of the tenant companies, the incubator now has a news group on the local network. The incubator management uses the news group to provide information to tenants, including announcements and the incubator newsletter, and has even presented a short series of lessons on calculating net present values.

Access to External Labs and Facilities

In many technical fields or industries, there may be a need to access state-of-the-art laboratory or testing facilities. This will often disadvantage a start-up company, which is typically undercapitalized with limited facilities and research laboratories. Incubators themselves rarely have more than rudimentary on-site equipment or facilities. Many incubators have developed creative partnerships with other institutions to meet this need, particularly in programs that focus on a single technical area. These may include rented or leased laboratory facilities at universities, brokered relationships with federal laboratories, or other arrangements.

The **Bio-Business Incubator of Michigan** shares space with the Michigan Biotechnology Institute (MBI), which is a major R&D program and facility located adjacent to Michigan State University. Incubator tenants have access both to the state-of-the-art ($16 million) facilities of MBI and to the laboratories of the university. MBI's 120,000 square feet contain the following facilities: a 20,000-square-foot industrial pilot plant; aerobic and anaerobic fermentation capacity up to 3,000 gallons; a 900-square-foot cold room for handling sensitive microorganisms; gas chromatography equipment; high-end computers; and a machine shop. As incubator tenants, entrepreneurs also get a university ID, which gives them access to library facilities and entry into other laboratories on campus. Laboratory space is leased to companies at a rate of $20 per square foot, which is competitive with other local space, although competing space in the community does not include access to the same range and scope of facilities. Additional equipment may be purchased for the exclusive use of the company, and the company is charged at the depreciable value of the unit.

Many of the novel or useful approaches employed by the **Rensselaer Polytechnic Institute (RPI) Incubator Center** are related to helping tenant companies access the technical resources of the university. Resources are both physical (in the form of laboratories and libraries) and intellectual (in the form of faculty and graduate student assistance).

On a case-by-case basis, RPI will negotiate the use of sophisticated laboratory equipment for tenants. Generally it accomplishes this by a telephone introduction to the administrator of the department in charge of resources. If a tenant is willing to use equipment during off-hours, the firm will be given access at no charge. Most of the tenants know the faculty in the involved department, and this can also be helpful in gaining access to equipment and informally working out arrangements. Some departments have a standard rate established, and any outside company can access equipment that is not being used for other academic or research purposes.

RPI also brokers the relationships between faculty consultants and tenant companies. Usually these arrangements are fee-based. Sometimes negotiations are easy, though at other times a little more creativity is necessary to gain access to the university. The latter was true when RPI established a university accounts number system for each of its tenants. University services are charged to the account number and then billed as a service charge to the tenant via its monthly incubator invoice. The account can be used to charge photocopies, graphic arts, catering, and other services provided through the university. Tenants can also use their account numbers to access several prototyping and research centers on campus.

The Center for Advanced Technology in Automation and Robotics (CAT) is a prime example of how the account number can be useful. CAT focuses on university-industry collaboration on projects related to automation and automated production processes. Many incubator tenants are scaling up from the "make-it-by hand" stage to more sophisticated production processes and manufacturing systems. Few tenants are familiar with that type of transition, and they may make contact with the center for assistance. The director of CAT will talk with the tenant about his or her needs and help develop a short proposal. CAT will assign a researcher and graduate students to analyze the problem; they will demonstrate a solution based on university equipment. Tenants will pay a small amount for the service via their university account. By utilizing university resources, tenants have access to cutting-edge technology at low or no cost. All of the tenants at RPI have used one or more of these resources, and they find the service invaluable.

The **Ohio University Innovation Center** has the status of a "program" within Ohio University. As such, many of the services and facilities of the university are available to incubator tenants through the account structure of the institution. That is, the incubator program can arrange for a particular service through its university account and can bill back the client. For example, a company can access the services of the radioactive materials officer, laboratory equipment or space, computers, or the use of animal care facilities. This use of university facilities stops at the point of actual standardized production. While the development of prototypes is appropriate, turning out low value-added products for market is not. This strong tie to the university has some drawbacks. For example, under Ohio law a university program (the incubator) cannot have a service arrangement with a company that involves a university trustee. This rules out using one of the best patent law firms in the state.

The University of Maryland Baltimore County **Technology Enterprise Center** (TEC) brokers access for its companies to specialized university laboratory facilities, academic computing facilities, animal lab facilities, and hazardous waste removal. UMBC also provides specialized labs and facilities that would be too expensive for the incubator to provide and certainly too expensive for the companies to obtain on their own.

The incubator manager brokers the use of facilities by directing the company to the appropriate faculty or department. To do so, the incubator manager calls the appropriate department chairperson or faculty member to arrange for use of the required facility or for the tenant to meet with this person to discuss the request. One of the biotech companies in the incubator has made use of fermentation equipment in the biochemical engineering department. Also, incubator companies can use electron microscopes at very moderate hourly rates.

The companies have access to the academic computing facilities on campus as well. This is especially useful to software companies. When they use the facility at off-peak hours, there is no cost to the companies. They also have access to the university's animal lab facilities.

TEC does provide wet labs on site. It has installed plumbing, sinks, ventilation connections, and the case work such as benches and tables. The companies pay for the hoods and other movable equipment, and they are entitled to take that equipment with them when they leave. The incubator has acquired surplus National Institutes of Health (NIH) and university equipment that it will lease to companies or sell to them at an attractive price.

The incubator tenants, especially the biotech companies, are also able to take advantage of the university's license for hazardous waste removal. They simply store their hazardous liquid waste in appropriate cabinets, and the university's transporter removes it periodically.

The Small Business Incubator at **Evanston Business and Technology Center** is located in the Northwestern University Evanston Research Park. In addition to its business support network, the incubator offers the advantages of the research park, with ready access to the programs and facilities of Northwestern University and the BIRL Industrial Research Laboratory that anchors the research park.

BIRL is a 130,000-square-foot, state-of-the-art facility for contract applied research and development. Owned and operated by Northwestern University and built with Department of Energy funds, the facility provides access to world-class scientists and engineers, many with industrial experience. Working on a contract basis, BIRL helps companies of all sizes to solve problems and capitalize on emerging opportunities.

BIRL specializes in materials and manufacturing technology, with a focus on technology transfer. BIRL is organized to conduct scale-up, pilot-plant construction, prototype production, and evaluation. BIRL's technical expertise includes wear and corrosion, structural materials, automated inspection, and process control. As an example, it can mock up the production process to apply a new form of coating technology. It is organized specifically to take a company from preproduction scale to a production application stage. One of its specific missions is to develop a production and manufacturing process for companies. Because of the involvement of students, it can do this at a lower cost and higher value

The incubator has been fairly successful in helping companies gain access to BIRL. Done mostly on a case-by-case basis, this ranges from structuring formal research relationships to arranging free lab time when students aren't using the facility. Incubator companies often use BIRL for access to the machine shop. BIRL has very sophisticated machine shop equipment and heavy moving equipment. Three incubator companies currently have contractual relationships with BIRL. Because of the expertise of some of the incubator companies, they have been invited to be involved in BIRL projects, which gives them access to facilities at low cost.

The incubator is also able to regularly "raid" the university for facilities and equipment that may be underutilized or available for use. For example, the incubator has been able to purchase used equipment from university facilities at very low cost for its companies.

In 1994, the State of Maryland began construction of the $25 million **Maryland Bioprocessing Center** adjacent to the Johns Hopkins Bayview Research Park. The Dome Corporation, which manages the **Alpha Center** biotechnology incubator, was instrumental in convincing the state to locate the project next to the Bayview Campus.

Individually, small biotech firms cannot afford their own facilities for preproduction FDA clinical trials, with the result that many cannot bring their products to market. In the past, many biotech companies in Maryland had to contract for this kind of activity out-of-state and may have had to give up equity. The state's interest in the project is to stimulate the biotech industry in Maryland and to keep the equity of those companies in the state.

The Maryland Bioprocessing Center provides shared facilities that meet FDA certification requirements during the critical stages of product development for new biomedical firms. It is a two-story, light manufacturing facility designed for biotech companies to produce drugs for clinical testing. Its construction was funded by the state, the City of Baltimore, and the U.S. Economic Development Administration. The Dome Corporation facilitated the project and is cooperating with the Center's management, as this will be a valuable resource for Alpha Center clients. A quasi-public corporation will manage the Center.

Tenants of the **Ceramics Corridor Innovation Center** have a relationship with the Center of Advanced Ceramics Technology at Alfred University. This is a "center of excellence" within the university, providing expertise of interest to many of the residents of the incubator. Incubator firms can exchange a negotiated percentage of common stock for affiliate membership in the Center. This functions in effect as a debit card against consulting services provided by faculty. Access to expensive specialized equipment (e.g., nondestructive testing, high temperature kilns) and/or partial rent subsidy may also be built into these arrangements. These deals are negotiated during entry into the incubator, although exit mechanisms and processes for buyout have been difficult to negotiate at the front end.

The start-up companies in the **University City Science Center**, located in Philadelphia, are able to arrange access to the laboratory facilities of the Science Center (used for contract research) and to those of the other research and development businesses located there. Many of the larger companies are willing to let start-ups use their facilities during off-hours.

The **Center for Innovation and Business Development** (CIBD) is located at the University of North Dakota in Grand Forks and has access to specialized R&D facilities. CIBD capitalizes on the presence of the Energy and Environmental Research Center both to provide services to client companies and as a source of new entrepreneurial ventures.

The Energy and Environmental Research Center (EERC) conducts applied research that bridges the gap between basic research and industry R&D. EERC employs 260 scientists, engineers, and technicians as full-time researchers. Originally established as a U.S. Bureau of Mines Lignite Research Laboratory in 1951, EERC was defederalized in 1983 and became a part of the University of North Dakota. EERC provides contract research and services to private industry and governmental agencies worldwide. In 1994, EERC attracted more than $20 million in contracts, more than two-thirds of which were with private industry. Research areas include clean energy and environmental technologies, groundwater monitoring and cleanup, waste utilization, contaminant remediation, plastic recycling, and extracting energy from waste. EERC has several contracts for technology development with small businesses and entrepreneurs. Contracts and consulting services include working on Small Business Innovation Research (SBIR) grant projects. In addition, contract work sometimes done by EERC with larger companies results in innovative technologies that have commercialization potential but which might better be developed by a start-up or spin-off company. In these cases, the incubator will get involved.

Equipment Deals

Technology-based entrepreneurs, particularly in certain technical areas, may need to access, on a relatively continuous or permanent basis, unique and expensive laboratory or testing equipment. Often this equipment needs to be dedicated to the use of one company. Therefore, in addition to brokering access to external facilities or having equipment available to all incubator tenants, programs have used a number of approaches to lease, purchase, or otherwise obtain special equipment for individual companies. Leasing is a useful means of obtaining expensive equipment, but start-up companies may have difficulty in obtaining leasing commitments because they lack credit and funds. Leasing companies, in turn, are often unwilling to handle small transactions because of the administrative costs involved.

The **Ceramics Corridor Innovation Center** confronted this issue quite early. The Center found that it was impossible for tenants to share key processing equipment, whether because of contamination problems from one user to the next, or due to widely differing applications, materials, and processes. As a result of this experience, the incubator will now acquire (buy or receive via gift) equipment that is needed for a particular entrepreneur as part of the initial lease agreement. (Some of this company-specific equipment is in effect sequentially dedicated; that is, it is part of an initial capital expenditure for the incubator that can be reused by subsequent tenants as commodity production equipment.) Equipment that is truly specialized is leased back to the company during its stay in the incubator, which agrees to purchase the equipment at some book value when the firm leaves. This approach has generated positive cash flow for the incubator (15 percent return annually on leased equipment), and also helps out the tenant who is unable to make initial front-end payments. Some of the equipment that is obtained for tenant use is from Corning, as part of its partnership with the Center. Corning allows the program to have access to equipment that is not fully depreciated, but which may be obsolete or inappropriate for the original project application. This equipment is centrally stored and managed, and is generally available to other units within the corporation. In addition, the incubator has the opportunity to look it over for tenant applications.

Philadelphia's **University City Science Center** is starting up an equipment-leasing program to help start-up companies obtain needed equipment by guaranteeing the company leases. The equipment leasing program will be operated in conjunction with the Ben Franklin Technology Center and a major leasing company. The leasing company is to provide an umbrella commitment of $500,000 to $1 million for a capital pool to be drawn down as individual company transactions are negotiated and closed. The leasing company will provide the capital and expertise, while the Science Center will screen participants and market the program. In addition, the Science Center will pledge additional security for each lease agreement, in exchange for the company agreeing to stay in Philadelphia during the lease term. The company will pay back the lease capital, with interest over a three-to-four year period and provide company stock warrants. The leasing company will receive a fee for each agreement, and the Center will receive equity in the company for each transaction.

This arrangement meets start-up companies' need to obtain financing for capital purchases and to be able to pay for the purchases over a number of years. It also involves a new industry (leasing) in the technology business development process. Finally, the program allows the Center to use its funds to assist start-up companies without spending the funds directly. Because part of the security for the lease would be the residual value of the equipment acquired, each dollar pledged by the Center will be leveraged at least one-to-one.

The act of bartering has been around for a long time. However, **NET Ben Franklin Technology Center** has given it a new twist. The Center has instituted an informal bartering system in which any leasehold improvement made to space is kept by the facility when a company leaves. Sometimes this is in exchange for a rent reduction. Up to 90 percent of the tenants receive Ben Franklin funds for their product development efforts. They are also allowed to use a small portion of those funds to do modifications to some type of process, which can include renovations to the space itself. Since the money for renovations has been provided by Ben Franklin, many companies do not have a problem with leaving equipment. The bartering system is utilized on a case-by-case basis. This practice is mutually beneficial because it can be costly for companies to move their equipment from the facility, and the equipment left behind for the incubator has residual value for the program.

In anticipation of tenant needs, the **University of Buffalo Foundation Incubator (UBFI)** has established an equipment leasing program for computers and telephone systems. The equipment leasing program began in December 1991. Leases are funded by the Technology Development Center (TDC) Foundation, an affiliate of the Western New York Technology Development Center, Inc., which manages the UBFI. The lease program does not run through the incubator's operating budget. No leases have been written off, and the TDC Foundation receives interest revenue from the leases. For each transaction, the Western New York Technology Development Center receives a one-time administrative fee of four percent, although that probably does not cover the actual administrative costs incurred.

Tenants may lease up to $25,000 of computer equipment, movable office partitions, and telephone equipment. The terms for the program are the following: all computer equipment must be IBM-compatible; the maximum lease term is 36 months; equal monthly payments are based on an interest rate of prime plus one percent; the four percent administrative fee ($100 minimum) is to be paid to the TDC at the closing; all equipment must be insured by the lessee; and the lessee may purchase the leased equipment at the end or during the term of the lease for an amount equal to the unpaid balance of the lease plus five percent of the original equipment cost. In addition, leases under this program are not subject to sales tax, and the tenant is responsible for maintenance.

Terms do not vary based on the type of equipment leased. Tenants may lease the equipment at any time, but the lease agreement states that the equipment must remain in the incubator. The tenant is usually allowed to move the equipment to a new location if the tenant graduates before the lease expires. If equipment is not purchased by the tenant upon expiration of the lease, the incubator will attempt to resell any returned equipment.

About one-third of the tenant companies at the University of Buffalo Foundation Incubator use this program. It is advantageous for tenants because there is no rigorous credit check prior to leasing the equipment. In addition, the interest rate is below market, and tenants are not charged sales tax because of the nonprofit, tax-exempt status of the incubator. To date, all equipment has been purchased by tenants upon expiration of the lease.

Incubator tenants at the **Port of Benton** in Richland, Washington, have access to U.S. government surplus equipment as well as that of State of Washington agencies. This practice allows the incubator companies access to valuable equipment at very reasonable prices.

As a publicly funded incubator, the Port of Benton incubator has arranged with the state to give its tenants the same purchasing status as the state itself for federal surplus sold within the state—first in line after the federal government. Incubator companies are given state tags, so they can tag the desired equipment before local governments, schools, or members of the public can have access. The incubator companies thus have an advantage in obtaining the equipment needed. Equipment from Hanford, Fort Lewis, and other sites in Washington is available for incubator companies.

Equipment obtained in this manner costs much less than market rates. There may be no charge at all other than processing costs. Government surplus equipment may save incubator companies upwards of 90 percent of the market cost.

The Port pays the bill for equipment picked up by tenants, who then reimburse the Port. By law, the Port must retain ownership of the equipment for 18 months, so they lease the goods purchased to the tenant during that period for $100 plus 10 percent administrative costs. After the 18 months, the lease may be renegotiated, or the tenant may buy the equipment from the Port.

Staff at the **Massachusetts Biotechnology Research Institute (MBRI) Innovation Center** at Worcester includes a staff member who can make purchases for tenant companies as part of the assistance provided to tenants. The Innovation Center will purchase equipment for tenant companies as part of their entry agreement. Such purchases include specialized equipment, lab supplies, and personal protective equipment. Entry agreements stipulate that the equipment will be repurchased by the tenant from the Innovation Center at its depreciated value upon graduation.

These various lease, purchase, and barter arrangements save start-up companies time and money and allow them to focus their efforts on research and business development, yet enable them to obtain needed equipment. They permit member companies access that is a notch above, in sophistication and performance, that which a start-up might otherwise enjoy. They also have significant budgetary and cash flow benefits for companies.

Chapter 8

Markets and Products

Defining markets, bringing products and services to maturity, and organizing sales and distribution structures are integral parts of any business. A recent study of 193 high-tech companies in North America indicated that companies that are successful at product development use market/customer research throughout a project and formulate early definitions of products, target customers, and value propositions (Deck 1994).

These crucial tasks associated with market definition and product development may become special challenges for technology-based start-ups. The limited resource base of small firms makes them more vulnerable to shifts in the overall market environment (Belich and Dubinsky 1995). Because the issues of business risk are compounded with the realities of technical risk, the entrepreneur may need a more intensive dose of services and assistance from the incubator. These services may go beyond business planning into more technical work. For example, highly complex technical products may be associated with issues of standards, may require prototypes that take more effort to build and/or engineer (as well as have more complex manufacturing processes and systems), and may be subject to issues of product testing and certification.

By assisting with these complex market and product tasks, incubators can provide a tremendous competitive advantage to new technology-based businesses. This chapter provides examples of these assistance activities that incubators are providing in-house or through partnerships.

Overview of Practices and Services: Markets and Products

We asked incubator managers to respond to a checklist of likely services and practices provided to client companies to help them understand and anticipate market needs; design, develop, and test appropriate products; and arrange for packaging, distribution, and promotion. For each practice or service, managers were asked to indicate whether they provided the service or practice directly, brokered or referred the service or practice, did both, or did neither. The checklist had the effect of providing a scale of intensity for services and practices provided in the markets and products area. The summary results are presented in Table 8.1.

Table 8.1: Market and Product Practices (valid percent responses)

	no, rarely/never	yes, by referral	yes, directly	both
develop/use marketing databases	18.5	46.3	29.6	5.6
provide formal market research	20.4	42.6	25.9	11.1
comply with federal, other standards	34.0	49.1	9.4	7.5
contract for manufacturing services	35.8	49.1	13.2	1.9
assist with product design	39.6	43.4	13.2	3.8
develop product prototypes	40.7	46.3	13.0	0.0
test and certify products.	42.6	50.0	7.4	0.0
use concurrent engineering	53.8	36.5	9.6	0.0

The most common practices in this area are the development and use of marketing databases and provision of formal market research. Both of these services are provided by referral more often than they are provided directly by the incubator. Thus, market research is not a strength of many incubators.

The least common practices include product testing and certification and concurrent engineering of products. When these services are provided, it is usually by referral. Incubators rarely have the ability to provide these services directly. In fact, all of the services in the markets and products area are provided more often by referral than directly by the incubators.

We performed comparative analysis for different incubator types. Table 8.2 (next page) shows the frequency of services provided by university and non-university incubators. No market or product practices were found to have statistically significant relationships with university affiliation of the incubator. Most practices in the area of markets and products were provided with similar frequency by university-affiliated and non-university affiliated incubators.

Comparing incubators in rural areas with those in urban areas, we found no practices in the area of markets and products to have statistically significant relationships with the incubator location.

Table 8.2: Market and Product Practices by Incubator University Affiliation (valid percent responses)

	no, rarely/never		yes, by referral		yes, directly		both	
	university	non	university	non	university	non	university	non
develop/use marketing databases	19.4	16.7	41.9	50.0	35.5	22.2	3.2	11.1
provide formal market research	29.0	11.1	45.2	33.3	16.1	38.9	9.7	16.7
comply with federal, other standards	40.0	22.2	43.3	61.1	13.3	5.6	3.3	11.1
contract for manufacturing services	40.0	22.2	50.0	55.6	10.0	16.7	0.0	5.6
assist with product design	40.0	33.3	43.3	50.0	13.3	11.1	3.3	5.6
develop product prototypes	41.9	33.3	41.9	55.6	16.1	11.1	0.0	0.0
test and certify products	45.2	33.3	41.9	66.7	12.9	0.0	0.0	0.0
use concurrent engineering	58.6	44.4	34.5	44.4	6.9	11.1	0.0	0.0

Table 8.3: Market and Product Practices by Incubator Location (valid percent responses)

	no, rarely/never		yes, by referral		yes, directly		both	
	rural	urban	rural	urban	rural	urban	rural	urban
develop/use marketing databases	23.1	17.1	30.8	51.2	46.2	24.4	0.0	7.3
provide formal market research	30.8	17.1	23.1	48.8	38.5	22.0	7.7	12.2
contract for manufacturing services	38.5	35.0	46.2	50.0	15.4	12.5	0.0	2.5
comply with federal, other standards	46.2	30.0	38.5	52.5	15.4	7.5	0.0	10.0
develop product prototypes	46.2	39.0	46.2	46.3	7.7	14.6	0.0	0.0
assist with product design	53.8	35.0	38.5	45.0	7.7	15.0	0.0	5.0
test and certify products	61.5	36.6	30.8	56.1	7.7	7.3	0.0	0.0
use concurrent engineering	66.7	50.0	33.3	37.5	0.0	12.5	0.0	0.0

BEST PRACTICES: MARKETS AND PRODUCTS

Some enterprises are involved in businesses that need to make an extra level of effort to mature the product. This may take the form of several types of practices: 1) prototyping and testing; 2) market analysis and research; 3) marketing tools; 4) international trade; and 5) developing marketing partnerships.

Prototyping and Testing

Two questions that confront tech-based new enterprises are: Will the technology work? and, Is there a market? Technology incubators often provide access to product design equipment and expertise, prototyping facilities, and test sites that get the products or services ready for the market.

Effective modeling, product design, and prototyping are all crucial to successfully commercializing a technology. While necessary, it is often difficult for start-up companies to obtain access to these capabilities readily and at a reasonable cost. Tech-based entrepreneurs also need empirical validation of the market value of their product. Feedback is crucial to ensure that the seeming technical elegance of the emerging product is workable in a lab or production setting.

Through two vehicles at Stevens Institute of Technology—the Design and Manufacturing Institute and a capstone graduate course in concurrent engineering—the **Technology Ventures Incubator** is able to offer its tenant firms assistance with concurrent engineering, product design assistance, and product testing

The Design and Manufacturing Institute helps the tenant do CAD/CAM for a product and takes it through to the actual prototype. The institute does concurrent engineering to make any design changes as the product progresses to prototype.

Another way the incubator utilizes Stevens for assistance is through a capstone graduate course in concurrent engineering. An individual incubator company serves as the total subject matter for the course. The class may rewrite the business plan, rename and redesign the products, and produce prototypes. The company is a part of the class, with the entrepreneurs present at class meetings. The work is closely monitored by the instructor. The class meets weekly as a group and additionally in work teams. All students have deliverables and deadlines. There is no charge to the incubator firm but a contractual arrangement is made, stating expectations for both sides. This assistance requires a large time commitment from both parties.

Through the Design and Manufacturing Institute, start-up companies get exposed to the idea of using CAD/CAM and concurrent engineering. By serving as a case study for the capstone graduate class, tenant firms get comprehensive business planning and concurrent engineering assistance, which leads all the way to the prototype.

Companies in the Calgary **Technology Enterprise Centre** have access to the Alberta Microelectronic Centre and the Alberta Research Council digital prototyping facility, both located in the University of Calgary Research Park within the same building as the Technology Enterprise Centre. These facilities give start-up companies access to sophisticated modeling, product design, prototyping equipment, and expertise at a reasonable cost.

Administered by the Alberta Research Council (a provincial agency), the digital prototyping facility constructs hard plastic three-dimensional product models from CAD files. This facility is run as a largely self-supporting contract facility, with applications to many technologies. While the technology is sophisticated, the cost can be as little as $20 per cubic inch of model, if a company does not need the model immediately.

Also on-site is the Alberta Microelectronic Centre, which develops electronic prototypes, application-specific computer chips, and related circuitry. This facility is home to the Centre's design group staff, who can provide product design assistance to companies. Fees for services, at $85 per hour, range from a few hundred dollars for a preliminary concept evaluation to hundreds of thousands of dollars for a major development project. Fees are set to recover the cost of services.

These on-site facilities and their staffs have proven very valuable to incubator companies in developing their products and constructing models and prototypes. Because they are on site, incubator companies have better access to these facilities than other start-ups would have, although they do not receive preferential treatment or reduced rates.

Tenant companies need access to specialized testing and certification of products and to proper laboratory facilities for testing. One of the tenants of the **Business Technology Center** of Columbus, Ohio, is a product testing and certification consultant and laboratory. This tenant can develop special deals with other incubator tenants and with the incubator itself.

The tenant company is in the business of product testing and certification of intrinsic safety switching and electronics. This firm sponsors tests through UL or other certifying organizations. While this service has not been frequently used by other incubator tenants, special deals can be arranged. After the company graduates, it may agree to offer a discounted fee structure to the incubator as a whole.

Although incubator companies do not need the service frequently, they can gain cost savings or develop other deals with the on-site testing and certification laboratory.

Technology-based products usually need to be field-tested by prototypical customers and/or end-users. In some cases, the incubator itself can organize or broker beta site arrangements. For example, some of the tenants of the **Long Island High Technology Incubator** are involved in products with markets in the research community (universities, federal laboratories, corporate R&D facilities). The incubator manager will match up companies with ongoing technology needs of universities, laboratories, or hospitals in the area. A referral will be made and the entrepreneur and the organization will work out the details. In some cases this will result in sales; in other cases, a beta site for product development. For example, an environmental company arranged for installation of a sewer effluent treatment system for reducing grease from kitchen operations. It served as the initial beta site and provided valuable feedback for the company's marketing approach.

Detroit's **Metropolitan Center for High Technology** (MCHT) organizes focus groups of individuals who might be good proxies for ultimate consumers. In addition, in the case of industrial products, it will get major companies in the region to test the prototype product on the factory floor and provide feedback to the entrepreneur. The incubator has devoted considerable time to developing a network of corporate executives who can help organize these market tests.

The **St. Louis Technology Center** also helps clients locate beta test sites for their technologies, using universities and companies represented on the incubator advisory board. The incubator manager brokers these arrangements, and both the hosting site and the entrepreneur benefit. The former gets early access to potentially valuable technology (which may also represent an investment opportunity), and the latter gets real-life product development guidance.

Because of the support network that the incubator has built, hard-to-find beta test sites in corporations and universities are often more easily accessible.

Market Analysis and Research

In early stages of development, new ventures need to rapidly acquire a full understanding of the market for their product or service. They need to understand the user, how purchasing decisions are made, the extent of the market, and the nature and share of competing products and services. Acquiring this information efficiently and accurately requires knowledge that individuals involved in start-up ventures seldom have. In later stages, when a venture is preparing to enter the market, assistance in developing strategies and materials to present products and services becomes an important need. Again, these resources are seldom available from within a start-up venture.

The **Long Island High Technology** Incubator of Stony Brook has a partner relationship with the Long Island Research Institute, which is a state-supported program designed to accelerate the commercialization of technology from universities and federal laboratories. One of the services offered is a market determination and technology assessment. This is available at a nominal cost to participants. (In some cases, the institute may take a small equity share.) Staff from the Research Institute meets with the inventor or technology source organization, reviews any prototypes that have been created, looks at business planning documents and may be involved in some primary or secondary data collection. The Institute prepares a report for the submitting organization.

Special university-based assistance programs often meet the need for market research and other business assistance. The **Manoa Innovation Center** in Honolulu has such a relationship with the Pacific Business Center program, operated out of the College of Business at the University of Hawaii. The center has the capacity to pull together teams of graduate students and faculty to meet the needs of entrepreneurial companies. This might include assistance with business planning, market research, loan packaging, joint ventures or management development. The initial meeting with the client company is free, after which the Center staff puts together a team of students and faculty. The incubator contracts for a specific work product (e.g., a market analysis) and works out cost-sharing with the client company. One of these miniprojects can be put together and launched on a fairly rapid turnaround, often within a week.

The **Springfield Technology Center** uses teams (two to three individuals) of business students from a local university. They typically conduct market research projects, working with several companies a year. The students are supervised by a faculty member and get course credit for the experience.

The **Office for the Advancement of Developing Industries** (OADI) incubator in Birmingham, Alabama has a marketing specialist on its full-time staff who is available to provide continuing assistance and support to OADI incubator tenants and associates. The specialist's time is allotted to tenants on a complimentary basis for an initial three hours of assistance and consultation. After this initial period, tenants can access time at very favorable rates ($25 per hour). The specialist has a variety of responsibilities that include performing market research, developing informal networks, preparing promotional materials and brochures, and assisting in the preparation of exhibits for trade shows. The marketing specialist has even accompanied member companies' exhibits to specialized trade shows to help in presentations. This broad range of generalized marketing expertise is available at favorable rates.

The availability of comprehensive marketing support and assistance at such favorable rates is a major asset to OADI tenants and associates. These services can be focused to the special needs of technology companies and can assist in the development of accurate and appropriate marketing strategies and marketing campaigns. They provide assistance which might not otherwise be available or, because of high cost, might not be fully utilized by people starting new ventures.

As a general rule, technology incubators accept only technology companies. In certain situations, though, it makes sense to lease space to a non-technology company that can provide service to other tenants. As a prime example, the **Technology Development Center** (TDC) in Baltimore, Maryland, leases space to a marketing and communications company, which is only tied to the other tenants by the services it provides. This early-stage company was admitted as an exception. However, given the availability of space and the entrepreneurial focus of the company, the arrangement was considered healthy for all parties. In return for approximately five hours of *pro bono* service per month to the other incubator tenants, the company's rent is reduced.

The anchor tenant arrangement is mutually beneficial. Not only do tenant companies receive a valuable service but vacant space is rented to subsidize the income of the incubator. While leasing space to non-technology companies can be valuable, incubator managers should check, prior to entry, the quality of service that the anchor tenant will provide. In this case, the strong references provided by clients of the marketing company made the decision easy.

To achieve business success, companies need quick access to a wide range of information. The **Colorado Bio/Medical Venture Center** (CBVC) has a biomedical business library to serve as an information resource on the industry and as a resource for start-up companies.

The biomedical library currently consists of written materials—reports, books, and journals—rather than databases. The CBVC has invested approximately $20,000-30,000 so far in the library. It is working to build a library that will to be much more proactive in its structure and function for the young companies, particularly in terms of market-related issues. The idea is to help firms with information on size of market, competition, distribution channels, technology, and financing. This is an active and ongoing project of the CBVC.

The Technology and Business Information Center (TBIC), located in the **Center for Applied Technology** (CAT), is a fee-based information service available to all businesses through a toll-free number. TBIC can provide access to information and specifically tailored searches needed to help in market analysis and product development.

TBIC offers the incubator tenants $50 of free usage per month. The company pays the fixed costs that the databases charge. Most searches take about 15-20 minutes, so this typically gives the company one search free of labor charges per month.

TBIC subscribes to three private vendor databases—Dialog, Business Research Service, and Knowledge Express—which gives clients access to more than a 1,000 different databases and information resources. TBIC also uses the Internet to dial into the National Technology Transfer Center (NTTC), EPA bulletin board, FedWorld, and other databases. In addition to global data access, TBIC also develops and maintains up-to-date information on South Carolina research that might not be readily available on broader data networks.

CAT advertises the service though its newsletter and trade shows. Pre-research discussions and estimates are given at no charge. The service can be used to:

- Obtain competitive information for strategic advantage;
- Track developments in science, technology, economics, politics, and more;
- Obtain contact name, address, and telephone number for a targeted prospect list;
- Locate new suppliers, manufacturers, or distributors;
- Identify market, industry, and international business trends;
- Track competitive importing/exporting data;
- Review patent literature and obtain copies of patents;
- Scan reviews on product alternatives;
- Get valuable market studies for reasonable prices;
- Identify recognized experts in specialized fields;
- Review patents of cutting-edge technologies; and
- Gain access to federal technologies.

TBIC is a resource for both incubator companies and businesses throughout the state. Because it is located in the incubator, tenant companies are aware of the service and better able to learn how they might use it to build their business. TBIC also circulates a monthly accumulation of newsletters and announcements in a three-ring binder to the tenants. Therefore, tenants have the opportunity to be exposed to a wide range of information about new technologies, markets, and regulations.

The **Arizona Technology Incubator (ATI)** has accepted an international marketing outreach company as a tenant. This marketing firm brokers deals internationally, primarily to the Middle East, Europe, and the emerging eastern European countries. This group uses offset moneys from multiple aerospace partners as financial leverage in its deals.

Export Assistance

The **Business Technology Incubator** houses Bradley University's International Trade Center and North American Free Trade Agreement (NAFTA) Opportunity Center (ITC/NOC), which assists central Illinois businesses in the international market.

Initial attempts to enter the international export market are difficult for any firm. Uncertainty about language and custom differences, packing and shipping regulations, and procedures, or monetary exchanges can keep start-ups from exploring important overseas markets.

The International Trade Center and NAFTA Opportunity Center provide export assistance to businesses that are interested in exploring foreign markets for their products and/or services. The International Trade Center (ITC) assists businesses, including incubator companies, through workshops, seminars, counseling, and student research projects.

The ITC helps assess a company's readiness to export, locate potential export markets, penetrate target markets, and develop an international business plan. It can assess export readiness using the CORE (COmpany Readiness to Export) software program, which helps companies identify areas they need to work on before starting an export program. Target markets and potential distributors are identified using various databases. The ITC helps the company identify U.S. and foreign government regulations, requirements, and other regulations. Business planning for international markets is conducted one-on-one at the center or as part of the International Business Student research program.

The NAFTA Opportunity Center will help businesses take advantage of NAFTA by providing them with information on Mexican and Canadian business opportunities, recruiting large firms to act as mentors for small exporting companies, and working with the Illinois Department of Commerce and Community Affairs (DCCA) to facilitate computer trade lead matches.

The ITC/NOC is funded by the SBA, DCCA, the Rural Economic Technical Assistance Center, the Central Illinois Higher Education Consortium, U.S. Dept. of Education, and Bradley University.

Since its inception, the International Trade Center has assisted over 500 companies, helping them achieve over $17 million in export sales.

Marketing Partnerships

Market and product development for an entrepreneurial venture may evolve out of business relationships or partnerships with other firms. These may include manufacturer-supplier relationships, production and marketing partnerships, or other arrangements. Incubators have been involved to a limited degree in fostering these arrangements.

In a company's product development effort it may make sense to find suppliers of certain components. Moreover, companies within an incubator may have to outsource as much as possible to keep costs down. In many cases, companies are unfamiliar with manufacturers or suppliers in their area. The **NET Ben Franklin Technology Center** developed Matchmaker Procurement Services, Inc. to provide assistance to companies in this situation.

In 1985, the NET Ben Franklin Technology Center and Meridian Bancorp decided to hire someone to set up a database system to organize and maintain information for its companies. That idea has evolved into a separate nonprofit economic development organization, housed within the incubator, designed to locate manufacturers as well as encourage local and national sourcing. Matchmaker Procurement Services, Inc. is run by an executive director who maintains a database of 3,000 area companies that wish to develop supplier relationships with other manufacturing companies. The staff identifies the needs of each company, searches the database, and selects three to four potential suppliers. The incubator's executive director also helps facilitate contact between the company and the supplier. However, each company makes the final determination on firms to utilize. The service is free to both incubator tenants and nontenants. Individuals must go through Matchmaker to receive services. It cannot be downloaded to personal computers.

Each supplier fills out a data sheet containing information on its capabilities, volume, current sales, type of service, and other characteristics. Typically, Matchmaker begins working with a firm several weeks before an order has to be placed. However, the organization can assist firms that have an immediate purchasing need. Once a match is made, the program receives a percentage of the sale from the supplier. This percentage is the main method of generating program income.

The database is continually updated through solicitations, Harris Directories, and referrals. The service is publicized through brochures and local speaking engagements.

Matchmaker has helped hundreds of Pennsylvania firms to develop purchasing contracts involving such products and services as screw machine parts, tubing, electrical connectors, microcomputer services, printed circuit boards, and pharmaceuticals. Because of closer communications and more frequent on-site meetings, Matchmaker has helped local companies that purchase locally to minimize inventories, shorten delivery leadtimes, and improve product quality and design. Moreover, the general community benefits through an increased number of retained or new jobs at the supplier firms.

Since its inception, Matchmaker has generated over $13 million in annual sales between manufacturers and suppliers.

The **Carleton Technology Innovation Center (CTIC)** uses the Business Opportunities Sourcing System (BOSS) to identify suppliers and technical expertise. BOSS is a computerized database that provides information on all of the companies in Canada. The database lists each company and its products or services by key words. Annually, BOSS publishes several directories, including the *Directory of Canadian Manufacturers/Products* and the *Directory of Computer Software and Services.* Service directories include *Consulting Agrologists, Management Consultants,* and *Consulting Engineers.*

The publication of company names in the directories does not imply any government endorsement of a company's capabilities. It simply reflects services advertised by each company. Information in the directories is also available on-line via microcomputer. This information is beneficial to start-ups who are trying to establish their own network.

Contracting manufacturing saves a company up-front costs, while retaining control over the final production stages allows the company to ensure quality. Marketing partnerships help companies obtain access to a given market without spending a lot of their own money on marketing. **High Technology of Rochester** advises start-up companies to consider manufacturing and marketing partnerships where applicable. These "virtual companies" are especially important in the early stages of the company. Even if the company does not have the facilities to do final assembly, testing, or shipping, it should have access to those facilities for some final testing. In marketing, if another company has a firm hold on a particular market, the start-up may be advised to form a strategic alliance with a larger company in order to have better access to the market without enormous expense and to avoid having to develop a sales force.

There is no formal process for facilitating these partnerships. When the incubator management determines that a partnership is appropriate, they will contact local firms that are likely to be interested. They will also contact businesses outside of the community through such channels as personal knowledge, university programs, and faculty, and through Batorlink, an interactive electronic network that is a member service of the National Business Incubation Association.

Creating "virtual companies" in the early stages, especially for manufacturing, saves the company up-front costs of production. These strategies help the company move ahead more quickly without large up-front costs.

Tools

Some programs have made successful use of tools to assist companies. Tools in this context might mean databases, guidebooks, checklists, and so on.

Commercializing Technology: A Hypertext Manual is an updated version of a popular manual created for the U.S. Department of Energy's Small Business Innovation Research (SBIR) Program. Originally written in 1988, the SBIR manual has been provided to countless SBIR awardees. Revised in 1994, the manual is a step-by-step guide through the commercialization process. The new version includes an extensive discussion on how to use commercial databases and Internet news groups to facilitate market research and marketing. A new chapter also discusses the conversion of defense technology for civilian applications. Templates for planning commercialization efforts, building commercialization teams, conducting market research, determining commercialization vehicles (license, sales, etc.), and other tasks are provided.

The manual is produced in the form of computer software by Foresight, Inc., a technical marketing firm that provides commercialization assistance to small and large companies, universities, federal agencies, and nonprofit labs. The manual has been formatted as a hypertext document to facilitate use. Templates can be easily downloaded by users. The cost of the manual is $95.

Contact:
    Foresight Science and Technology, Inc.
    1200 W. Sims Way, Suite 201
    Port Townsend, WA 98368
    Tel (206) 385-9560
    E-Mail 3446234@mci.com

The Marketing Plan: Step-by Step is published nationally and is available through the **Center for Innovation and Business Development** (CIBD) at the University of North Dakota. The publication was written by a business consultant who is an alumnus of CIBD and edited by the director of CIBD. The center provides business and technical support services to hundreds of individuals and businesses a year who have product ideas.

Although there are numerous guides and theories about writing business plans, there have been very few publications to help entrepreneurs with marketing plans.

The marketing plan book, published in 1992, is targeted to new and expanding ventures with new products, technologies, or services but with little or no market history. It was developed specifically for manufacturers launching a product *who* don't need a business plan for financing but who do need a well-developed marketing strategy. The book is a step-by-step guide with seven chapters to help entrepreneurs with researching, analyzing, writing, and implementing an effective marketing strategy, with lists of common mistakes to avoid.

An introduction gives an overview of marketing concepts and the marketing process. Chapter one sets out marketing guidelines for both start-ups and existing companies. The rest of the guide is made up of 20 modules, each representing a component of the marketing process. There are internal audit modules used to assess the company's position and determine how the product or service will be priced, packaged, distributed, and serviced. External audit modules deal with what is happening in the marketplace. Other modules deal with marketing objectives, strategies, tactics, the budgeting process, and sales projections. Communications modules relate specifically to advertising, public relations, promotions, sales and customer relations. There is also a module for execution and evaluation.

Each module is an exercise that will result in a section of the marketing plan. The guide tells the entrepreneur what to do but not how to do it. For each section, it details the suggested length, the objective, a series of questions that must be answered, a suggested sequence of presentation, subheadings to include, and common mistakes to avoid.

The guide is a valuable tool used by CIBD in working with people bringing a product or service to market. It is most useful when someone goes through the process with experienced entrepreneurs who can help them face the facts of the marketplace and learn more about what they don't know. The Center has sold approximately 18,000 copies since 1992 at a cost of $30 plus shipping. CIBD receives royalties from the publisher.

The popular *Guerrilla Marketing* series by Jay Conrad Levinson offers entrepreneurs an "insider's edge" in marketing and advertising their products. The series includes the following texts:

Guerrilla Marketing: Secrets for Making Big Profits from Your Small Business (1993) is an updated edition of the first best-seller in this series. This new edition discusses how to identify and reach the fastest-growing markets, develop a creative marketing program, select marketing methods, save money, and obtain free market research. The book discusses all types of media and gives tips on what to use for particular situations. It also advises on the best ways to use trade shows, exhibits, and fairs and explains how to obtain free publicity.

Guerrilla Marketing Excellence: The Fifty Golden Rules for Small Business Success (1993) contains rules to guide the entrepreneur's thinking, effectiveness, marketing materials, and actions. Each of the fifty sections begins with a golden rule such as Golden Rule #7, "Design your business to operate for the convenience of your customers and make it very easy to do business with you." The rest of each section provides specific methods for following these rules. Section topics include how to use "magic words," humanity, and humor in marketing, and target marketing to reach particularly important clients.

The Guerrilla Marketing Handbook (1994) is coauthored by Seth Godin, a marketing expert and recognized author of business manuals. The handbook provides ways to unlock the secrets of direct mail, cut advertising costs, generate word-of-mouth, expand market share, increase telephone sales, and reposition the competition. The book is divided into two parts. Part one, "Choosing Your Marketing Tools," offers 73 low-cost, high-impact ways to market. These include traditional advertising techniques such as Yellow Pages and newspaper/magazine ads, mini-media such as business cards and doorhangers, targeted media such as customer mailing lists and inserts, promotional techniques, telephone marketing, and nonmedia marketing such as choosing a business name and attracting customers with word-of-mouth. The second part of the book is an appendix of resources, including sample newspaper advertising rates, other business and marketing books, and radio, television, and cable network directories.

Guerrilla Advertising: Cost-Effective Tactics for Small Business Success (1994) shows small businesses how ads must be integrated into the total marketing strategy to maximize their effectiveness. The book stresses the need to know one's audience, its needs, the competition, the general character of the market, and the results one can realistically expect. The book is full of anecdotes and advice from successful advertisers. Also explored are topics such as how to stay within a budget, how to polish a look and pitch, and how to adapt tactics to appropriate media.

Guerrilla Marketing Online: The Entrepreneur's Guide to Earning Profits on the Internet (1995) is coauthored by Charles Rubin, a computer hardware and software expert. This book helps readers get oriented to Internet culture, develop knowledge about the audience that uses the Internet, apply Levinson's marketing techniques to the Internet, discover low-cost ways to market on-line, and stay ahead of the competition. The book discusses which traditional marketing tactics will backfire on the Internet. Strategies outlined include electronic storefronts, e-mail, forums and newsgroups, and marketing with information.

Contact:
Houghton Mifflin Co.
215 Park Avenue South
New York, NY 10003
Tel (800) 225-3362 Fax (212) 420-5850
Guerrilla Marketing web site: http://www.sedona.net/crubin

CHAPTER 9

STRUCTURE/ OPERATIONS

Separate from the services and programs that are offered to tenant companies are the underlying structure and operations of incubators. While the purpose of this study was *not* to focus on these aspects of incubation, we were taken with some interesting and presumably novel examples from the study sample. Some of these examples are probably unique to technology-oriented ventures and incubators, while others have more general implications for business development.

BEST PRACTICES: STRUCTURE/OPERATIONS

The best practices described in this section have been grouped into seven categories: 1) innovative incubator organizations—getting others involved; 2) building a supplier base of new enterprises—from large corporation to incubation; 3) incubator organizations—for-profit variations; 4) early stage facilities—only the newest need apply; 5) incubator operations—rental strategies; 6) incubator operations—beyond the walls; and 7) growing more than new businesses. These surely will not exhaust the variety of technology business incubator structures and operations but should provide insight into their processes.

Innovative Incubator Organizations: Getting Others Involved

Virtually all of the incubator programs in our study sample were resource-limited—whether those resources were financial, intellectual, or logistical. Some have been particularly innovative in forging partnerships with external entities. These relationships may be expressed in novel structures, support networks, or various associations or consortia. The following are examples.

The **MGE Innovation Center** was developed and is operated as a joint venture of the University of Wisconsin-Madison's Research Park and Madison Gas and Electric (MGE), the local utility company. The Innovation Center was founded to promote research and development of new growth-oriented companies in Wisconsin, to facilitate connections between the University of Wisconsin-Madison and new technology-oriented companies, and to provide a supportive business environment for start-up technology companies in the Research Park. MGE developed a partnership with the university because it wanted to help promote the University Research Park to attract, retain, and create business-es, especially technology businesses, in its customer area. Founding the incubator in the research park grew out of these goals.

MGE originally leased space for the incubator from the research park for a three-year period. The utility contributed lab equipment to equip the facility and subsidized the costs of operating the Innovation Center. Now MGE's contribution is in the form of a yearly operating contribution of $25,000 that is matched with $25,000 provided by University Research Park, Inc. annually for five years. The Wisconsin Department of Development provided a grant of $250,000 to expand the laboratory capa-bilities of the Innovation Center. The incubator is owned by University Research Park, Inc. which is responsible for approving leases, marketing the incubator, and setting its policies. The incubator facili-ty is managed by Venture Investors of Wisconsin, Inc. which is a venture capital fund focused on financing growth companies in Wisconsin. Venture Investors also provided early contributions to the incubator. The fund provides tenant companies with financing, business advice, and referrals. Both MGE and Venture Investors of Wisconsin have representatives on an advisory board to University Research Park that reviews incubator applicants.

Because the three-year pilot project was successful, this partnership is being continued. University Research Park is able to provide desired incubator management services through Venture Investors of Wisconsin and obtains financial support from MGE.

Support of ongoing operational expenses can be a chronic problem for technology business incu-bation programs. One solution is to adapt a relatively common fundraising approach—to market sup-porting corporate memberships in the incubator program to companies in the area.

An example is the approach taken by Miami's **Center for Health Technologies** (CHT). CHT has three levels of corporate participation: corporate "members" pay $2,500 a year; "partners" pay $5,000; and "trustees" $10,000. Corporate members may include bankers, lawyers, and accounting firms, as well as executives in research or product development from major companies in the health industries and academic institutions that support the health technologies. Given the health technology focus of the incubator, there are also some industry-specific member companies. These include a company that does consulting in federal Food and Drug Administration regulatory affairs and another that pre-pares companies for third-party reimbursements on their products. In order to be successful at this type of membership arrangement, it was essential to have 501(c)(3) status for the incubator, which was enabled by state legislation. CHT currently has 30 corporate members that not only provide a steady core of funding but also provide a network of contacts that can help early-stage companies. For exam-ple, a client company may be in the critical stage of product development and may need a larger part-ner for either technical assistance or financing. Summary packages about client entrepreneurs are cir-culated among the corporate members. Thus, one of the advantages for corporate members is access to interesting deals, and the members build support for the incubator in the community. The goal for CHT is to have 10 trustees and 100 other corporate members, which would provide base operational funding of more than $350,000 for the incubator.

Other incubator programs find it useful to employ the expertise of an industry network in assist-ing incubator companies. This practice may be especially useful when the incubator can bring that expertise to bear upon a particular technology field. The **Colorado Bio/Medical Venture, Carleton**

Technology Innovation Center, and **Chicago Technology Park** all have formed networks in the local biotech industry. These alliances help to provide incubator companies with both specific assistance and a better view into the industry from a "real world" perspective. These organizations may also serve to provide financial support to the incubator and are potential partners for incubator companies.

The **Colorado Bio/Medical Venture Center** (CBVC) has organized a Bio/Medical Friends Group as a trade association focused on the biomedical industry in Colorado. Approximately 60 companies and individuals form a core network including CEOs of biomedical companies in the state, venture capitalists, accounting and legal firms, insurance companies, bankers, and injection molding companies, to name a few.

In many ways, the Group acts as a "chamber of commerce" for the Colorado biomedical industry. It provides financial support to the CBVC, organizes special programs, and works to educate the public, media, and government about the biomedical industry. As part of a membership organization, members pay an annual contribution based on the size and characteristics of the company. Contributions and fundraising help to defray the operating expenses of the CBVC. Approximately 20 percent of CBVC's annual budget or $60,000 comes from the Group. Specifically, funds are used for video conferencing, the newsletter, or other activities; however, most of the contributions are not earmarked.

The Bio/Medical Friends Group also provides strategic insight and access to valuable resources not otherwise available to CBVC and its client companies. Through the Group, the CBVC organizes working teams of senior executives who lend their expertise to start-up companies. Two volunteer committees have been formed to educate state and community leaders about the importance of the biomedical industry to Colorado and the key issues affecting it.

CBVC is constantly working to build this network through personal contacts and a monthly newsletter that is faxed to all biomedical CEOs in the state. In addition, CBVC has conducted surveys of the biomedical industry to establish ongoing programs. Through these activities, the network extends beyond the 60 core members.

The approach that launched the **Arizona Technology Incubator (ATI)** was that of a public/private partnership—a large network of public and private sponsors who have donated over $1 million to the incubator as of early 1995. In order to secure this sponsorship at the outset, the board of directors of the incubator made calls to individuals whom they thought might be interested in contributing. The director then met with each potential sponsor individually. ATI currently has more than 26 direct sponsors, such as the Arizona Public Service Company and the City of Scottsdale, and more than 51 in-kind sponsors. These contributors not only provide financial support for the incubator, they also help publicize it to potential tenants. ATI's vision of a public-private partnership, close ties with a major university, and a direct source of capital for companies is the core of success of the incubator and a successful model for technology incubation.

Ottawa's **Carleton Technology Innovation Center** is capitalizing on the region's strong research base in medical devices and biotechnology. The center has established the Medical Engineering Industry Research Affiliation (MEIRA) to assist start-ups in these fields.

In May of 1994, the University of Ottawa and Carleton University combined with local industry to launch Canada's first research association for the medical device industry. MEIRA is a concept that is industry-driven. It is designed to provide companies with a supportive "guild" environment, in order to nurture their growth by providing shared resources without threat to their commercial freedom.

MEIRA's objectives include giving industry a strong voice in directing the research programs; providing technical assessments; providing R&D support both to start-ups and those seeking lateral growth; working with the university and regional technology transfer teams on health technology projects; collecting and transferring relevant news about local and global trends in medical devices and techniques; providing showcases for developments at appropriate venues and meetings; fostering an active and receptive audience at the two universities; and attracting new faculty members with an interest in health technology.

Industry contributions to MEIRA are between $2,000 and $5,000 per year, depending upon the size of the company and the turnover in the medical field. This money will be matched over the first five years by a government grant program.

Companies in the health technology industry in the Ottawa region and elsewhere will benefit from this initiative to provide considerable resources to firms both small and large. To date, it has enrolled more than 45 faculty members from the fields of medicine, engineering, and science. It also has targeted 47 regional companies, more than half of which have five or fewer full-time employees.

The **Chicago Technology Park** created the Illinois Alliance for Biotechnology to help biotech companies network with each other and access financing sources such as venture capital. With the help of state grants, the Chicago Technology Park put together this association of biotechnology companies and local investors interested in biotechnology. The primary purpose of the alliance is to bring large and small companies together, to foster mentoring, and to encourage collaboration. The alliance encourages collaboration among large and small biotech firms to bring new products into production. For instance, large pharmaceutical companies realize that new products come out of small companies more readily than from their own labs but that large companies are more able to take the products through the approval process and bring them into production. The alliance maintains a mailing list consisting of 350 sources.

The Illinois Alliance for Biotechnology is helping to create a biotech focus in the area. Consultants from various companies in the alliance have provided technical support to small companies for free or for deferred payments. Through networking in the alliance, the Argonne National Laboratory has helped small firms develop cooperative research and development agreements (CRADAs). It also informs investors about investment opportunities in local biotechnology companies.

An incubator may draw upon a variety of community resources through other means. One solution launched by Detroit's **Metropolitan Center for High Technology** was to establish an endowment for the incubator.

Working with several Big Six accounting firms and local legal assistance, the incubator established a legal structure to receive endowment funds. These monies will be dedicated to operation support and special projects. The incubator expects the fund to grow to $1 million within three to five years and is now approaching individual contributors, major corporations, and foundations for support. The endowment can accept gifts of cash, real estate, bequests, or anything with long-term value.

Some innovative organizational strategies draw not on corporate resources but on other relevant forces in the community. Incubators can turn to federal labs, universities, and local government economic development organizations as sources of both funding and other support.

The **High Technology Development Corporation (HTDC)** in Hawaii is a state agency that has pursued a deliberate strategy to "capture" and manage the business-creation potential of major federally funded research centers. The approach is either to colocate or to facilitate close working relations among incubators, private industry, and educational institutions.

For example, within a research park on Maui, a fiber optic communications link was installed between an incubator and a national Department of Defense (DOD)-funded supercomputing center. The colocated incubator has become the wide area network "point of presence" for Hawaii users desiring to access the supercomputing center's computing and telecommunications resources. In addition, HTDC has a memorandum of understanding with the supercomputing center to provide Hawaii's incubators and technology training centers (incubators without walls) access to the supercomputer and the national information superhighway. Other DOD projects managed by HTDC include a Center of Excellence for Research in Ocean Sciences, the Hawaii Electric Vehicle Demonstration Project, and the Electric Vehicle National Data Center—projects totaling $10 million per year. HTDC's strategic objectives are to create business opportunities, reduce the cost of entry into the market, and make it easier for businesses to stay in business in the state.

The **University City Science Center**, Philadelphia, Pennsylvania, is owned by a consortium of 28 area universities, hospitals, and research institutes that created the Science Center in 1963. The Science Center was developed in order to stimulate the economic revitalization of an area of Philadelphia through the development of a research park.

Each of the 28 organizations purchased nearly $500,000 in stock in the initial development of the Center, but they do not make continuing contributions. The Center's earnings are reinvested into the Center, enabling it to be self-supporting.

While several of the founding universities are liberal arts institutions, most of the Center's interaction is with the research-oriented universities. Those universities nearest to the Center, especially within walking distance, are also more likely to produce spin-off companies that locate in the Center. Incubating start-up technology businesses is one of the Center's activities.

Shareholders hold an annual meeting to update the partners, and some shareholders are represented on the Center's board of directors. As a neutral party, the Center can bring the universities and other organizations together to develop joint programs.

By retaining locally the commercializable research of the universities and attracting new businesses to the area, the Center has achieved its mission of economic revitalization. The Center seeks to keep incubated businesses in the research park, and many have stayed there. One incubated company has even purchased space on-site. The Center has also served to unite the universities leading to other collaborative programs.

Another example of an interesting corporate structure involves a partnership between a university and a local economic development organization. The director of the **North Central Idaho Business Technology Incubator** is also the executive director of the county's Economic Development Council (EDC). This relationship gives incubator tenants access to the resources of both the local EDC and the university that owns the incubator, the University of Idaho.

The incubator/EDC director's time is allocated equally to each organization. This relationship allows resources to be shared and creates a synergy that benefits both organizations. Essentially, this two-in-one structure gives incubator tenants expertise that neither a local EDC nor a university incubator alone could provide. The university's technology transfer and intellectual property management arm, the Idaho Research Foundation, is an incubator anchor tenant. The foundation can answer tenants' questions on an as-needed basis, including technical, commercialization, and basic patent questions. The EDC serves as a vehicle for bringing together all the local economic development interests, including city and county governments, the university, and the business community. The incubator facility itself was built by a U.S. Department of Commerce Economic Development Administration grant, a state grant and a local match.

This relationship is especially useful in a rural area, combining local resources to provide incentives for start-ups to stay in the county. The EDC provides interaction with the rest of the business community and can serve as a pass-through agent for state and federal programs, such as the U.S. Department of Commerce Trade Administration, which offers an EDC-hosted workshop on exporting that is open to both incubator companies and other local businesses.

The EDC has brought together various local economic development interests to work on projects including the incubator, a business/technology park currently in development, and a microloan/equity fund for early-stage businesses. The incubator has supported 19 businesses in the past five years, producing approximately 100 new jobs.

Building a Supplier Base of New Enterprises: From Large Corporation to Incubation

Innovative technologies are often products of entrepreneurs within major corporations. Corporations also need to develop a strong local supplier base. Quite often, these corporations find it expensive to subcontract work outside of their operating area. Therefore, it is important to develop local capacity through small businesses.

The **Technology Deployment Alliance** of Palm Beach County, Florida was organized to find common solutions to these issues by deploying existing nonproprietary technologies, attracting a local supplier base, and identifying capital sources.

The Alliance includes a number of worldwide business leaders. Corporate members include Pratt & Whitney, IBM, W.R. Grace, Motorola, Florida Power and Light, Sensormatic, and Energy Partners. The MacArthur Foundation, Southern Technology Application Center, Florida Atlantic University (FAU), FAU Small Business Development Center, University of Florida, Northwood University, United Technologies Technology Center, and the Business Development Board of Palm Beach County are all institutional or foundation partners. The deployable technologies from the participating corporations represent multi-billion dollar assets. Each Alliance member or "technology source company" establishes an internal office and an interface person to work with the **Technology Deployment Center (TDC)** to fulfill its mission. The TDC is the nonprofit organization that focuses on finding partners for technology and linking them with capital for commercializing, licensing, and helping ideas proceed to production. In return, the TDC may hold an equity position in the venture or receive a royalty payment for marketing the idea successfully. The TDC uses different strategies for different marketing niches.

Each technology source company receives training in a four-phase process to help identify the path to commercialization. The four phases are technology inventory and characterization, technology matching, business case development, and spin-off approach identification. During the technology inventory, source companies catalog "releasable" core technologies. These core technologies are derived from a company's product line or from scientists at the company. Companies do not want to "give away" their competitive advantage, so a one-page inventory is performed. The company's interface person and management have prepared criteria to determine if a technology is releasable. It generally describes the technology and clarifies the level of maturity. It also asks the following questions:

- Will the technology require more development?
- Will the technology require a lot of the technologist's time?
- What is the desired outcome for the end-user?
- What is the benefit?

If the technology is deemed not releasable, then it is filed away by the source company until it may be released. Once the database of these core technologies is built, the interface person screens and classifies each core technology based on its strategic importance to the company. The interface person decides if the company prefers to own or just influence the technology. If a technology is determined to be releasable, it proceeds to a more detailed analysis called technology characterization.

This characterization involves use of a very detailed seven-page instrument. Categories include:

- How far the technology is beyond the state of the art;
- Research requirements;
- Technical risks;
- Licensing constraints;
- Technical tasks that need to be completed;
- Intellectual property status;
- Business characteristics; and
- Commercialization issues and path selection.

An internal team from the source company reviews all of the information. It is logged, and a legal release form is signed that gives the TDC 90 days to develop a business partnership for the technology. The remaining three phases require input from the TDC.

The technology match phase is market-driven. Core technologies from all of the Alliance members are stored in a database at the TDC. It builds a matrix of technologies in rows and possible markets in columns. When several rows intersect one column, the TDC notifies Alliance members about the possibility of business partnerships. This is a low-cost method of predicting success. A meeting is hosted by the TDC for the potential partner team members, including the capital sources. During this meeting, the team determines whether it should proceed to the next phase—the business case.

The TDC recognizes the potential market application or product that can be created from a particular technology. The TDC and team partners conduct a verification of the technology in the form of the business case. The business case is composed of the technical assessment, the market assessment, conclusions, and recommendations.

Once the business case is developed, the partner team determines the best spin-off approach: licensing, joint venture, or start-up. When the business development approach is selected, the start-up is given appropriate business resources, facilities, and capital. In addition, a management team is hired with the approval of the business case partners. This team is usually hand-picked by the technology source company where the idea originated.

Completion of the four-phase process does not guarantee that the technical source company will contribute significant resources to the project. Completion of the process can take anywhere from six months to one year.

There is no set fee structure for membership in the Alliance. Many in-kind contributions are made. Moreover, Alliance members are not always the technology source companies. Alliance members may also be partners that will benefit from leading edge technology.

The comprehensive nature of the Alliance adds unique strengths to business development strategies, bringing TDC in touch with worldwide opportunities for deployment of a variety of technologies.

Incubator Organization: For-Profit Variations

Not all for-profit incubators are created equal. While they share the common goal of financial gain, there is much variation in organizational structures of for-profit incubators. **Trilogy Systems, Inc.** and **Laboratory Associated Businesses, Ltd.** both operate as cooperatives, with tenants acting as owners. The **Technology Development Center** in West Sacramento, California, has two principals who invest in tenant companies.

Trilogy Systems, Inc., of Mountain View, California, a for-profit incubator formed as a cooperative by retired and semi-retired engineers, has a unique arrangement for tenants. The incubator offers facilities and support services to companies without rent or fees for the first year in return for equity and future financial reimbursement when the company begins earning revenues. Both companies formed from members of the cooperative, and outside companies that are accepted into the incubator enter into a buyback agreement with Trilogy Systems, Inc.

The incubator was formed as a direct result of a 1991 San Jose newspaper article that stated that those over age 50 and unemployed would end up flipping burgers. The cooperative was an answer to the problem of displaced workers who were in early retirement but has now expanded to other entrepreneurs.

Trilogy Systems, Inc. was initiated by a newspaper ad placed by two successful business owners who had recently retired and decided to form an engineering cooperative. The ad was directed to retired and semi-retired professionals and technicians looking for productive outlets. Interested individuals were instructed to meet at a local restaurant. The group that met decided to form a cooperative, toward which each party contributed $1,000. The group found a manufacturing facility and formed Trilogy Systems as a for-profit corporation. The goal of the original group was to develop commercializable products and services from within the cooperative. Trilogy now accepts tenants who were not part of the founding group, and each new tenant can purchase a $1,000 share of the corporation.

The incubator operates on an equity-based arrangement, taking 18 percent equity ownership in each tenant firm. The incubator takes the position of chair of each tenant firm's board.

Companies sign an extensive memorandum of understanding up-front, with time and quality benchmarks. The firms operate on one-year contracts with the incubator. The incubator expects six months of building followed by revenue in the second six months. If a company reaches its first-year benchmarks, it has the option of staying in the incubator for a second year but will begin paying a discounted rent and some shared bookkeeping costs. The second year objective is to move the firm into profitability. When a company reaches profitability, the incubator wants it to begin buying back its equity on a monthly basis, at a valuation based on a set formula.

The incubator will retain three percent at the end of the three-year buyback period with periodic valuations based on owner equity. The incubator steps down from the tenant company's board at the end of five years. The three percent the incubator retains is undilutable but can be bought back through negotiation. The incubator staff members, as shareholders, do not receive a salary but own equity in the companies.

The incubator owns a piece of each company; thus, the staff has a personal investment in the success of each firm. The goal of Trilogy shareholders is to make a small investment, help create jobs, and gain the opportunity for a good return on investment through this structure.

Similarly, **Laboratory Associated Businesses, Ltd.** is a for-profit corporation that provides laboratory space to emerging biotechnology and medical testing companies. The Madison, Wisconsin-based corporation owns the 40,000-square-foot building and much of the laboratory equipment that is available to tenants. A separate corporation has started up several of the tenant companies and invested in others. Laboratory Associated Businesses gives the tenants free rent for up to six months, then phases in full rent as the company is able to pay it. Eight of the 10 tenants own some stock in the corporation. Because of this, they are interested in the growth and upkeep of the building.

The **Technology Development Center** (TDC) of West Sacramento, California, is a for-profit incubator that takes stock options in all of its companies, both tenant and non-tenant. The incubator was founded by the president and CEO to invest in high-growth companies, in order to make long-term gains.

TDC assists the development of companies by providing seed financing, management support through its associates program, and other support services (see Chapter Four: Management). The principals (the president and the CEO) hope to achieve long-term gain through the ownership of stock options and royalty agreements in the incubator companies. High growth is defined by projected revenues of $10-20 million in five years.

Since the incubator was founded in 1990, 15 companies have been started, and four companies have graduated. Most of the companies have attained some level of success. However, the principals have not yet cashed out of any of the companies, so gains have not yet been fully realized.

The **Wichita Technology Corporation** (WTC) is nominally structured as a not-for-profit, but the organization takes an equity share in all of the companies in which it is involved. This is, in effect, an exchange for the services and activities involved in pulling the deals together. In addition, WTC has a 20 percent equity share in each deal put together by its seed capital affiliate, Wichita Holdings. Above and beyond the corporate involvement, the senior management, and staff of WTC also have small equity shares in any investment made by the corporation, in addition to their salaries. These structural and financial relationships tend to motivate the organization to function in more of a business-like manner.

Early Stage Facility: Only the Newest Need Apply

Operating like a for-profit incubator by investing in its tenants with the hope of returns, the **Massachusetts Biotechnology Research Institute (MBRI) Innovation Center**, Worcester, has taken an innovative approach to building businesses.

With very limited space, the MBRI Innovation Center focuses its efforts on serving the needs of very early-stage companies. It provides extensive early-stage support and financing, including capital investment, to companies that are expected to graduate from the facility after a brief tenancy.

Focusing on early-stage companies maximizes the number of start-ups the small facility can serve. MBRI focuses on launching biotechnology start-ups because of the strengths of area research institutions in biotechnology and the desire to build a regional biotechnology industry.

The MBRI Innovation Center facility is only 7,000 square feet, so it is unable to support companies once they begin to grow. Instead, the Innovation Center focuses its efforts on companies in the early stage, before they begin to expand. Innovation Center services include providing seed financing, office and lab space, equipment purchasing, and business assistance such as developing funding proposals and business plans. This structure allows the entrepreneurs (from both industry and research environments) to develop their businesses and their technologies simultaneously. Tenants need only a business plan executive summary to enter the facility and do not need to be incorporated. Companies remain in the Innovation Center an average of six to 24 months.

Once in the Innovation Center, research projects enter the first of four development stages: prestart-up, capital funding, investment and reinvestment. In the first stage, the researchers have access to advanced molecular biology and biochemistry laboratories, isotope and glass wash rooms, and administrative personnel to assist in day-to-day operations. Business support is offered through a network of preferred vendors to assist with legal, financial, and business planning.

In the capital funding phase, companies are assisted in obtaining equity financing. In many cases, the initial seed money comes from MBRI's affiliated venture capital company, Commonwealth BioVentures, Inc. As the venture develops, it moves to the next stage of capital investment by going public or being purchased. In the final stage of the development process, MBRI will invest a portion of its return in basic research grants to academic and research institutions, thereby stimulating new research and potential new Innovation Center enterprises. Preference for the grants will be given to the nine public and private research and academic universities across the state that are affiliated with MBRI. While no grants have yet been made, this stage is anticipated as part of MBRI's development process.

Incubator Operations: Rental Strategies

Among the challenges faced by incubator managers are those connected with the businesslike management of the space and physical assets of the facility. Getting an affordable facility, filling it with tenants, and ensuring that those tenants have access to incubator services for as long as needed (but no longer) are recurrent concerns faced by incubator managers.

One important issue is that of rent: How much to charge? How can it be susidized? What creative arrangements can be worked out with cash-limited tenants? Some incubators have donated facilities and can thus charge a limited monthly rent. Others exchange rent for equity stakes in client companies. Several incubators have developed sliding rent scales, and there are various combinations of rent vs. lease arrangements. To the extent that space *per se* becomes less important than services, fees paid by client companies will reflect more of the latter, in a bundling arrangement. In the following practice descriptions, all of these combinations are illustrated.

The **First Flight Venture Center**, located in Research Triangle Park, North Carolina, is managed by the North Carolina Technological Development Authority, Inc. (TDA), a private nonprofit corporation chartered by the North Carolina General Assembly.

The TDA was established to stimulate job creation across North Carolina through supporting small business. The First Flight Venture Center is one of 14 small business incubators cosponsored by the TDA; however, it is the only one directly managed by the TDA.

Along with chartering the TDA to serve as the development agency for technology-based small businesses in the state, the State of North Carolina deeded the current First Flight Venture Center facility to the TDA with the stipulation that it revert to state ownership should it cease to be operated as a small business incubator. While the operating expenses of the facility—including staff salaries and benefits and recurring operational costs—are completely paid from rental incomes, additional funding for improvements and expansions must be raised through state appropriations and/or private sources.

The greatest benefit to the operations of the incubator from this arrangement was the ability to tenant the building immediately and therefore generate revenues from the start, without the debt service that would have been incurred with the purchase of a facility. Thus, the First Flight Venture Center was able to maintain competitive lease rates without losing significant dollars during the lease-up phase.

The **Boulder Technology Incubator** has an arrangement with the two private developers who own the incubator facility. Both owners provide space rent-free to the incubator. Although the incubator pays no rent, it pays common area maintenance fees, taxes, utilities, and insurance, among other costs, so that the building owners have no out-of-pocket expenses for the facility.

This arrangement gives tenants access to space at below-market rates. The private developers are acting on enlightened self-interest; the incubator is bringing in companies that will likely graduate and relocate in nearby industrial parks that are owned by the developers.

The **University City Science Center** will help its tenants meet capital needs by taking equity in lieu of rent in some cases. The Center will make this decision, on an *ad hoc* basis, in order to ensure that the company will stay on-site in one of the buildings owned by the Center. When equity is taken, the Center takes a more active role in monitoring the company. In the cases where equity has been taken, the Center has not yet cashed out of the companies.

The **Austin Technology Incubator (ATI)** uses a sliding-scale rent policy. The primary purpose of this strategy is to provide the lowest rent possible to the neediest companies in their first year of tenancy and to give the more successful and mature companies a gentle push into the open market. Currently, the first year rate is 65 cents per square foot per month; the second year rate is 80 cents; the first six months of the third year is $1; and the final six months of tenancy is $1.30. ATI originally had a flat rental structure for all tenants but quickly found that it was hard to get successful tenant companies to leave the incubator. This was especially worrisome as the incubator's purpose is to grow fledgling companies, not subsidize financially secure ones. This sliding scale also helps prepare the tenant companies for the realities of life outside the incubator. As the company reaches its third and final year in the incubator, the rental rate ATI charges is near market rate, and in the final six months it meets or exceeds market rent. This strategy helps minimize the shock of complete independence and forces tenants in their last year of incubation to operate in a more fiscally realistic manner.

The **St. Louis Technology Center** uses a monthly license agreement for use of space and services in place of a lease arrangement; the Center does not require tenants to sign leases. Tenants sign a license agreement upon entry which outlines monthly fees for the use of the space and services and indicates that they are free to leave or can be asked to leave at any time without notice. Tenants are billed one month in advance for the use of the space and 15 days beyond the end of the month for the use of services. If the incubator staff sees that the client is having problems such as debt-to-equity ratio trouble and does not follow the center's recommendations, the tenant may be asked to leave. The incubator has never asked anyone to leave but has nudged businesses out after they became fully developed and no longer needed the services of the center.

A month-to-month agreement in place of a lease relieves clients of financial obligations and keeps them in a flexible frame of mind necessary for business growth. Since a company can leave at any time if it does not like the services the incubator is providing, it has a stake in getting maximum benefit from those services. The incubator also retains more legal flexibility, since a lease gives clients an interest in the property and a license agreement does not.

One of the dangers of the typical incubator operation is that the real estate aspects of the operation may overshadow the more essential service aspects of the program. One solution is to separate these functions in arrangements with the entrepreneur.

The **Metropolitan Center for High Technology** has gotten away from the concept of leasing space. It charges a flat tuition fee of $300 per month for all program services plus 100 square feet of office space. If the company needs more space, the additional space is prorated based on what the incubator pays in its lease to the building owner. This enables companies to budget a constant cost item that includes all the services and a variable cost item (rent) that is linked to company growth. This, in a sense, reverses the pricing structure of many incubators. It enables companies to receive assistance at a relatively low cost when they need it most, in the early stages of business development.

The **Office for the Advancement of Developing Industries (OADI) Incubator** in Birmingham, Alabama, provides a program of services to "associate" companies that are not tenants of the incubator but have need for various services that the incubator provides to its regular tenants. Associate companies may be going through early-stage development and are not yet ready to begin operations in the incubator. The **Technology Enterprise Centre** (TEC) in Calgary, Alberta, has a similar arrangement called the Corporate Identity Program.

New business ventures go through stages of development as they grow. Most start "in the garage or in the basement" and involve a single individual pursuing development of a product or service. Often, the success of a venture emerging from this seed stage is due to access to basic support services and expertise found in a business incubator. OADI and TEC have recognized this need and have developed support programs for early-stage associates, preparing them to grow to the point at which the incubator facility will be beneficial to them.

The OADI associates program provides new ventures access to a range of infrastructure services, also available to incubator tenants at reduced rates, because space, light, and heat are not being used by the associate companies. Incubator management keeps in touch with associate companies on a regular and systematic basis to monitor their progress toward becoming tenant members or bypassing incubator tenancy and moving to the next stage of development. There is a modest annual fee ($250) charged to associate members.

The TEC Corporate Identity Program requires a month-to-month commitment of $50. For this fee, the program clients receive access to all of the incubator's services except office and laboratory space. These services include a mailing address, receptionist services, and access to a conference room. Corporate Identity Program clients also have access to the entrepreneurial development elements of the incubator program, including training workshops, counseling, informational meetings, and the opportunity to exhibit in the twice-annual Mini-Trade Show (see finance and capitalization).

The Corporate Identity Program is growing, in part because it is also open to entrepreneurs whose start-ups are failing and who can no longer afford office space because they need to reduce their operating costs.

The **Tri-Cities Enterprise Association** utilizes an affiliate tenant program that allows non-tenants to access the resources of the incubator. For a $95 monthly retainer fee, affiliates can utilize secretarial services, meeting facilities, telephone, 24-hour voice mail, and commercial-grade office equipment. They receive Internet access and an e-mail address as well. Affiliate tenants, often brand-new businesses or prestart-ups, sign an affiliate tenant agreement that specifies services to be received, as well as outlines restrictions such as when the conference room is available. The affiliate tenant agreement can be set up on a month-to-month arrangement or for a longer period.

Incubator Operations: Beyond the Walls

Incubators in some areas must also provide outreach to clients not located near the incubator who may not be able to readily take advantage of incubator services and activities.

Hawaii's **High Technology Development Corp.** has already developed or is developing facilities on several islands to be linked through remote conferencing capabilities.

Incutech Brunswick, Inc. operates an outreach program for firms outside Fredericton that cannot locate in the incubator building. Strategies for outreach programs are especially important to incubators that serve large geographic areas, areas with low population density, and other places where the incubator is not easily reached by current or potential entrepreneurs. The innovative approaches to outreach work best where they are matched to local needs and resources.

Incutech Brunswick, Inc.'s outreach program helps non-local entrepreneurs start businesses in their own communities. The incubator will subsidize the entrepreneur's rent at 33 cents per square foot per month and provide all other incubator services such as mentoring and listing on Incutech's World Wide Web home page. The incubator manager and a board member will go on-site periodically for mentoring sessions and offer the company advice on financing, strategic planning, marketing, and other areas relevant to new technology businesses.

Growing More Than New Businesses

The **Port of Benton**, located adjacent to the Department of Energy's Hanford site in Richland, Washington, focuses its incubator activities on companies that eventually will purchase facilities developed by the Port. The goal of the Port district is to develop the area through developing industrial parks, not just businesses. This goal derives from the function of port districts to stimulate business and industrial development. The policy allows the Port of Benton to keep incubator companies on site, even after they begin to grow.

Once a company is large enough to grow out of the incubator, the Port will sell the land and the building to the tenant. This sale does not displace any other companies, because by the time the company is ready to purchase the facility, it has already "taken over the building." The profit from sales of facilities is used for improvements to Port facilities and for new buildings. The Port continually purchases undeveloped land in order to continue developing the largely rural 1,500-square-mile port district. The Port of Benton currently has five industrial sites, with incubator facilities at four of the sites. The Port facilities are both general use and specialized, including a shared kitchen/food processing facility.

Tenants are both high-tech and agricultural in nature. Incubator companies must be new businesses and not compete with existing businesses in the area. They also need to have a reasonable chance of success to be admitted to the incubator program. Although the tax-subsidized rents are tied to the companies' income, tenants are not forced to leave the incubator after a set period of time. Rather, the Port wants companies to stay on-site and purchase the land and facility. In essence, the companies do not graduate. Because they can stay where they are, growing companies are not hindered by having to find a new location and can focus on managing their growth rather than on relocation. Three buildings have been sold to incubated companies since the incubator program was started in 1978. The end result is an area with more developed land and more businesses owning industrial facilities on the tax rolls.

CHAPTER 10 # NEXT STEPS

In this chapter, we will not attempt a summary of the previous nine. The content in this book has been too disparate, the entries too dense, and the style too practical and operational to yield a sweeping big picture. In Chapter 1 we noted in passing some of the limitations of the study and of the final product. In this chapter we would like to build on those brief comments and discuss some of the next steps that should follow from this effort.

As we see it, there are three unanswered questions or remaining challenges to address as logical follow-ups. First is the problem of how to position this book in a community of readers and users so as to maximize opportunities for *change*. Second is how to address some of the *methodological* limitations of this project through additional primary research and/or secondary analysis. Third is the question of how to maintain this guidebook as a living resource, through *updating and expanding* the entries, so that program evolution in the field of technology business incubation can be captured in the future. Obviously, solving this last problem will also help to address issue number one.

Taking Action: The Inherent Problem of the Text

An early vision of the final version of this project was to create a "cookbook" of technology business incubation that would enable a reader to simply pick through the operational guidance therein and replicate a practice or strategy in another setting. By any measure we have taken a long step toward that goal; there are more than 250 strategies, practices, or tools described in this volume.

However, like cookbooks of a traditional culinary variety, this document is only as good as its ability to promote action. If existing incubator programs are improved or new programs launched as a result of this volume, then the project will have been a success. Otherwise, this will become one more rapidly outdated chunk of text.

The problem, of course, is that text does not inevitably lead to action, no matter how specific the guidance that it provides. In fact, the descriptions of best practices and strategies assembled here are still not in the step-by-step, do-it-yourself level of detail that we originally (and perhaps naively) hoped to achieve. In effect, we have compiled a large number of case vignettes, with varying degrees of operational specificity. Given that we have described more than 250 strategies, practices, or tools, a true cookbook format would have required a volume of a few thousand pages. It would also have stressed the patience of our incubator manager informants far beyond the breaking point.

We believe that the probability of action and change can be enhanced, however, if we simply build upon the analytic base presented here and take a few more relatively painless steps. In the next few pages we would like to present some preliminary thoughts about "actioning" the content of this book.

A Best Practitioner's Network

Despite the presentation in this book, it would be a mistake to think of best practices, strategies, and tools as somehow existing in a disembodied program space. Each of them represents some individuals' creative genius, applied to the task of improving the process of technology business incubation. In effect, not only is there a catalog of best practices, but also a yet unrealized network of best practitioners. These individuals represent a valuable resource for converting the results of this project into real changes in programs.

One long-established finding of the innovation literature (Fairweather, Sanders, and Tornatzky, 1974; Tornatzky, Fergus, and Avellar, 1980) is that complex program change is rarely realized through the dissemination of written materials alone. If a substantive consultant or an organizational change agent is added to the mix, however, the probability of seeing program innovations adopted and implemented increases considerably. The value of external help seems to be most apparent during the implementation stage of innovation, when changes in organizational practice are being negotiated. Organizations may decide to adopt a programmatic innovation, but the nitty-gritty of implementation is often the major stumbling block.

In the context of this project, the best practitioners who lie behind our best practices should be considered an implementation assistance resource. We encourage the readers of this book to contact programs of interest, find out who are the key players, and try to lure those people into lending you a hand. We also encourage the best practitioners alluded to in this volume to have some forbearance and patience and to make yourselves available for some peer-to-peer advice-giving.

We also believe that there is a large-scale project lurking here in the background. Suppose that a third-party entity organized a national consulting/assistance bureau to coordinate this change process? External resources permitting, such a project could defray travel costs or consulting fees for best practitioners, or promote teleconferences on implementing a category of service (e.g., being involved in seed funds), in which the best practitioners would be the star attractions. A need also exists for best practitioners to take some time out and collectively reflect on the nature of their practice. Although many of these things already occur informally, for example at technical conferences and in normal professional networking, they take place at a relatively low level of intensity. A three to five-year outreach effort, focused on the burgeoning technology business incubator field, might significantly pick up the pace.

Archives of "Stuff"

Many of the practices and strategies described in this book—and all of the tools—have some physical artifact attached to them. While many practices are simply patterns of behavior on the part of program staff, other practices have a fair amount of tangible materials embedded in them. For example, a client selection procedure may involve a set of forms or checklists, a training program for tenants may include a set of videotapes, and an approach to crafting cooperative research agreements may use some standard protocols for intellectual property understandings. Obviously, all of the commercial tools that are described in this book involve some physical thing that is bought and sold.

In conducting this project, the research team made an effort to acquire samples of these various physical artifacts. (We gradually came to refer to our collection as "stuff.") Although the collection of stuff is by no means complete, having in hand a sample of the physical paraphernalia that is linked to a practice aided us immeasurably in understanding how the practice, strategy, or tool actually worked. This was particularly so when we could compare stuff that was related to different discrete practices, presumably performing the same function. In effect, the team could do some comparison shopping using the samples.

We believe that the change process could be significantly accelerated if there were a central archive of such materials, with multiple copies of each. This would be accessible to incubators attempting to adopt a new practice or tool. Samples could be examined on a short-term lending library basis and then mailed back to the repository. This could be a natural service for an appropriate third-party organization, perhaps supported by grant money or by small user fees. Based on our experience, most best practitioners are quite willing (when pressed a little) to provide such materials free or at cost. For commercial vendors, it is in their business self-interest; for others, it is a matter of professional pride.

Tool-Making

Best practices that are predominantly embodied in the behaviors of program staff at one or a few sites will always remain in the realm of art. They will also necessarily be tied to particular personalities and practitioners and as such will be difficult to replicate in other places. While some of best practices will always reflect art or clinical judgment, we believe that the field could gain much by trying to forge tools from the others—in short, by making the unique accessible and even mundane.

Following up the previous section, we would like to focus a bit more attention on practices that are almost entirely physical artifact. That is, the *tools*. The list of these is fairly large, ranging from commercial software to books, to simple forms or checklists. Some of these are commercial products with the backing of the manufacturing, marketing, and customer service functions of the vendor company. Others are more informal in their product status, being used as tools exclusively within the program where they were invented.

One of the best ways to improve the performance and operations of technology business incubators, *and* to accelerate the change process would be increased "tool-making" based on best practices and strategies. We also believe that the benefits of tool-making are particularly enhanced when practices-as-tools become commercial products.

How would this be accomplished? First of all, it would mean adopting a tool-making mindset, with increased discipline in documenting and operationalizing in a step-by-step manner how things are done. Then it would involve an attempt to capture the practice/art in some form of tangible tool or tools. As suggested by this book, such tools can take many forms and involve various kinds of media. Finally, the tools would be widely disseminated or marketed to the world. For those tools that have applicability outside the small population of the incubator world, a potential exists for building commercial products that could be sold to businesses. Many of the tools described in this volume are of that nature. Taken to its logical end point, a second or third edition of this book a few years from now might be more a catalog of vendor-provided tools than a guidebook of practices.

This raises the issue of who should do the tool-making. In some cases, entrepreneurial incubators themselves might to be developers—particularly if they are for-profit organizations. As an alternative, some companies that already have a portfolio of business software might be logical candidates for tool-making projects. Other potential tools will only be appropriate for incubators as users (and thus have a limited market) and might be developed by NBIA or another third-party organization using grant funds.

It should be noted that this tool-making vision is being realized in other allied settings. For example, in the last 10 years there has been a tremendous growth in manufacturing or industrial *extension* programs. These programs provide assistance to small companies in improving manufacturing systems and business practices. Since there are upwards of 300,000 small companies that are potential users of such programs, there is by necessity a high client volume. However, manufacturing extension programs have made increasingly effective use of decision tools, and that use is being actively promoted by federal agency funders. For example, the Manufacturing Extension Partnership (MEP) of the National Institute of Standards and Technology (NIST) has been a strong supporter of tool development efforts, not only in the context of its Manufacturing Technology Centers programs but also through special project initiatives. A project funded by the Appalachian Regional Commission (ARC) has involved the creation of a "tools catalog" (Southern Technology Council, 1995) of decision aids suitable for manufacturing extension practice. The Modernization Forum, which is the nonprofit professional association for the extension field, has developed its own inventory of existing tools and is actively promoting the development of new ones.

While manufacturing extension is not the same as technology business incubation, we believe that the incubation field can learn much from manufacturing extension and other venues about the use of tools. We also believe that tools—particularly commercial tools—create their own dynamic for program change. After all, best practitioners have few incentives to share their practice secrets, and professional pride can only go so far. On the other hand, tool vendors have a business interest in getting their tools sold and used. Good vendors also have customer support and service organizations; in effect, the cost of technical assistance is built into the price. If this happens on a widespread basis, qualitative changes in service delivery will result.

EMPIRICAL VALIDATION AND SORTING

While much has been accomplished in this project, in a few areas limitations of time and resources precluded using the optimal research methodology. One was the approach that was used to define "best" among the many practices, strategies, and tools used by technology business incubators. That is, best practices were self-defined by the incubator manager informants ("tell us what has worked for you, in terms of a particularly novel or useful approach"), with essentially no external or empirical validation.   In addition, not all of the practices that were described ended up in the book. The research team eliminated several practices that seemed to be relatively common in their usage across the sample. Furthermore, there was no attempt to quantify practices, in terms of various dimensions or attributes, other than the simple checklist that was used in each practice domain or area.

A second methodological limitation was completely out of our control. No common impact or outcome data gathering was used across the sample of incubator programs. Although many of the programs were involved in their own customized data gathering, such as for evaluation purposes, there was no commonality across the sample. Some past efforts have been undertaken to provide common measures across the incubator community (e.g., the NBIA state-of-the-industry surveys), but those have focused more on operational issues of incubators generally, and their treatments of outcomes or impacts on clients has been limited to looking at graduation rates, business failure rates, and the like. To our knowledge, no uniformly formatted national database has been compiled on the business performance of incubator client companies or graduates involving data collected at the level of the enterprise across a large sample of incubator programs.

Given these issues of data and method, we would like to make some proposals about how this project and others like it could be even more useful in the future.

Toward Performance Benchmarking

We believe that the technology business incubator community could benefit from a long-term effort to benchmark program performance. When we say performance, we are thinking in terms of impacts on and outcomes for client companies. If common performance metrics were available across the country, the ability to sort out best practices would be considerably easier. Qualitative, reputation, and self-nomination approaches to defining "best" could be supplemented by statistical-based analysis. For example, one could correlate the use or nonuse of a particular practice or class of practices with a range of performance metrics. The checklist data gathered in this project could have been used as predictor variables in such an analysis. At the individual program level, assuming that different client companies get different mixes of services, it would be relatively easy to examine the relative effects of specific service categories on client success. The biggest obstacle to this kind of empirical sorting is the absence of a set of reliable, quantitative outcome and impact benchmark metrics.

The first step in building a performance benchmarking system would be to get consensus on that small set of metrics and measuring approaches. This should be relatively easy to do, assuming there is agreement on the underlying theory and process of enterprise incubation. A group of practitioners (in this case incubator managers) can usually get quick agreement on what "variable domains" should be assessed. We would argue that performance measurement should be tilted toward *client* outcomes, rather than incubator outcomes (such as the number of clients served) which do not directly address business development success. For example, the group might decide that some sort of measures need to be devised in the areas of client firm growth, profitability, and the development of business systems. Others might be specific to technology development.

The next steps become more technical in terms of questionnaire creation and the manipulation of data into metrics, and without going into excessive detail, a few rules of thumb are in order. For one, it is essential that any measurement devices or questionnaires be relatively easy to use and not demand a great deal of program or company record-keeping. Many performance measures will need to be gathered directly from current and former client companies, and the time demands on entrepreneurs must be considered. Nonetheless, participating in such data collection could and perhaps should be a condition of service delivery. In addition to being part of a program-wide performance benchmarking database, such firm-level information could also be used in client oversight and periodic review.

It is also important—if at all possible—to develop measures and metrics that are relatively standard across incubator programs. These could be adjusted by other dimensions such as program size, type of client served (very early-stage, preenterprise clients vs. companies well into product development), or industry focus. In this area, benchmarking practices in manufacturing or other established businesses can provide a good starting point for modeling. Many of the more useful benchmark metrics are in the form of business ratios, in which two or more specific variables are combined into something that is more meaningful for the user. For example, the percentage of raw material (e.g., sheet steel) that ends up as scrap has particular relevance in manufacturing. In the area of university technology licensing, the Southern Technology Council (Tornatzky, Waugaman, and Casson, 1995) has developed metrics in which the typical measures of gross patents, licenses, and royalties are "normalized" in terms of the size of the research portfolio of the institution. Thus, rather than using royalties *per se*, the metric became royalties divided by total research dollars, which is the equivalent of a rate-of-return index. Similar metrics could be devised for the technology incubator field and collected at both the program and client company levels.

Of course a precondition for standard, comparable measures is that a large number of organizations will participate in an ongoing performance benchmarking effort. The value of performance benchmarking is directly related to the size of the study sample. With a larger study sample, norms can become established and individual programs can compare themselves to them. In the university-industry technology transfer example cited above (Tornatzky, Waugaman, and Casson, 1995) virtually every major research university in a 14-state region was in the study sample, and individual institutions could examine their relative standing on each of seven performance metrics. In the technology business incubator field, one would need to get a minimum of 20 to 30 programs involved, with 20 to 30 client companies sampled from each; otherwise the data would be too unstable. As the study sample increases, there is also greater potential for comparisons within a subgroup. For example, a manufacturing benchmarking service with which we are familiar (Industrial Technology Institute, 1995) has data from more than 600 companies on more than 40 measures and practices, which makes it possible for a single customer of the service to compare its metrics against other companies of the same size, product mix, and customer base. More than 1,400 companies have received customized reports on how their company compares to others in their industry.

Another important task when developing performance benchmarking is to get longitudinal involvement by participants. It is extremely useful to examine time trends, and this is virtually impossible if institutions move in and out of the study sample. A three-year commitment from participants is desirable.

Finally, although we are trying to benchmark the performance of incubator *programs*, we are gathering many of the critical outcome measures from *client companies*. Since it would be difficult and expensive to gather such data from all client companies, across all incubators in the study sample, it will be necessary to devise a sampling strategy. This could be simple random sampling. However, because there is great heterogeneity among client companies, as well as among incubator programs,[6] it might be useful to stratify the sampling of companies in terms of one or more dimensions (e.g., size, stage of development, area of technology).

Empirical Validation of Practices

Once a system of performance benchmarking is established and a set of outcome and impact measures defined, it becomes possible to validate the usefulness of various practices and strategies. Although it is difficult to establish the impact of a specific and unique practice unless a within-program experimental test is designed (see below), it is possible to establish a research design to examine the effect of *types* of practices on client company outcomes. That assumes one has a study sample of sufficient size (see above), a reliable and valid way to benchmark performance outcomes, and an approach to measuring the use of various types of practices.

How to measure the use of practice types? In this project, we used a simple crude checklist procedure, in which the unit of analysis was the entire program. Program managers were asked to indicate whether or not they had used various practice types with any clients, and whether they had delivered the practice directly or via referral. While that approach was adequate in this first project, it could be improved in two ways. One is to be more precise about the unit of analysis for data-gathering purposes. In order to quantify the impact of a particular type of practice, it will be necessary to examine its use across a range of *individual* client companies. That means gathering data at the case level *and* across a number of service provision engagements between programs and client companies.

A second area for improvement lies in the measurement of "use." The procedure used in this project was, in effect, a nominal level of measurement (yes-no, did it happen?). Better statistical analysis can be realized if we can measure use in a ordinal manner (more or less), and analytic precision can be obtained if we can to get to a true ratio scale of measurement.[7] In short, we need to be able to measure "how much" of a practice or practice category is being delivered to (and used by) client companies.

If we could achieve the optimal levels of measurement, sample, and statistical analysis, it would indeed be possible to analyze via correlation techniques, the effects of various practice variables. This would clearly improve the empirical "sorting out" of best practices that was begun in the current project.

There is another much more laborious and costly way to examine empirically the effects of various practices. It is much more methodologically correct and eliminates most of the ambiguity about inferences of cause and effect. This method entails a true experiment, in which the effect of a single practice (or two or more concurrently) on a client company outcomes can unambiguously be assessed. This usually involves the precise administration of a "treatment" to one group (in this case, companies) and the absence of that treatment to a comparable group or "control." Comparability is assured by random assignment of experimental units (individual companies) to either the experimental treatment or control groups. Again, this volume is not the appropriate place for a full discussion of this methodological approach, and classic texts have been written on the subject (Cook and Campbell, 1979; Fairweather and Tornatzky, 1977). Nonetheless, the point to be made is that there are quite robust methodologies to empirically sort out practices and treatments, and we are poised to move beyond the useful but incomplete analysis conducted in this project.

The Needed Mega-Project

As should be obvious from the above, we believe that a fairly large and quantitative data collection project represents a logical follow-on from this report. Such a project would subsume performance benchmarking, as well as sorting out the relative impact of practices and/or types of practices. It would need to be large, in terms of the number of programs and client companies involved, and longitudinal. We are not suggesting that this needs to become an ongoing preoccupation of the field, but should be at least a one-time event that might be replicated in another few years. One logical venue for such an effort might be something akin to the state-of-the-industry survey conducted by the National Business Incubation Association (NBIA) and last done in 1995. A similar study could involve an expanded survey design (at least focused on technology-oriented programs), as well as a different approach to outcome measurement with an eye toward performance benchmarking. Any takers? Obviously, to move forward on such an ambitious undertaking would involve identifying both research partners and funding sources.

UPDATING AND EXPANDING

When this book went to press, the project team knew that our documentation of best practices, strategies, and tools could be neither exhaustive nor completely up-to-date. We know that many of the programs have gone on to improve and/or expand the practices that they discussed with us. It was incomplete because the group of programs that we studied was a sample and not the entire population of technology business incubators in North America as of 1995. What we have assembled is a snapshot in time, with not everything in the picture.

Given those realities it is appropriate that we close this edition of our catalog of best practices with a consideration of how we will produce the next edition, and how we can do that either as a continuous process or through an intensive period of data collection, much along the lines of what has been accomplished here. In effect, how can we update, expand, and qualitatively improve this reference work over the next few years? Several issues are pertinent to that task.

The Logistics of Data Collection

This product involved about three-fourths of a "person-year" of effort, over about an 18-month calendar time frame. That effort included study design, instrument creation and field testing, phone interviewing, quantitative data analysis, documenting cases and practices, and a lengthy process (with participants) of correcting and refining practice descriptions. It also required staff qualities and competencies (that increased over the project), including knowledge about entrepreneurial behaviors and the various practice categories examined in the study, as well as listening and interviewing skills. This is not a process that can be done by shipping questionnaires blindly around the country.

Although there might be some increased efficiencies in a repeat engagement, a safe estimate would be that a comparable wave of data collection for new entries would encompass a similar level of effort. If we assume that there are another 50-plus technology incubators that were untouched by this project, and that they *should* be added to the study sample, then it would take another significant chunk of work to add new entries. This need not be done in a single, intensive project period. This could be a natural project for a quarter-time research assistant position, over two to three years.

We do believe that updates will be somewhat less onerous. Given that we now have a base product, we should easily be able to poll sources of current entries for additions and/or corrections. Such information would be relatively routine in nature and would demand the same degree of qualitative interviewing and analysis that was used with initial entries. This function might also be accomplished via telecommunications, if the participating incubator programs were pulled into an on-line discussion group or equivalent. For example, an ongoing "best practices" or "tools" on-line discussion group could be convened. The outputs of this group would simply need to be downloaded and processed for updated information.

Alternative Presentation Media

In this project we have not explored presentation media other than printed text. However, there are good reasons to believe that a future version of a best practices catalog might be packaged in other forms. For example, in its current version the document is not easily searchable other than in the time-honored manner of consulting the index and table of contents and plowing through text. However, if the material were available in an electronic form, with appropriate search tools, it might be a more useful resource.

We also believe that there is an unexplored opportunity for nontext media. To the extent that the content of this resource becomes more "tool-based" (see above), it will become increasingly useful to have visual information on the tools themselves. In addition, as more of the content is made up of commercialized products, it will become more appropriate to include purchase forms and procedures in the resource. All of this points to multi-media on-line versions of a future best practices resource and/or periodically updated CD-ROMs. Obviously, a next edition of this resource needs to evaluate these options.

Incentives for Participants

When we began this project it was not obvious how participants (particularly incubator managers) would benefit, relative to the costs in time and effort of providing information, sharing materials, and reviewing documentation. No doubt some were hesitant about sharing "trade secrets" with others, with no obvious compensating results. Those concerns are still out there and will only be resolved as this book is used by individuals and organizations in the technology business incubation field. We are confident that the incubators in our study sample will see this book as a resource to compare their efforts against their peers, gleaning several new ideas.

From the perspective of the project team, we had a fairly simple calculus in mind. We assumed that every incubator that we talked with would yield at least three to six novel and useful practices that could be shared with others. If every incubator could derive eight to 10 good new ideas out of the aggregate product, then for most programs the incentives for participation would be positive.

This intuitive analysis of costs and benefits has some implications for future updates and expansions of the document. These should only be done if we believe that there will be significant value added to the new product, relative to the one that we have now and to the costs of adding that new content. Unfortunately, the team has no simple approach for determining when that point will be reached. As the current book gets into wider circulation, we trust that the field itself will judge when a new version is needed, and that some new project team will be assembled to meet the need.

At any rate, as we close this project in late 1995, we feel that an important and valuable addition to the professional literature on technology business incubation has been realized. When we launched the project 18 months ago there was no existing best-practice analysis in the technology business incubation field, and now there is a useful resource document. We look forward to feedback from our colleagues over the next several months and will continue to ponder the "what's next" questions of improving practice in our field. It is now possible to go forward—intelligently—in many good directions.

APPENDIX A

ENDNOTES

1   This is financing which is contingent upon an order received by an external vendor (e.g., of equipment), with money coming from the vendor.

2   University-affiliated incubators were those incubators found to have a formal relationship with a university. Incubators without a close, formal relationship were categorized as nonuniversity incubators. Valid responses were based on a sample of 33 university-affiliated incubators and 21 nonuniversity incubators.

3   A statistical level of $p \leq .05$ was used in all analysis.

4   Rural incubators were defined as incubators in cities with a 1990 population of less than 50,000. All incubators located in cities of greater than 50,000 population were counted as urban incubators. Incubators in Hoboken, New Jersey and Stony Brook, New York are also classified as urban, due to the urban/suburban nature of these locations, despite having populations less than 50,000. Valid responses are based on a sample of 13 rural incubators and 41 urban incubators.

5   The best practice descriptions associated with access to laboratories and equipment are found in the chapter on physical infrastructure. We will confine our discussion here to less tangible approaches and practices.

6   In terms of research design considerations, in this situation, one unit of analysis (client companies) is "nested" within another (programs). As has been discussed in several statistics texts, this creates interesting analytical issues.

7   This is not a chapter reading for a research design or statistics course. The reader should consult an appropriate text for greater detail on the nuances of various levels of measurement precision.

APPENDIX B

PARTICIPATING INCUBATORS

CONTACT THESE INCUBATORS FOR MORE INFORMATION...

Advanced Technology Development Center
430 10th Street, NW, Suite N-116
Atlanta, GA 30318
(404) 894-3575   Fax (404) 894-4545

Akron Industrial Incubator
526 S. Main Street
Akron, OH 44311
(216) 375-2173   Fax (216) 762-3657

Arizona Technology Incubator
1435 N. Hayden Road
Scottsdale, AZ 85257-3773
(602) 990-0400   Fax (602) 970-6355

Auburn Center for Developing Industries
1500 Pumphrey Avenue
Auburn, AL 36830
(205) 821-2561   Fax (205) 826-1659

Austin Technology Incubator
3925 W. Braker Lane, Suite 400
Austin, TX 78759
(512) 305-0000   Fax (512) 305-0009

BioBusiness Incubator of Michigan
P.O. Box 27609
Lansing, MI 48909-0609
(517) 336-4660   Fax (517) 337-7904

Boulder Technology Incubator
1821 Lefthand Circle, Suite B
Longmont, CO 80501-6740
(303) 678-8000   Fax (303) 678-8505

Business and Technology Center
Idaho State University Research Park
1657 Alvin Ricken Drive
Pocatello, ID 83201
(208) 236-2936   Fax (208) 233-5960

Business & Technology Center
1220 Potter Drive
West Lafayette, IN 47906
(317) 494-1727   Fax (317) 494-0130

Business Technology Center
1275 Kinnear Road
Columbus, OH 43212
(614) 487-3700   Fax (614) 487-3704

Business Technology Incubator
Bradley University
1501 W. Bradley Avenue
Peoria, IL 61625
(309) 677-2852   Fax (309) 677-3386

Carleton University Technology Development
    and Commercialization Office
1125 Colonel By Drive, DT 1524
Ottawa, ON, CANADA K1S 5B6
(613) 788-2517   Fax (613) 788-2521

Center for Applied Technology
511 Westinghouse Road
Pendleton, SC 29670
(803) 646-4000   Fax (803) 646-4001

Center for Business Innovation
4747 Troost Avenue
Kansas City, MO 64110
(816) 561-8567   Fax (816) 756-1530

Center for Health Technologies, Inc.
444 Brickell Avenue, Suite 224
Miami, FL 33131-1404
(305) 377-7323   Fax (305) 377-7325

Center for Innovation & Business
   Development
P.O. Box 8372
University of North Dakota
Grand Forks, ND 58202
(701) 777-3132   Fax (701) 777-2339

Ceramics Corridor Innovation Center
109 Canada Road
Painted Post, NY 14870
(607) 962-6387   Fax (607) 962-0645

Chicago Technology Park
2201 West Campbell Park Drive
Chicago, IL 60612
(312) 633-3434   Fax (312) 829-4069

Colorado Bio/Medical Venture Center
1610 Pierce Street
Lakewood, CO 80214
(303) 237-3998   Fax 303-237-4010

CYBER Center
1600 Pennsylvania Avenue
York, PA 17404
(717) 846-2927   Fax (717) 854-9333

Dome Corp.
333 Cassell Drive, Suite 4000
Baltimore, MD 21224
(410) 550-2284   Fax (410) 550-2285

Enterprise Development Center
240 Dr. Martin Luther King, Jr. Blvd.
Newark, NJ 07102
(201) 643-5740   Fax (201) 643-5839

Evanston Business & Technology Center
1840 Oak Avenue
Evanston, IL 60201
(708) 864-0800   Fax (708) 866-1808

First Flight Center, Inc.
P.O. Box 12076
Research Triangle Park, NC 27709-3169
(919) 990-8558   Fax (919) 990-8561

GENESIS Technology Incubator
Engineering Research Center, Rm 366
University of Arkansas
Fayetteville, AR 72701-1201
(501) 575-7227   Fax (501) 575-7446

High Technology of Rochester
5 United Way
Rochester, NY 14604
(716) 224-2500   Fax (716) 224-8119

Idaho Innovation Center, Inc.
2300 North Yellowstone
Idaho Falls, ID 83401
(208) 523-1026   Fax (208) 523-1049

Incutech Brunswick, Inc.
P.O. Box 69000
Fredericton, NB, CANADA E3B 6C2

Iowa State Innovation System (ISIS)
Suite 600 Bldg. #1, ISU Research Park
2501 North Loop Drive
Ames, IA 50010-8283
(515) 296-9900   Fax (515) 296-9910

Laboratory Associated Businesses, Ltd.
1202 Ann Street
Madison, WI 53713
(608) 251-3005   Fax (608) 251-3007

Long Island High Technology Incubator
25 East Loop Road
Stony Brook, NY 11790-3355
(516) 444-8800   Fax (516) 444-8825

Manoa Innovation Center
2800 Woodlawn Drive, #100
Honolulu, HI 96822-1843
(808) 539-3600   Fax (808) 539-3611

MBRI Innovation Center
Mass. Biotechnology Research Institute
One Innovation Drive
Worcester, MA 01605
(508) 797-4200   Fax (508) 799-4039

Metropolitan Center for High Technology
2727 Second Avenue
Detroit, MI 48201
(313) 963-0616   Fax (313) 963-7606

MGE Innovation Center
University Research Park
565 Science Drive
Madison, WI 53711
(606) 238-5054

Montgomery County Technology Enterprise
  Center
Suburban Maryland Technology Council
2092 Gaither Rd., Suite 220AA
Rockville, MD 20850
(301) 258-5005   Fax (301) 208-8227

NET Ben Franklin Technology Center
115 Research Drive
Bethlehem, PA 18015
(610) 758-5262   Fax (610) 861-8247

North Central Idaho Business Technology
  Incubator
Moscow-Latah County Economic Dev.
  Council
121 Sweet Avenue
Moscow, ID 83843
(208) 885-3801   Fax (208) 885-3803

Office for the Advancement of
  Developing Industries
1075 13th Street South
University of Alabama @ Birmingham
Birmingham, AL 35294-4440
(205) 934-2190   Fax (205) 934-1037

Ohio University Innovation Center Program
20 East Circle Drive, Suite 190
Athens, OH 45701
(614) 593-1818   Fax (614) 593-0186

Port of Benton
3100 George Washington Way
Richland, WA 99352
(509) 375-3060   Fax (509) 375-5287

Rensselaer Polytechnic Institute Incubator
  Center
1223 Peoples Avenue
Troy, NY 12180
(518) 276-6658   Fax (518) 276-6380

Rutgers Technology Help Desk and Incubator
100 Jersey Avenue, D-1
New Brunswick, NJ 08901
(908) 545-3221   Fax (908) 545-0120

Software Business Center
8845 Long Point Road
Houston, TX 77055
(713) 932-7495   Fax (713) 932-7498

Springfield Technology Center
300 E. Auburn Avenue
Springfield, OH 45505-4703
(513) 322-7821   Fax (513) 322-7874

St. Louis Technology Center
9666 Olive Blvd., #305
St. Louis, MO 63132
(314) 966-9979   Fax (314) 432-1250

Stevens Technology Ventures Business
  Incubator
610-614 River Street
Hoboken, NJ 07030
(201) 216-5366   Fax (201) 420-9568

TDC, Inc.
M/S 707-21
P.O. Box 109600
West Palm Beach, FL 33410-9600
(407) 796-2123

Technology Advancement Program
University of Maryland
335 Paint Branch Drive, Rm 1100
College Park, MD 20742
(301) 314-7803   Fax (301) 314-9592

Technology Development Center
2545 Boatnan Avenue
W. Sacramento, CA 95691
(916) 375-6500   Fax (916) 375-6508

Technology Development Center
1414 Key Highway, Suite 300
Baltimore, MD 21230
(410) 528-1546   Fax (410) 727-6460

Technology Enterprise Center
  University of Maryland Baltimore County
5202 Westland Blvd.
Baltimore, MD 21227
(410) 455-1220   Fax (410) 455-6822

Technology Enterprise Center
100, 3553-31 St., NW
Calgary, AB
CANADA,   T2L 2K7
(403) 282-0464   Fax (403) 282-1238

Trilogy Systems, Inc.
505 E. Evelyn Avenue
Mountain View, CA 94041
(415) 961-1681   Fax (415) 961-5949

University City Science Center
3624 Market Street
Philadelphia, PA 19104
(215) 387-2255   Fax (215) 382-0056

University of British Columbia Research
  Enterprise
2194 Health Sciences Mall
IRC Building Room 331
Vancouver, BC, CANADA V6T 1Z3
(604) 822-8996   Fax (604) 822-8589

University of Buffalo Foundation Incubator,
  Inc.
1576 Sweet Home Road
Amherst, NY 14228
(716) 636-3626   Fax (716) 636-3630

University of Iowa Tech Innovation Center
100 Oakdale Campus #109 TIC
Iowa City, IA 52242-5000
(319) 335-4063   Fax (319) 335-4489

University Research Park
1265 WARF Building
610 Walnut
Madison, WI 53705
(608) 262-3677   Fax (608) 265-2886

Virginia Biotechnology Research Park
MCV 127
Richmond, VA 23298-0127
(804) 828-5390   Fax (804) 828-8566

BIBLIOGRAPHY

Abrams, Rhonda M., *The Successful Business Plan: Secrets and Strategies*, 2nd Edition, Grants Pass, Oregon: The Oasis Press, 1993.

Belich, Thomas J. and Dubinsky, Alan J. "Factors Related to Information Acquisition in Exporting Organizations." *Journal of Business Research*, 1995, 33, pp. 1-11.

Birch, D. *The job generation process.* (Unpublished manuscript.) Cambridge, MA: MIT Program on Neighborhood and Regional Change, 1979.

Brett, Alistair, Gibson, David V., and Smilor, Raymond W. (Eds.). *University Spin-off Companies: Economic Development, Faculty Entrepreneurs, and Technology Transfer.* Totowa, NJ: Rowman and Littlefield, 1990.

Bruno, Albert V., McQuarrie, Edward F., and Torgrimson, Carol G. "The Evolution of New Technology Ventures Over 20 Years: Patterns of Failure, Merger, and Survival." *Journal of Business Venturing*, 1992, 7, pp. 291-302.

Buss, Dale D. "Coping with Faster Change." *Nation's Business*, March 1995, pp. 27-29.

Camp, Michael S. and Sexton, Donald L. "Trends in Venture Capital Investment: Implications for High-Technology Firms." *Journal of Small Business Management*, July, 1992, pp. 11-19.

Carnegie Commission on Science, Technology, and Government. *Science, Technology, and the States in America's Third Century.* New York: Carnegie Commission, 1992.

Cook, T.D., and Campbell, D. *Quasi-Experimentation: Design and Analysis Issues for Field Settings.* Boston: Houghton-Mifflin, 1979.

Deck, Mark. "Why the Best Companies Keep Winning the New Products Race." *R&D Magazine*

November 1994, pp. 41-51.

Eisinger, Peter K. "State Venture Capitalism, State Politics, and the World of High-Risk Investment." *Economic Development Quarterly*, May 1993, pp. 131-139.

Fairweather, G.W., and Tornatzky, L.G. *Experimental Methods for Social Policy Research.* New York: Pergamon Press, 1977.

Harris, C.S. *High technology employment growth: Considerations of firm size.* (Unpublished paper.) Washington, DC: Brookings Institution, 1984.

Health Care Technology Institute. *The Dialogue of Device Innovation: An Overview of the Medical Technology Innovation Process.* Washington, D.C.: Health Care Technology Institute, 1993.

Kearns, Shelia M. "Technology Alliances for Competitiveness." *Technology Knowledge Activities: Leading-Edge Technologies and Alliances*, Summer 1994, pp. 33-41.

Kinni, Theodore B. "Strategic Thinking." *Industry Week*, August 15, 1994, pp. 17-18.

Kozmetsky, G. "The Coming Economy." In F. Williams and D. Gibson (Eds.), *Technology Transfer: A Communication Perspective.* Newbury Park, CA: Sage, 1990.

Ladin, Lawrence. "Capital ideas for high-tech firms." *Wall Street Journal*, June 13, 1994, pp. 16 (A).

Mansfield, E. " Academic Research and Industrial Innovation." *Research Policy*, 1991, 20 (1), pp. 1-12.

Mokyr, J. "Punctuated Equilibria and Technological Progress." *The American Economic Review*, 1990, 80 (2), pp. 350-354.

National Business Incubation Association. "NBIA's New Directory of Incubators and Members Shows Continued Growth." *NBIA Review*, September/October 1993, 4.

Southern Growth Policies Board. Commission on the Future of the South, 1986. *Halfway Home and a Long Way to Go.* Research Triangle Park, NC: Southern Growth Policies Board, 1986.

Southern Technology Council. *Turning to Technology: A Strategic Plan for the Nineties.* Research Triangle Park, NC: Southern Growth Policies Board, 1990.

Spragins, Ellyn E. "A New Deal." *Inc.*, January 1991, pp. 121-122.

Stevens, Mark. "Strategic Partnerships." *D & B Reports*, November/December 1992, pp. 50-51.

Tornatzky, L.G. and Fleischer, M. *The Process of Technological Innovation.* Lexington, MA: Lexington Books, 1990.

Udell, Geral G. "Are Business Incubators Really Creating New Jobs by Creating New Businesses and New Products." *Journal of Product Innovation Management*, 1990, 7, pp. 108-122.

U.S. General Accounting Office. *University Research: Controlling Inappropriate Access to Federally Funded Research Results.* Washington, D.C.: U.S. Government Printing Office, 1992.

Index

S

sample — 5, 7-8, 13, 54, 138, 155-160

Small Business Administration (SBA) — 23, 27, 104, 133

Small Business Development Center (SBDC) — 15, 24, 48, 58, 61-62, 89, 96-98

Small Business Innovation Research (SBIR) — 10, 18, 32-33, 44, 47-48, 64, 101-102, 122, 134

scholarships — 64

Senior Corps of Retired Executives (SCORE) — 32, 61, 66, 83, 132

seed capital — 9-10, 14-15, 146

seminars — 24, 32-3, 44, 63-64, 91, 96-99, 132

shareholders — 142, 145-146

Shingle Out Session — 108

skunk works — 44

software — 28, 35, 45, 50, 66, 71-72, 74, 81-73, 99, 101, 103, 113-774, 116-778, 120, 132, 134-136, 154

space — 3, 16, 31, 33, 41, 43, 49, 57-58, 60, 63, 73, 78-79, 81, 89, 91, 112-113, 116-119, 123, 131-132, 138, 142, 146-149, 153

Southern Technology Applications Center (STAC) — 47

state government — 16, 18, 24, 33, 36

strategies — 1-8, 63-64, 78, 85, 102, 130-131, 134-136, 138, 141, 145-146, 150, 152-158

Strengths, weaknesses, opportunities, threats (SWOT) analysis — 98

T

technical milestones — 85, 87

technology executive breakfast — 69

technology month — 29

technology transfer — 8, 41-45, 50-51, 102, 110, 120, 131, 141-142, 157

tools — 3, 7, 29, 40, 72, 78, 82, 90, 92, 99, 100-103, 135, 154-155, 159

training — 2-3, 19, 24, 28-29, 32, 39-40, 52-54, 62-66, 75, 80, 87, 96-99, 111, 117, 142, 149, 153

tuition — 63, 149

U

UBC Research Enterprises — 17, 39

undergraduate students — 92-94

university — 2-8, 10, 12-13, 16-20, 22, 24, 28, 30-33, 36-51, 53, 56, 59-60, 62-63, 65-66, 68, 70, 73-74, 76, 79-81, 84-86, 90-98, 100-104, 106, 108-112, 114, 116-124, 126, 128, 130, 132-135, 138-143, 148, 156-157, 160

urban incubators — 11, 38, 54, 87, 113-114, 161

V

venture capitalists — 9-10, 16, 22, 28-30, 32, 34, 71, 76, 91, 140

venture fairs — 23-24

venture forum — 10, 30, 70

video toasters — 116

virtual companies — 134

virtual licensing office — 110

volunteers — 27, 59-62, 64, 66-67, 72, 75-77, 83, 93-94, 116, 140

W

Wall of Fame — 81

white board — 74

workshops — 30, 32-33, 61, 63-64, 71-72, 78, 96-100, 132, 143, 149

work-study — 94